T0336030

Introduction to Game Programming using Processing

This is an introductory textbook focusing on games (specifically interaction and graphics) as a pathway into programming. It empowers readers to do basic programming, prototyping, game creation, and other highly interactive applications, all from scratch and without any prior programming knowledge.

Using the popular programming language *Processing*, this book describes, explains, and demonstrates the basic and general programming principles and mechanisms used in typical game algorithms and concrete game projects. Chapters cover basic graphics, text output, loops, data types and variables, movement, time, audio and sound, debugging, classes and objects, event-based programming, real-time input controls, computer speed compensation, animation, tiling, scrolling, collision detection, basic AI, and much more. Additional support materials such as code examples and demo programs are available to download from this book's webpage.

This book is a great resource for students and aspiring professionals looking for an approachable entry into game programming.

Daniel Cermak-Sassenrath is former Associate Professor at the IT University, Copenhagen, member of the Center for Digital Play, and co-head of the Games Group. He teaches in the Game Design track programme. Daniel has taught university courses since 2002 and introductory courses to programming for design students since 2010.

Introduction to Game Programming using Processing

For Designers, Artists, Players, Non-Tech People and Everybody Else

Daniel Cermak-Sassenrath

CRC Press
Taylor & Francis Group
Boca Raton New York London

CRC Press is an imprint of the
Taylor & Francis Group, an **informa** business

First edition published 2024
by CRC Press
2385 NW Executive Center Drive, Suite 320, Boca Raton FL 33431

and by CRC Press
4 Park Square, Milton Park, Abingdon, Oxon, OX14 4RN

CRC Press is an imprint of Taylor & Francis Group, LLC

© 2024 Daniel Cermak-Sassenrath

ISBN: 978-1-032-38622-5 (hbk)
ISBN: 978-1-032-38613-3 (pbk)
ISBN: 978-1-003-34591-6 (ebk)

DOI: 10.1201/9781003345916

Typeset in Times LT Std
by KnowledgeWorks Global Ltd.

Access the Support Material: www.Routledge.com/9781032386225

Contents

Foreword

There are a few reasons why I am excited about this book.

First of all, it is the distillate of the material for Daniel's course Programming for Designers. About ten years ago, before I started my career at IO Interactive, I was the TA on that course – and as such, exposed to some of the earliest iterations of this book's contents. Back then, it came in the format of weekly booklets, each featuring a short story centred on programming superhero Commander Hex C0d1ng. While Hex himself did not make it into the text you now hold, his – and Daniel's – enthusiastic, can-do attitude certainly did.

Second, speaking as a technical, and former lead, level designer, I can attest to the value of computational thinking in game design; if not as a foundation for readable, scalable scripting or communication with programmers, then as a universally applicable toolbox – a structural, logical mindset for clarity, brevity and exactness in design, production and everything.

Third, learning code can be hard; programming languages, computer science and mathematics are, by their very nature, abstract and often obtusely formal fields. By focusing on creative, interactive applications with fun or artistic expression at their centre, programming becomes tangible and goal-oriented – and, even if you are not a game designer, creation can be a strong motivator.

That brings me to Daniel himself. The last time I saw him, he was hunched over some obscure contraption set up in a corridor of the IT University of Copenhagen, meant to demonstrate an academic point. On most other occasions, I will find him in his office, covered in half-disassembled electronics, 3D-printed doodads and musical instruments. If you picture an inventor's workshop, that is it.

And this is exactly what makes this book special: Its fiercely pragmatic, creative and solution-oriented author who understands the value of motivating learning with concrete applications. After ten years in the making, this book is the manifestation of that mindset, a repertoire of creative and technical nuggets on programming for everyone.

With that said, I will take no more of your time; please go right ahead, try things out, take them apart, learn code and make something fun!

Toke Krainert
Senior Technical Level Designer, IO Interactive,
Copenhagen, October 2023

Preface

This is the book I wish I had when I started out to learn programming, in the mid-1980s. It would have changed my life. Back then it was tricky to learn such an obscure skill. There was no Internet, of course, and the few resources that were available to me were pretty inaccessible. For instance, I had the technical documentation for *BASIC* which listed and explained all commands of the language in alphabetical order. Over time I acquired some programming books, but all of them were pretty stiff, and I didn't even know how to start. None of them worked for me. The magazines of the day were glorious; some focused on hardware and many on games. In my recollection, at least, the magazines that focused on programming, mostly featured long listings of program code; but typing-in many pages of, at the time, incomprehensible gibberish, did not appeal to me. Some of my friends had computers and were also interested, but they knew even less than me, and I had no idea. Having a computer was seen, in the best case, a weird hobby, and otherwise as a social stigma (not as a career move, as happened a decade or two later, and not as an ubiquitous part of modern life, as today).

Today, computers have won – many people carry one (or several of them) on them at all times, many attend to it day and night, and a myriad of productive and unproductive applications exist, and it is almost unthinkable to live without it. Access to education about digital media is abundant; school courses, books and online resources cater to many various and specialised interests.

Games have been a great attraction of home computers in the 1980s, and for many non tech people, they were the first point of contact with the novel medium. A considerable number of these people were, in fact, children. For many of them, games became a pathway into programming. Collins (2022) comments that 'children in the 1980s might have become interested in computers because of games, but the nature of computers at the time meant that many of them got into programming almost by accident'. Digital games are still, and probably more than ever, a popular path into competent computer use.

In the last 20 years, there has been an unbelievable cultural and economic boost to the field of digital media. Where only a handful of geeks were interacting with computers before, ignored by a worried (in the case of gamers) and scared society (in the case of hackers), there are now billions of ordinary people and members of the general public using and playing with computers. But it appears, after several decades of strong innovation, exponential growth, upward mobility and several spectacular and unusual careers (for instance, of early IT entrepreneurs whose names are well-known today), that a gap is widening between the increasing professionalism of the producers with specialisations of sophisticated skills, and the end users and consumers of digital media. Digital media becomes more mainstream, and *at the same time*, the distance increases between the producers and the increasingly numerous, diverse and likely less tech-savvy users. This division between the pros and the amateurs has happened with other technologies before, for instance, with the motor car.

Tech is becoming increasingly like rocket science – far removed from and closed to the general public. It is even dangerous; sharing self-written programs is almost made impossible in some recent operating systems. The operating system informs the user: This software was downloaded from the Internet and is not signed by an official developer registered with the computer manufacturer – so, no, sorry, you can't run this. Let's delete it (Figure 0.1)![2] In today's digital media, users better leave their hands off the machine and buy and use software that is made for them. The early days, when digital culture was fuelled and propelled forward and inspired by ideas (and illusions) of societal progress, individual freedom, participation, and a better future for all through the digital computer, of everybody making and sharing software collectively and for free, seem to be over for most people. But competent computer use needs programming. The medium of the computer can arguably only be understood, appreciated and fully utilised when users have at least basic knowledge about what computers can do and how they work.

FIGURE 0.1 The OS protects the users from themselves: Downloaded programs which are not officially signed by developers registered with the manufacturer cannot be run (the OS (wrongly) claims that the file was corrupt, and offers to delete it; *macOS* 12.6)

This book is an attempt to support non-tech people such as designers, artists, players, other non-tech people and the interested public, to start programming, hopefully, in a fun and accessible way: Games as a pathway into programming. It empowers readers to do basic programming, prototyping, creating games and other highly interactive applications, and to talk competently with tech people. This is also an entry-level introduction to programming with examples in the popular language *Processing*. Basic and general programming principles and mechanisms are described, explained, demonstrated and applied in typical game algorithms and concrete game projects.

Acknowledgements

The book is based on my course *Introduction to Programming for (Game) Designers* that I have been teaching for more than ten years, first at the Creative Technologies programme at Auckland University of Technology (AUT) in New Zealand, and then at the Games' Programme at the ITU in Copenhagen, Denmark. I got the idea to turn the course materials into a book when I heard that students were passing around the course materials to their friends who were not taking the course but were keen on learning programming.

I'd like to thank the many students who have been taking the course, from within and without the ITU, for their enthusiasm and energy that have kept the course (and me) going. Also, my co-teachers along the way, for their invaluable contributions and company, the many TAs for their essential work, and everybody else who supported this project over the years. Finally, Will Bateman at Routledge/CRC Press for believing in the book and his friendly and professional support to make it happen.

Acknowledgments

Introduction

Outline

- Motivation
- A Very Brief History of Programming
- Programming Needs Diversity
- How this Book Works

Here we discuss what
this is all about

Motivation

The computer has entered all areas of people's lives, media and culture – with digital games and their popularity being one of the very visible expressions of this trend. Because of their lack of technical expertise, non-tech people regularly have limited possibilities to participate in and contribute to the creation of the digital world, and their innovative ideas might never be known or realised. To know something about programming is arguably the only way to use a computer to the full extent and a key skill to substantially participate in and contribute to the brave new digital world.[1] This book aims to offer an accessible pathway into fun, meaningful, skilful and competent computer use. It offers a potentially disruptive change of perspective, and participants will experience the world of digital media in a different way, and be able to participate and contribute in ways they could not before.

Learning to program appears desirable for multiple reasons. It is an inspiring and powerful way of creative and artistic expression. It is clearly much in-demand in today's and tomorrow's job markets. Basic programming knowledge is an asset in communication: Project work benefits from non-tech people being able to understand and effectively negotiate with all team members, including the tech people, and to appreciate their roles and contributions.

This book approaches and presents programming from a hands-on, non-tech, application-centred perspective. It is all about the *application* of programming in practical, genuine design challenges; not about gathering abstract knowledge, to be used in the future in some other context; but hands-on skills, to be used here and now. The book aims to facilitate the making of projects people *want to have*. And this does not imply little learning or learning on a low level. But learning that centres on motivation and builds on curiosity.

Arguably, the most interesting things to program are *interactive systems* for people to use productively, express themselves and play with each other.[2] The computer has been used and it is still often used as a tool to model other media, e.g. to paint pictures and to cut movies. But increasingly, the computer is coming into its own, and people start to question its uses and experiment with it, and interact with it in novel, provocant, and playful ways that were unimaginable before, and which have no precedent.

The book integrates the endeavour to learn programming with a focus on (digital) games. The audience this book addresses is people interested in games who have no previous experience in coding: Students of Game Design and other (design) students, DIY indie game designers, freelance design professionals, game enthusiasts, but also ordinary people just wanting to learn to program.

Learning to program is not just learning another program or tool; it is a meta-skill similar to learning the principles of a universal language; people will be able to read one another's programs and create their own, share, discuss and collaborate.

Readers of this book:

- Gain an understanding of general programming principles, paradigms and practices, with an emphasis on graphics and interaction;
- Acquire hands-on programming skills in *Processing*, a modern, popular, well-supported, *C*-based language;
- Build up their own collection of game-related routines (such as real-time input, collision detection, hardware-speed independence, tiled graphics, scrolling, frame-based animation and basic game AI); and
- Create their own, custom game-making tools (such as a pixel art drawing program, and a tiled 2D level editor).

Programming as a Design Skill

Programming is a very useful design skill; for me, it is very similar to how I design and build (other) stuff. I trust readers are able to transfer their (previous, various) knowledge and approaches to this field. Programming as a design skill is:

- Similar to other skills, e.g. sketching, writing, using *Photoshop*, *Illustrator*, *Director*, dancing, singing, sports and foreign languages;
- A way of expression that goes beyond (or is simply different from) static representations and (human, live) performances;
- Required in some exciting areas of design such as interaction design and parametric design; and
- As useful as reading, writing and math; for instance, for animation, scripting and websites – and for creating games!

Programming is a unique way to test and communicate ideas about interaction. A player can then *do* it himself or herself, and experience it first-hand, directly and immediately, and not just *imagine* doing it. It is a difference like hearing about the scene in *Pulp Fiction* where the guy in the car gets accidentally shot and watching it oneself. One can't quite compare one experience with the other.

What Programming Can Do

With programming, people can actually create *functional artefacts*. The created software might neither be a finished, sellable product nor reach professional standards, but it works and can be demo'ed, tested, and given away.[3]

One can simply sit down with any computer (and probably a network connection) and start coding. One does not need anybody's permission, expensive hard- or software, machines, tools, literature, or to be at a specific location. Many languages, development tools, libraries and assets such as graphics are available for free. One can do it alone, if necessary; after a few hours or a night one has created something that was not there before, and it (hopefully) does something novel, different, useful, dubious, exciting, beautiful or fun!

What programming can do:

- To have the first shot at an idea, one can use interactive programs to *communicate one's vision*
- Quickly *prototype*, test and find out if an idea is any good
- Competently communicate with and *understand programmers*, e.g. as part of a project team
- To use game engines (such as *Unity*), game makers and tools (such as graphics programs) effectively through *scripting*

- Everybody *likes* people who can program
- It will get one a *better* and a better-paying *job* if one can program (for which this book might be a starting point)

But most of all, it is tremendously *fun!*[4] It is a kind of magic, but a kind that everybody can command. It is a tricky *challenge*, it allows, invites and is based on *exploring* and *discovering* what can be done (not reading the manual), it is *uncharted* territory. When I program, I can make a digital artefact that was not there before. I can *try out*, have *control* over what happens, *test* it, see (i.e. *experience*) what it is and what it is *doing*, how it can be *used* and *misused*.

Programming and the Physical World

Programming is *not watching dots on screens*, and try to make them do something else. I can totally understand if someone feels that this is pointless and far from exciting. *Arduino* boards (introduced in the early 2000s) make it fairly easy to *mess with the physical world* (Figures 0.2 and 0.3)! Buttons, potentiometers, LEDs, motors, sound, GPS location, acceleration, weight, temperature, humidity, light, colour, pressure, distance, flex, vibration, tilt sensors, etc., can be used or controlled.[5] The *Arduino* interface uses (almost[6]) the same programming language we use for screen-based stuff, *Processing*. The programming of artefacts in the digital world and in the material world will turn out to be quite similar.

FIGURE 0.2 Various *Arduino* projects: A sensorised boxing bag, a multi-legged walking robot, and a self-driving slot car (photos by the author)

FIGURE 0.3   More *Arduino* projects: A mobile phone theremin, a wave measuring device, and an air quality sensor (photos by the author)

A Very Brief History of Programming

Computer use changed its character remarkably during the (short) history of the medium. It transformed from a task for technicians to operators to users to consumers. The necessary levels of individual and collective expertise and the costs of hardware went down, the number of people and the range of applications up.

The idea that machines can be anything else than 'on' or 'off' has only been around since the 1950s. The new academic discipline of Cybernetics (which later turned into Computer Science), which was started and essentially defined by Norbert Wiener, introduced the concept of (automatic) feedback loops. Feedback loops are the basis for what we know as *human-computer interaction* (HCI) or *interaction design*; an ongoing, real-time, open-ended process, an exchange between a person and a machine.

First, programming was an expert's job effectively done by swapping out, etc. electric parts; today, the pervasive availability of the hardware invites programming by the end user. In retrospect, it might seem amazing or astonishing, how many things were not there and needed to be invented and made and refined in a long iterative process, and how rough the conditions for people using computers were for a considerable stretch of time (e.g. access to a computer, assembler, batch processing, data storage, availability of software). Compared to today, very few people were working with computers or developing them, all of them are total experts and specialists.

Many advances described here happened in academic, commercial or even military labs. New ideas and techniques were not immediately communicated, and moreover, it was often not immanent what was an advancement and what was not. Developments happened in parallel and overlapped each other by several years (e.g. use of tubes), and inventions were occasionally made almost simultaneously in different places. Immense gaps separated abstract concepts of computing from technical research, experiments and inventions from military, commercial and (much later) private use. The moment in time, when an innovative development became commercially available and successful, rarely corresponded to the order of invention (e.g. the local network was developed in parallel with the mouse and a windowed interface, but it took more than a decade for it to make its way to a widespread application by the end user). Magic was not involved in the emergence of the modern computer. It was all mundane, iterative advances and progress, sometimes in brilliant and surprising leaps, but often painstakingly slow and basic.

In the last 100 years or so, the development of the computer has exploded. But not only from a technical perspective but also, and more relevant here, from a user perspective. Using a computer meant for a long time, programming. And programming could mean changing gears, plugs, punching cardboard, or entering number codes, commands and more sophisticated structures. The computer user was an operator. Individuals only own (personal) computers since the 1980s, and commercial off-the-shelf application software has only around for a bit longer. Early on, there was no gap between tinkerer, inventor, developer and user, because everybody who ever came near a computer was a highly-trained expert (the experts never went away, and are still around; they just became very few compared to the vast number of (novice) users). Soon, a new class of knowledge workers emerged, computer programmers, specialising in creating software. The gap started to widen when professional (i.e. non-technical) experts (e.g. business people) started to use computers in the late 1950s, and attempts to spread the wisdom (*BASIC*, *LOGO*) did not meet with large-scale success. The gap reached its widest point probably by the end of the 1990s, after the massive booms that the video gaming (in the late 1970s), the personal computer (in the early 1980s) and the popularisation of the Internet (from 1995) triggered. The gap is still immense, and unlikely to disappear completely, but it is getting smaller: Ordinary people are learning to move beyond using the computer by clicking (or tapping) on pretty icons; they script, fab, mod, code and hack. This happens because it is easy and fun, and people have (easy access to) the technical equipment and the competencies, and are probably also disillusioned with commercial offers and being spied upon. Now end users and even school children code – programming for all.

Programming has become quite a general skill[7]; this was proposed since at least the 1970s (e.g. by Alan Kay), and there have been a number of programming languages aimed at novices, and intended as introductory paths into programming, such as *BASIC*, *LOGO*, *Pascal* and *Java*. *Processing* is a language made from a similar perspective and proves to be quite popular. Now, arguably, as before, the time has finally come.

First, the development of programming faced fundamental and hard technical challenges, but beginning from the 1980s the challenge was no longer about raw computing power, speed and resource management, but the ease of use came into focus. First professionals started to use the computer, e.g. in engineering and business, followed then increasingly by ordinary people. And these ordinary, non-tech people are precisely the target group that limited, reduced, simplified languages such as *Processing* and scripting addresses. Programming is today on the verge to become a ubiquitous skill, taught, learned and used as part of a general curriculum, an additional way of expression, and learning, of engagement, experimentation, similar to math and writing.

What is already clear is that it is now possible to do things with computers that were only fantasies before. And we are still finding out what this new medium is.

Programming Needs Diversity

I speculate that much of the digital world has been created by middle-aged white men; not only specific hardware or software artefacts such as the *Apple* computer (Steve Jobs, Steve Wozniak, Ronald Wayne), the mouse (Doug Engelbart), the *Linux* operating system (Linus Thorvalds), the *C* programming language (Dennis Ritchie), many games and productivity software, but also the overarching structures and paradigms of interaction with and application of digital media (such as the modern *PC* at Xerox Parc, and the Internet by the US military). Generally less recognised, so far, are the contributions of women to the technological progress in computing and programming[8].

While also the area of game design is certainly male-dominated, there are several notable examples of female game designers; the most high-profile, in my view, could be Roberta Williams, who invented the graphic adventure and designed many very successful games (for instance, the *King's Quest* franchise, with her husband Ken) and Brenda Laurel and her company *Purple Moon*[9]; other female designers of famous games include Mabel Addis (The Sumerian Game), Danielle Bunten Berry (*M.U.L.E.*), Dona Bailey (*Centipede*), Rebecca Heineman (*Bard's Tale* series), Sheri Graner Ray (*Ultima* franchise), Ellen Beeman (*Wing Commander* games), Kellee Santiago (*Journey*), and Kim Swift (*Portal, Left 4 Dead*)[10].

The existing conventions of the digital world are just that, conventions, which people have agreed upon for various reasons and in various circumstances, and not invariable laws of nature. The people who made (and make) the decisions might not be representative of (or aware of or interested in) the people who are affected by them. The digital world could have developed very differently than it has, and it can certainly develop in any direction in the future.

Diversity and inclusion with regard to, for instance, people's age, gender, sexual orientation, religion, ethnicity, nationality, professional experiences, academic education, knowledge, skills and (dis-) abilities can arguably benefit both the processes and the results of collaborative activities. Phillips [2014] notes that '[d]ecades of research by organizational scientists, psychologists, sociologists, economists and demographers show that socially diverse groups [...] are more innovative than homogeneous groups' and 'better [prepared] than a homogeneous group at solving complex, nonroutine problems'.

For instance, in an economic context, it is regularly reported 'that businesses with more diverse workforces perform better on a whole range of measures' (Blackman 2017). In a two-year study on 180 publicly traded companies in four large Western countries, Barta et al. (2012) observe that '[c]ompanies with diverse executive boards [with regard to gender and nationality] enjoy significantly higher earnings and returns on equity'. A 2014 Gallup poll 'of more than 800 business units from two companies representing two different industries – retail and hospitality – finds that gender-diverse business units have better financial outcomes than those dominated by one gender' (Badal 2014): A '14% higher average comparable revenue' in the retail sector, and a '19% higher average quarterly net profit' in the hospitality sector (ibid.). A McKinsey study 'of 1000 companies in 12 countries [finds] that organisations in the top 25% when it comes to gender diversity among executive leadership teams were more likely to outperform on profitability (21%) and value creation (27%)' [Catalyst 2018].

Ashcraft and Breitzman's (2012) '30-year study of US patents in the IT industry' observes that mixed-gender teams 'produce patents that get cited by other researchers 30–40% more often than average' (Blackman 2017). On a board of directors, 'deep-level diversity', that is, 'differences in background, personality, and values' [...] contributed to a higher degree of creativity' (Catalyst 2018). Other observed benefits for businesses include retaining talent (ibid.), maximising productivity (ibid.), as well as reducing groupthink and enhancing decision-making (ibid.). Cognitively diverse teams 'solve problems faster' (ibid.). Mixed-gender corporate boards are reported to '[h]ave [f]ewer [i]nstances of [f]raud' and [...] are associated with more effective risk-management practices' (ibid.).

There might be various problems and trade-offs associated with creating and maintaining diversity at the workplace. For instance, 'individual employees may prefer less diverse settings' (Dizikes 2014) because 'more homogeneous offices have higher levels of social capital' (Sara Ellison qtd. in ibid.). But MIT economist Ellison (qtd. in ibid.) also points out that the 'higher levels of social capital are not important enough to cause those offices to perform better'. While '[t]he employees might be happier, they might be more comfortable, and these might be cooperative places, but they seem to perform less well'. Progress towards diverse work settings might be slow. In 2019, 'Google's [t]ech [s]taff is [o]nly 4.8% African American [...] [and] only 1.1% [...] is Hispanic, and only 33.1% are women' (Wholley 2019). Diversity programs in business might be 'designed to preempt lawsuits by policing managers' thoughts and actions' (Dobbin, Kalev 2016) rather than actually to prompt a change in corporate culture.

If digital technology, which is already used in many or most areas of life in First World societies, is to be inclusive and to speak to various groups of users, the participation of a mix of diverse players in the creation of it might become increasingly urgent. We arguably need more non-tech people coming into digital media to help us out. With mostly geeky (male) nerds developing everything, one can only get so far –

The important bit is that you yourself actually
start programming something today.
Everything is possible to those who try

How this Book Works

This book can be read in sequence, front to back; the topics build on each other. It can also be read selectively; references to relevant topics in other parts of the book (e.g. pointers to previous chapters, that one may not have read) are given.

It is attempted to connect the topics with each other as much as possible, to make clear how the ideas interface with each other and how they are used in concert and in context. Every concept is introduced together with concrete, typical or exemplary applications. Explanations are kept short and are immediately connected to code. Almost all code snippets in the book are complete programs, not only parts of larger programs that readers would need to puzzle together to see a result.

Part of learning to program is also to learn to talk about it, using the correct terminology, for instance, when communicating with team members who are tech experts such as programmers. Thus, while at the start of book, a somewhat loose language is used, to pick up the reader who might be unfamiliar with geek lingo and who might be put off by it; during the book, the language becomes more precise and correct with regard to terminology. Precise terms are usually used throughout, but given the choice between absolute correctness and high readability, readability is regularly prioritised.

Topics (structures, concepts) are introduced bottom up: First, they are demonstrated in concrete typical or exemplary applications, and only then are they discussed and explained. An understanding of the principles and concepts and possibilities of programming emerges for readers but is not presented to them up front in the form of a lecture.

Bonus Features and Online Resources

In addition to the explanations in textual form, the book contains a fair number of (mostly short) code snippets. All **Code Examples** from the book are accessible online and available for download. Ideally, readers have a (networked) computer handy and immediately try things out while consulting the book; but it is also possible to go to the beach and read the book offline and by itself.

In the text, two kinds of exercises are offered: **In-Text Exercises** directly pick up aspects discussed in a particular section; solutions are given at the end of the chapter. The in-text exercises should inspire readers to program something on their own.

At the end of the chapters, more extensive **Chapter End Exercises** are given; these exercises relate chapter content to exemplary uses, allow readers to check their understanding, and challenge the readers to become active to modify and extend the given material.

On the book's website, **Demo Programs** are available as an additional, online-only resource. The programs provide entry points for readers who are motivated by concrete applications. They are tightly related to the book content (and are usually based on it), but connect and integrate content from different book chapters and demonstrate its meaningful application in concrete contexts.

For instance, demo programs show the use of real-time controls in a simple two-player action game such as *Space Invaders*, classes for bricks and a paddle for a *BreakOut*-style game, and the program structure of a basic *Frogger*-style game. The programs can serve as starting points for readers to modify and experiment with code and also as starting points for readers' own projects.

Also online is **Buggy Code**, that is, programs that need fixing; the code contains bugs that readers can find and correct. The code that needs fixing speaks to readers who prefer (designed, quiz-like) challenges to free-form experimentation.

The bugs are based on my own programming experience and observations during many years of teaching programming courses. For concrete info on finding and fixing programming errors, see the sections 'The Process of Debugging' and 'Common Errors' in Chapter 23.

Multiple **Links** are given on the book's website that connects to learning resources outside of this book (e.g. *Processing*'s own video tutorials, *OpenProcessing*, *Arduino* Projects at *Instructables*, math for collision detection, an audio library, game programming patterns, and graphics resources). There are various styles of learning and teaching; readers should pick and use the resources that they prefer and which work best for them.

Where are the Games?

This book explains programming *for* and *with* games. It may appear as if the book was quite generally programming focused, and that it takes rather long to give concrete examples of real game features. Certainly, the examples feature games as early and quickly as possible. But some basics need to be established before games can be meaningfully made.

This book is not a tutorial, for instance, where one concrete game is made, and outside of this specific case the reader is lost. The book explains how programming works, with the example of games and with a view towards making games. The learning happens systematically, from the ground up. The material is appropriately and carefully structured and organized, building on the experience of teaching introductory programming courses to designers for more than ten years. Readers learn and understand everything they do. First the basics of programming, and then we make games (or other cool stuff), as soon as possible!

If in Doubt, Do It

This book is intended as an *introduction* and as an inspiring first point of contact with programming for non-tech people[11] with a specific focus on game programming. The book explains the raw basics of (any) programming for readers who have not done a line of programming ever before, and the functions, tools and concepts popularly used in game programming.

Programming needs to be done by oneself; yes, one can work with friends, and this can be a lot of fun, and I welcome and recommend that later, but learning programming is like learning to ride a bicycle: One *has* to do it oneself! Not watch somebody – none of one's mates and not me. *Readers should program something they want to have now*, really anything. Don't wait; look things up, try things out, and start today!

The book shows stuff and explains it, but readers need to do it, themselves – see it run, toy around with it, break it, fix it, feel the magic –

The best way to get it done
is to do it now

Notes

1. 'There is a need for learning how to code, if we are not going to be programmed ourselves.' (Marckmann 2019:69)
2. Warren Sack (2019) maintains that interaction had initially been an integral and even central part of computer science, and was only de-emphasized when computer science developed a strong if not exclusive focus on algorithms, promoted, for instance, by Donald Knuth.
3. If the software proves to have, e.g., commercial potential, it can then be re-implemented from scratch (e.g. by professional programmers). Probably a fair bit of commercial software starts that way.
4. 'I sometimes forget one of the main reasons I like programming, and that's that programming is fun. People can talk all they want about problem solving and helping others to accomplish tasks, but for me it's all about realizing that I can do it, and that's always been a fun thing. Granted, there's some code to write

because some user (somewhere) needs a new feature, or there's a bug to be tracked down and squished, but the main reason I like programming is that it's, well, fun.' [Paul Barry, October 24 (2011, presumably), qtd. in blogs.oreilly.com/headfirst/2011/10/programming-is-fun-again.html (December 8, 2015)].

5. *Make: magazine* (www.makezine.com) and *AUTODESK Instructables* (www.instructables.com/Arduino-Projects) are great starting points.

6. See the section 'The Choice of Programming Language' in Chapter 1.

7. This observation appears to apply, very roughly, to the US, Europe, South East Asia and Australia.

8. See, for instance, www.hackerearth.com/blog/developers/top-women-programmers-history, www.computerscience.org/resources/most-influential-women-computer-science, mashable.com/article/unsung-women-in-tech or www.fullstackacademy.com/blog/remarkable-women-programmers (all September 2, 2023).

9. For info on some female game designers connected to Atari, including Brenda Laurel, see the AtariWomen project (www.atariwomen.org/stories).

10. Read more: Jason W. Bay. 17 Most influential women game developers. Blog post, www.gameindustry careerguide.com/influential-women-game-developers (December 11, 2021).

11. For a well-written and comprehensive book on *Processing* from an art and design perspective see the books by Reas and Fry (e.g. 2014); and for tech people there are many excellent computer science books on all kinds of programming languages.

1

The Process of Programming

Outline

- What is Programming?
- The Choice of Programming Language
- Programming First Aid

What Is Programming?

By itself, the computer does nothing. To control this technical medium and to elicit some interesting behaviour from it, humans have to give it explicit instructions. For practical purposes, instructions are written down, in multiple programs, in languages that the computer can read. The practice to create such programs is called programming.

Programming tries hard to be accessible. Programming languages are made for humans, not for machines. High-level languages are specifically made to be suited to what humans want to do with computers[1]. They are tools designed by people for people to use, and they have come a long way already towards the user. Specifically, programmers do not need to learn to talk, write or think like machines, to instruct or use computers. Modern languages do what they can to make it easy for humans to use them. They aim to be close to how humans act and think and not to emulate or reproduce how machines function. The translation between such programming languages and the actual machine code (which is, in fact, pretty incomprehensible) is then done automatically under the hood.

There are only a handful of programming structures; mainly these are: *Loops* to repeat operations, *checks* to make decisions based on particular conditions and *variables* to store data. For people to interact with programs, there is often some form of *output* (e.g. text, graphics, sound) and *input* (e.g. keyboard, mouse, joystick, sensors). Only what is formulated in its programs happens, the computer does not suddenly start to do weird (or wonderful) things by itself. Programming is quite mundane:

- It is all written down
- It is not magic
- Computers are dumb[2]

Multiple Aspects of Programming

Just as *making music* is not *playing notes*, and *math* is not *calculation*, programming is not making a list of commands and letting it run. Programming involves typing-in commands but also regularly includes many other aspects that are as essential:

- Selecting a language[3]
- Creating reasonably elegant code
- Reading (other people's) code

DOI: 10.1201/9781003345916-1

- Scoping and structuring programs
- Choosing data structures
- Selecting and competently using tools (such as language functions and additional libraries)
- Making of custom functions and tools for specific purposes
- Organising the handling and moving of data in the program (such as level layouts, enemy positions and user data)
- Optimising programs for specific applications and contexts (e.g. speed, network bandwidth and robustness)
- Communicating with team members (e.g. designers, programmers, business people, clients)

To emphasise one aspect, that might be specifically similar to other design practices: Programming means to *create the tools along with the artefacts*, in one seamless process. Programming is not only or even primarily concerned with picking and using pre-made functions (except for the most trivial tasks) but mainly with the construction of systems. Programs are developed in iterative processes which oscillate between creating code and using it to make artefacts. Programming is a multi-faceted process of making and adapting and testing and fixing and re-using.

How Programming Concretely Works

The general public might only have a vague idea of how programming works, and representations of programming in popular media might not be specifically accurate. For instance, it might be assumed that programming happens fast, code is written top-to-bottom in one go, and software works immediately and reliably. All of these assumptions are dubious. Readers should not assume they do something wrong if the actual process of programming they experience is different.

The creation of code is usually a goal-directed process, but this process is also often chaotic, piecemeal, spontaneous, opportunistic and partial. Often, the person programming knows how to implement some things the software should do but not others. Some parts of a program are more complex than others. Development of some parts of a program might progress faster than other parts; that might mean that one particular feature of a program works really well but nothing else. The ideas or need for some functions or features might only emerge during the development phase and are then integrated into the existing framework, one part or function at a time. Often, the addition of more features necessitates the re-implementation of (other) parts of the program, because the incorporation of the various programme parts with each other is non-trivial.[4]

Programmes usually do not run (at first, anyway). Even short programmes can contain and often do contain an astonishing number of bugs. Programming is, to a considerable degree, fixing bugs. It takes much effort to find some or most of the bugs, and then some more effort to fix them. Fixing them usually introduces new bugs, too. Debugging is part of the process and the challenge, and much effort regularly is spent on it (see the section 'Programming First Aid' and the section 'The Process of Debugging' in Chapter 23). This applies to novice as well as to seasoned programmers. I usually find numerous bugs in my code and am then regularly surprised that my programs did anything at all, with all those bugs in them.

In most cases, new software is built based on existing software. The program structure of a new project is often new, but people still have their favourite code such as sets of classes and functions they have developed over time, and like to bring them to new projects. That code is a great asset because it makes little sense to develop everything from scratch every time. However, it is of course also a limitation, that might hinder truly innovative approaches, if the same code is taken from project to project and (similar) structures are reproduced.

Programming is, in many cases, a team effort. Either code is collaboratively developed by a team of people, or code is passed on from one person to the next, e.g. in a company. Or, the person who developed a program gets back to it after some time (weeks, months or years), and needs to make sense of it, again[5].

Much software gets re-developed (or re-implemented) eventually, at some point. That usually happens when the program structure is no longer fit for the purpose, and effectively prevents future development. The reason is that at the point in time when a program structure is usually decided on, that is, at the start of a new project, it is often pretty unclear what the precise requirements for the programme are and which issues will emerge over time. Also, then, over time, many features are often added to a program, and the structure gets overloaded, and an increasing level of effort has to be made to integrate new features and to maintain the old ones, and to keep everything working together. Thus, at some point, it is less trouble to re-implement a project with the experience and benefit of hindsight. Sometimes the re-development of a program includes the port to another (for instance, more modern) language.

Particularly when starting out, even trivial programs take a considerable amount of time to be developed; and even the professional development of software often takes longer than anticipated.

Arguably, programs remain unfinished; there is always more to do, add, include or test. There is no obvious endpoint when a game or application is done. Usually, software gets released at some point, and then, later, more advanced incarnations of it are iteratively released as well (e.g. as bugfixes, updates or as new program versions, occasionally over many years). For games, there are often new features and contents released over time (such as levels or characters).

The Choice of Programming Language

This book is an introduction to programming. The *Processing* programming language is used, but understanding general programming is the focus. The book empowers participants with an understanding of the basic and general concepts while it avoids both a follow-me-blindly tutorial approach and language-specific functions and features. Participants are thus able to transfer and apply the insight they gain to the programming language or scripting tool used in their next project, design team or job.

As a first programming language for a non tech audience, *Processing* (Figure 1.1) is well-suited:

- *Processing* is free, platform-independent, stable, regularly updated and available for many computer systems. It can be downloaded (from processing.org) or might be already installed;
- It can do graphics and interaction out of the box, and no setup of libraries is required;
- It can be used with *Arduino* boards for easy hardware access (e.g. buttons, sensors, LEDs, motors)[6];
- It has a vibrant online community, especially for beginner-oriented, introductory stuff and
- It is based on *Java* and very similar to widely-used and industry-relevant languages such as *C#*, so skills can readily be transferred[7].

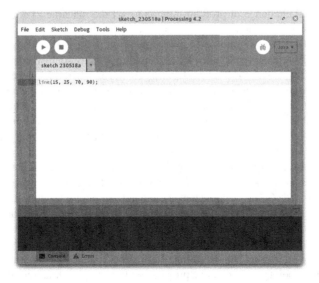

FIGURE 1.1   The *Processing* language is used as a vehicle to learn (general) programming (pictured: Version 4.2, *Linux*)

It is to be expected that for many years, *Processing* will continue to play a role in learning programming and as a preferred language for artists and designers.[8]

Many of my colleagues support the use of *Processing* for an introductory course and book on game programming, but several have questioned it. Thus, some reasoning is given here. Many people who code have their favourite programming language and occasionally are quite opinionated on the topic, and some have kindly shared their views and recommendations about the best programming language to use in this endeavour. There has not been a consensus, not even close. All the currently popular languages (as well as several scripting languages and game engines) have been proposed and argued for, with the vote roughly evenly split.

Various other languages are used in teaching (such as *JavaScript, Python, C#*). *Processing* is popularly used in artistic and design projects and rarely in game design. Certainly, it is not a language used in the game industry. Professional game development happens in *C++* or *C#*. *Python* is the new hot thing but not made for highly interactive applications (there is a game library, of course, and it does work), and syntactically quite different from *C*-style languages. *C* and *Python* are also typically employed in Computer Science programmes. *Java* and *JavaScript* are also available, possibly with decreasing popularity. And there are new (e.g. browser-based) scripting languages every few years.

Also popular are versatile game engines such as *Unity, Unreal* and *Godot*, and they can only be used to full (or any) effect with coding. Arguably, one can teach and learn programming within an engine. The question is, is this representative of general programming, and can it be transferred to other (scripting) tools and 'proper' languages? And the answer is, yes. And there is no shortage of resources (courses, books, online videos and fora) of various qualities.

It might be a matter of preference to favour one or the other approach: Programming within engines might have impressive initial results (e.g. engines usually have physics engines, and with very little coding anybody can make something that moves and can be shot). Programming outside of engines, on the other side, affords more freedom and requires the programmer to take control because very little (if any) structure is given. In my (own, rough) assessment, programming in engines is reading documentation and finding out what one can do with elaborate pre-made engine structures and functions; while programming outside of engines is laborious fiddling with tiny snippets of code (and reading some documentation) and trying to make meaningful things happen.

A reason to favour learning (and teaching) programming without engines is, that it is more universal: Learning programming in an engine creates a substantial reliance (technically and psychologically) on that engine. Take away the engine, and the learner hits a wall; he or she can do nothing. Somebody who learned programming without an engine can (almost) start from scratch with a blank screen; and also use an engine with very little preparation.

Probably the essential challenge of programming is to get the machine to do exciting and complex things while instructing the machine with rather basic and clunky commands. I remember how disappointed I was when I started to programme and was only given those relatively low-level and open commands. I was expecting words but was given letters. Instead of using sophisticated future tech, I had to build things up myself. For novel, original work, skills are needed, and this may apply to programming to the same degree it applies to other areas of design. The trade-off between convenience and control is well-known. Of course, there are programming techniques and tools that require less practice and skill to produce desirable results than textual programming. There are many digital tools for prototyping and communicating ideas for interaction, that require very little programming knowledge. One can use tools such as *Director*, game makers and website editors such as *FrontPage*, or subvert tools such as *PowerPoint*. But of course, without programming, one is left to follow and accept what these programs offer. Tools often focus on a specific kind of interaction (such as a genre, e.g. *Adventure Game Studio*[9] and the online *Retro Arcade Creator*[10] game maker), and have in-built behaviour that cannot be changed. In other words, a platform game maker makes the same game every time. The reliance and dependence on pre-made work not only channels, scopes and limits a tool's expressive power but also one's own ideation and creativity. Using a text-based programming language such as *Processing* requires some effort and practice to build up interesting behaviour but offers a very high level of control[11].

Of course, at different points in the creative process and for different situations, different methods and tools are useful. Programming certainly adds a tool to the box that significantly empowers designers.

Programming First Aid

The practice of programming regularly includes problems and bugs and things going wrong, and dealing with these issues is part of it. What can be done, if things don't work?[12]

- Take a break, do something else for a minute, talk to a human (about something else);
- Check what is going on in the program and make things visible: Use `println()` or `text()` to output variable contents[13] or graphics, to confirm the internal (e.g. collision detection) logic corresponds to what one assumes or observes;
- Explain the code to somebody else[14];
- Assume it will work eventually, comment it out for now, and come back to this issue later;
- See if anybody with coding skills is around who can help or
- Search the Internet, or more specifically, online fora[15] for an answer to the question or problem. Likely, other people have encountered it before. If nothing helpful can be found, post a question to the forum.

Notes

1. There are certainly languages that are fairly removed from applications such as assembler, and old code (e.g. *Fortran*) is and will be around for decades, but today much is done in languages that humans can read – chances are, as a designer living in the 21st century, all code one will ever see, is fairly user-friendly (e.g. *C*-based).
2. Computers are not capable of any complex operations; what they are tremendously good at, is to repeat simple things rapidly and very often. Specifically, computers can store and retrieve data, and a lot of presumably 'intelligent' behaviour of the computer is actually searching and retrieving data. *Google* search results and (some) poker-playing programmes are examples.
3. Section, The Choice of Programming Language is a discussion of why *Processing* was selected for this project, and the most prominent features of *Processing* are listed.
4. The typical process of iteratively developing programmes is demonstrated in the section 'Grids' in Chapter 12 and in the section 'Eye and Math Examples' in Chapter 14.
5. Thus, if one works in a team, but also if a person works alone on a project, it is useful to avoid overly wonky or idiosyncratic ways of coding.
6. *Arduino* uses (a subset of) *C++* actually, but for basic applications, the differences between *Processing* and *C++* are marginal (class use is different, e.g.).
7. For instance, the *Unity* engine uses *C#* for scripting.
8. Theoretically, one can program anything in *Processing*; practically, it is a bit limited (which is not a bad thing for learning) and for serious stuff (such as 3D graphics) too slow.
9. www.adventuregamestudio.co.uk (Jan 24, 2017)
10. www.sploder.com/free-arcade-game-maker.php (Jan 24, 2017)
11. In computer science lingo *Processing* is called an imperative programming language, because it states *how* the computer should do things; opposed to declarative languages which state *what* the computer should do.
12. For more info on debugging, see the section 'The Process of Debugging' in Chapter 23.
13. On console output, see Chapter 3.
14. The important part is the explaining; the other person does not need to be an expert, or even to say anything at all.
15. Such as the forum on discourse.processing.org (May 21, 2023).

2

Hello Game World!

Outline

- Hello World
- First Interactivity
- Pixel Graphics
- A Brief Look at Colours

*Now we see what parts a program
is made of and get some graphics
on the screen fast*

Hello World

Programming code is a piece of text, similar to a shopping list or cooking recipe. The computer reads and executes each item (i.e. command) when (and if) it reaches it, starting at the top. The machine looks at one spot at a time, line by line, command by command, does exactly what the code says, at best remembers what happened before, but has no idea where things are going and what is coming next.

Often, texts on programming start with a program that prints 'Hello World' on the screen, so the user can try it out and see that something is happening. Because *Processing* is all about graphics, this text starts with graphical output, a line:

```
line(20, 70, 80, 20);
```

Start *Processing* on the computer and type or copy this command[1] into *Processing*'s window.[2] Then press the *Play* button (showing a circle with a triangle, it looks like a play button on a cassette recorder) or press Ctrl-R or Apple-R, and a little window with a black line on a grey background should appear:

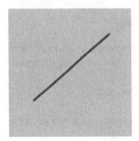

The line is drawn between two points: (20, 70) and (80, 20). The coordinate system origin (0, 0) is located in the top-left corner of the window.

Modify the two pairs of coordinates and the line will be drawn somewhere else.[3] Add more line() commands (with different coordinates) and several lines will be drawn.

DOI: 10.1201/9781003345916-2

With just a few commands similar to the `line()` command, it is possible to draw some simple graphics on the screen; such as a large eyeball (Code 1).

Code 1

```
size(480, 240);
strokeWeight(4);

background(255, 255, 255);

fill(60, 120, 190);
ellipse(230, 90, 400, 400);

fill(0, 0, 0);
ellipse(229, 88, 250, 250);

fill(255, 255, 255);
ellipse(180, 40, 70, 70);
```

There are many things one can already draw like this; and for the moment it is fine to understand code as a kind of list or recipe (and it is, actually, for instance, in the examples Code 1–Code 15). But, as will become obvious soon, the code is different. Lists and recipes are usually read from top to bottom and each line or item in-between is attended to. But code can include decisions (i.e. which code to execute depending on e.g. user action), repetition (e.g. keep repeating part of the code a number of times), variables (to store data) and structures (such as functions and classes). While it happens that code is executed line by line and every command once, and from top to bottom, it is a rather rare exception.

Here are more examples to try out, such as a rainbow (Code 2).

Code 2

```
size(480, 240);
noStroke();

background(0, 0, 0);

fill(255, 0, 0);
ellipse(240, 240, 480, 480);

fill(255, 128, 0);
ellipse(240, 240, 400, 400);

fill(255, 255, 0);
ellipse(240, 240, 320, 320);

fill(0, 255, 0);
ellipse(240, 240, 240, 240);

fill(0, 0, 255);
ellipse(240, 240, 160, 160);

fill(255, 0, 255);
ellipse(240, 240, 80, 80);
```

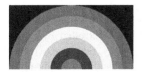

If one wants something more artsy-looking, that is possible, too (Code 3 and Code 4).

Code 3

```
size(640, 200);
noStroke();

background(235, 230, 230);

fill(245, 215, 0);
triangle(110, 20, 20, 180, 200, 180);

fill(90, 130, 210);
ellipse(310, 100, 160, 160);

fill(230, 70, 70);
rect(440, 20, 160, 160);
```

Code 4

```
size(400, 400);
noStroke();

fill(137, 67, 221);
rect(0, 0, 200, 200);

fill(178, 64, 233);
rect(200, 0, 200, 200);

fill(240, 71, 28);
rect(0, 200, 200, 200);

fill(2, 168, 88);
rect(200, 200, 200, 200);

fill(232, 175, 20);
rect(50, 50, 100, 100);
rect(250, 50, 100, 100);
rect(50, 250, 100, 100);
rect(250, 250, 100, 100);
```

Some things can now already be observed: There are different graphical output functions such as line(), rect(), triangle() and ellipse(), maybe more; they are somehow controlled by numbers (called arguments) in parenthesis; and there are other functions such as fill(), noStroke() and strokeWeight() that change the way the (following) objects are drawn (equivalent to picking up a drawing tool such as a coloured pen). The order in which functions are called is important, that is, later ones draw over earlier ones on the screen; colours are written in RGB values, red being, for instance, (255, 0, 0). Things can be drawn within and without the window.

Functions

Functions carry out actions, e.g.:

- Draw shapes
- Set colours
- Calculate pixel coordinates

Functions are either language-specific (such as size() and background()), provided by libraries (e.g. sound or network) or programmer-made. We'll be making lots of functions here in the book[4] – some specific to a project, others that are used in many projects. Often, programmers have a bunch of functions they have made over time, and which they re-use often.

A function has a name, which can be anything; it only needs to be unique.[5] Often (i.e. by convention) the name is spelled in lowercase letters or in a mix of (mostly) lowercase letters and some uppercase ones, as in noStroke(). Functions can take arguments, which follow after the function name in parenthesis and are separated by commas. Many functions require arguments, but some do not.

Now let us revisit some of the code from the examples above. The first function that is called in Code 1 is

```
size(480, 240);
```

size() takes two arguments to set the window size. The first argument defines the dimension of the window in pixels in the x-direction, the second argument in the y-direction.

The function

```
strokeWeight(4);
```

takes only one argument to set the width of the contour lines of graphic objects (e.g. rectangles and ellipses).

And the function (called in Code 2)

```
noStroke();
```

does not take any arguments; it just sets the contour line width to zero.

Functions can have any number of parameters. These parameters can also be (almost) anything, e.g. numbers or words. For the most common functions (such as line()) one probably remembers the parameters, but often one simply looks them up in the documentation or uses an IDE feature similar to auto-completion to be reminded (see the section 'The *Processing* IDE' in Chapter 23).

In *Processing* (as in many similar languages[6]), each statement (such as a function call or a variable assignment) is ended with a semicolon (not e.g. with a line break). In the following example, the computer reads two function calls, each of them terminated by a semicolon:

```
size(200, 200); strokeWeight(3);
```

This would work fine, but is hard to read for humans. As a general rule, always place statements in separate lines:

```
size(200, 200);
strokeWeight(3);
```

Case Sensitivity and Whitespace

For the computer to read and execute code, commands and everything else need to be spelled correctly, and typos are a popular source of bugs (luckily, these are usually straightforward to spot and to fix).

But *Processing* is also *case sensitive*. It makes a difference if one writes

```
size(200, 200);
```

which is correct (if one wants to invoke the function for setting the window size), or

```
Size(200, 200);
```

which is not.

However, whitespace can be inserted or omitted in some places:

```
size(200,200);
strokeWeight   ( 3 ) ;
x   +=   50;
```

These examples compile, but the code might be hard to read (and look unconventional); not everything that is possible is advisable to do.

Whitespace is not permitted within function names and operator symbols:

```
stroke Weight(3);
x+ =50;
```

What is meant is

```
strokeWeight(3);
x += 50;
```

First Interactivity

The examples above demonstrate that the computer can do some stuff when instructed to do so, such as drawing graphical shapes. But so far, the programs are not interactive. We will come back to the topic soon, but already now programs can be fitted with basic interactivity. Code 5 shows how a rectangle can be moved about the screen with the mouse.

Code 5

```
void setup()  //runs once at program start
{ }
void draw()  //runs repeatedly after that
{
  rect(mouseX, mouseY, 20, 10);
}
```

The structure works like this: The code in the first function, which is called `setup()`, is run once on program starts, and the second function `draw()` is run repeatedly after that until the program stops.[7] In Code 5, nothing is done at program start (because `setup()` is empty; although we might add something like setting the window size or colouring the background), but then (in `draw()`) the mouse pointer coordinates are used to draw a rectangle at the current position. When the mouse pointer is moved, rectangles are drawn at various places (as in the example's screenshot).

In Code 6, the `setup()` function sets the window size (once, at program start) to 320 by 240 pixels. In `draw()`, first, the background is (re-) drawn all the time, so the graphical output looks much cleaner than in Code 5; then the `mouseX` and `mouseY` variables are used to draw a line and a circle: The variables are used as an endpoint for the line (which starts at `(160, 0)`, which is the top-middle of the window) and as a centre point for the ellipse (which is round, so it is a circle).

Code 6

```
void setup()
{
  size(320, 240);
}
void draw()
{
  background(220, 110, 0);
  line(160, 0, mouseX, mouseY);
  ellipse(mouseX, mouseY, 60, 60);
}
```

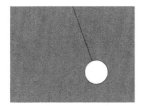

While most of the code snippets in this first part of the book omit the `setup()` and `draw()` structure, do experiment with it, and with interactivity! The mouse pointer coordinates are readily available in the variables `mouseX` and `mouseY` and can be used to control not only the position where something is drawn but also, e.g. its size, colour or line thickness.

The first rule of programming:
To get the job done

Pixel Graphics

Today's popular computer screens are made up of grids of little, rectangular elements called *pixels* (Figure 2.1). All the pixels on the screen or in the display window are controlled by the program.

The function call

```
size(100, 50);
```

sets the window size to 100 by 50 pixels (Figure 2.2).[8]

Each of the pixels in the display can be accessed by the program. While the above examples drew rectangles and ellipses, it is also possible to draw a single pixel[9]:

```
point(x, y);
```

FIGURE 2.1 A 1987–8 *Ms. Pac-Man* arcade machine (branded as *Super Pac Gal*; left); and a screen detail showing individual pixels on the scratched and misaligned CRT (right; photo by the author)

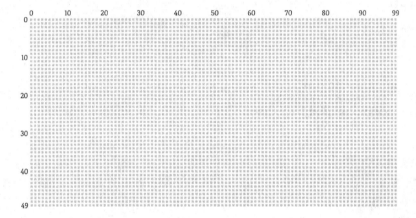

FIGURE 2.2 100x50 pixels window

FIGURE 2.3 How it really looks: Close-up of a 100x100 pixel window with some graphics

Computer people tend to re-invent the world. For historical reasons,[10] on computers, coordinates always start in the upper-left corner of the window/screen (Figure 2.3). Note that everything in computers is numbered starting from 0, and thus the pixels are numbered from 0 to 99 in the x-direction, and from 0 to 49 in the y-direction.

Exercise: Which kind of output do the following programs (Code 7) produce?[11]

Code 7

```
size(100, 100);

point(10, 10);
point(50, 10);
point(90, 10);
point(10, 50);
point(90, 50);
point(10, 90);
point(50, 90);
point(90, 90);
```

Code 8

```
size(100, 100);

point(50, 10);
point(30, 30);
point(70, 30);
point(10, 50);
point(90, 50);
point(30, 70);
point(70, 70);
point(50, 90);
```

Code 9

```
size(100, 100);

line(20, 20, 80, 20);
line(80, 20, 80, 80);
line(80, 80, 20, 80);
line(20, 80, 20, 20);
line(20, 20, 80, 80);
line(20, 80, 80, 20);
```

Code 10

```
size(100, 100);

line(25, 25, 25, 35);
line(75, 25, 75, 35);
line(25, 75, 75, 75);
line(25, 60, 25, 75);
line(75, 60, 75, 75);
```

Code 11

```
size(100, 100);

line(10, 50, 30, -10);
line(30, -10, 90, 10);
line(90, 10, 70, 70);
line(70, 70, 10, 50);
```

Code 12

```
size(100, 100);

ellipse(50, 50, 100, 100);
line(-100, 50, 200, 50);
rect(-10, -10, 120, 120);
point(-20, 50);
point(100, 100);
```

Code 13

```
size(100, 100);

line(10, 10, 90, 90);
line(10, 10, 10, 90);
line(10, 90, 90, 90);
point(50, 50);
point(10, 90);
ellipse(90, 10, 0, 0);
```

Here are the parameters of the graphical functions that were used in the above examples, plus two others: The quad and the Bézier curve.[12]

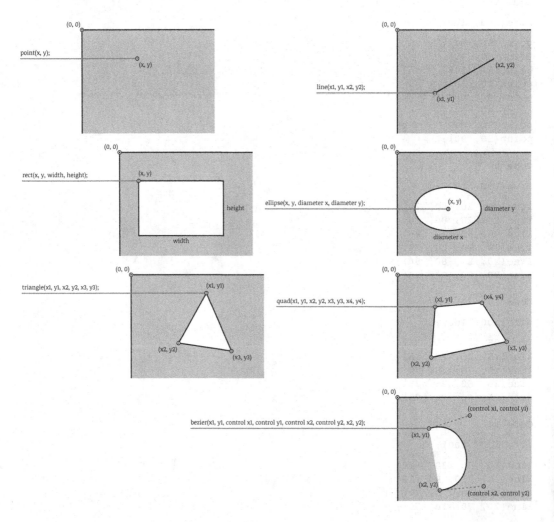

The ellipse, for instance, mixes as parameters: Coordinates and the size of it in pixels; it could even include a colour or a name – anything can be given as a parameter, there is no law against that (of course, one would need to write one's own function for that to work).[13]

Bézier curves are much used in drawing programs such as *Illustrator* and *Corel Draw* (Figure 2.4). Bézier curves are defined by anchor points and control points. Each anchor point has one (if it is an start/end point) or two control points associated with it. The curve goes through (or starts/ends at) the anchor points and curves towards the control points.

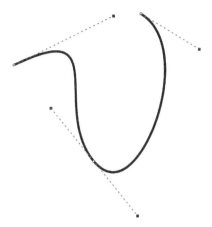

FIGURE 2.4 Bézier curve with control points in a typical (vector-based) drawing program

Processing's function draws a curve between two anchor points. It takes eight parameters:

```
bezier(x₁, y₁, control x₁, control y₁, control x₂, control y₂, x₂, y₂);*
```

The two anchor points are given first and last, with two control points in-between (Code 14–Code 15).

Code 14

```
bezier(40, 20, 20, 45, 20, 80, 70, 60);

stroke(160, 160, 160);
line(40, 20, 20, 45);
line(70, 60, 20, 80);
```

Code 15

```
bezier(80, 20, 20, 25, 80, 90, 20, 80);

stroke(160, 160, 160);
line(80, 20, 20, 25);
line(20, 80, 80, 90);
```

Use a (vector) drawing program to get a feel for Bézier curves – many popular, commercial programs use the same thing as *Processing*; also, try this interactive example (Code 16):

Code 16

```
void setup()
{
  size(200, 200);
}
void draw()
{
  background(12, 244, 22);
  bezier(40, 20, mouseX, mouseY, 10, 110, 160, 140);
  line(40, 20, mouseX, mouseY);
}
```

Drawing Order

Computers execute one command after the other, and this also applies to graphical output. As is visible in some of the examples above (for instance, in Code 1), on pixel displays, a shape that is drawn later occludes shapes drawn earlier. This is often very useful (e.g. it makes drawing a rainbow quite simple using circles, Code 2), but it can also be problematic (for instance, the last flower petal to be drawn occludes the first, so they do not look all the same (Figure 2.3).

When a graphical object is not visible, and one expects it to be, it may be because it is drawn outside the display window, it is obscured by another object or is too small (or big) or is drawn in an unexpected colour (for instance, it might have the same colour as the background or might be transparent).

Try it out:

Code 17

```
ellipse(50, 50, 40, 50);
rect(25, 55, 50, 25);
```

Code 18

```
ellipse(25, 50, 10, 10);
ellipse(75, 50, 10, 10);
rect(25, 40, 50, 20);
```

A Brief Look at Colours

If two things are certain, they are that the world is made up of pixels and nature defines colours as red/green/blue (RGB) values. Both observations are incorrect, of course and were not widely shared before everybody got a computer in the 1990s (and after).

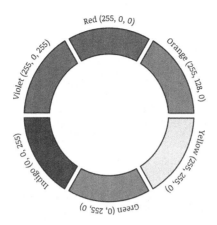

FIGURE 2.5 RGB colour codes

RGB is but one way to represent colour. It is not the only way, and also not the way to achieve the ideal alignment with the colours humans can see. But it is technically convenient and became the default model in screen-based computer graphics (as opposed to print). *Processing* uses by default the RGB model to define colours (alternatively, it can be switched to the HSB model[14]). A colour is given as a triplet of whole numbers, with each number going from 0 to 255; for example, maximum red is (255, 0, 0) – the red component of RGB is set to 255, green to 0, and blue to 0. For some other popular colours, see Figure 2.5.[15]

In the RGB colour model, black is (0, 0, 0), white is (255, 255, 255) and middle grey is (128, 128, 128). *Processing* offers a shortcut for grey values, and that is, to only use one value to describe a shade of grey (Code 19).

Code 19

```
noStroke();

fill(0);
rect(0, 0, 100, 20);

fill(64);
rect(20, 20, 80, 20);

fill(128);
rect(40, 40, 60, 20);

fill(192);
rect(60, 60, 40, 20);

fill(255);
rect(80, 80, 20, 20);
```

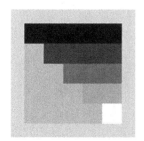

The stroke() function sets the colour for the contour lines, and the fill() function for the fill of the following shapes. The settings remain valid until a new setting occurs. The default values are white fill and black lines (Code 20).

Code 20

```
strokeWeight(5);
ellipse(25, 25, 25, 25);

stroke(64);
fill(192);
ellipse(75, 25, 25, 25);

stroke(192);
fill(128);
ellipse(25, 75, 25, 25);

stroke(128);
fill(64);
ellipse(75, 75, 25, 25);
```

Processing also offers transparency. Transparency is a quick and easy way to make graphics look like a million dollars. Transparency can be applied in the same way to fills and lines.

The transparency value is added as a forth (when colour is used) or second parameter (greys) to commands such as fill() and stroke(). 0 means transparent, and 255 means opaque (Code 21 and Code 22).

Code 21

```
noStroke();
background(255);

fill(255, 0, 0, 128);
rect(10, 10, 80, 20);

fill(0, 255, 0, 128);
rect(10, 70, 80, 20);

fill(0, 0, 255, 128);
rect(10, 10, 20, 80);

fill(255, 255, 0, 128);
rect(70, 10, 20, 80);
```

Code 22

```
noStroke();
background(255);

fill(0, 64);
triangle(10, 80, 10, 10, 80, 10);

fill(0, 128);
triangle(20, 10, 90, 10, 90, 80);

fill(0, 192);
triangle(90, 20, 90, 90, 20, 90);
```

Analogue to the stroke which is disabled with noStroke(), the fill can be disabled with noFill() (Code 23).

Code 23

```
noStroke();

fill(255, 0, 128);
ellipse(0, 50, 80, 80);

fill(0, 128, 255);
ellipse(100, 50, 80, 80);

fill(128, 0, 128);
ellipse(50, 0, 80, 80);

fill(0, 128, 0);
ellipse(50, 100, 80, 80);

strokeWeight(35);
stroke(0);
noFill();
ellipse(50, 50, 120, 120);
```

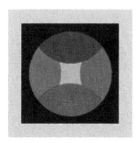

Solutions

Code 7: Points form a square box.

Code 8: Points form a Diamond.

Code 9: A square Box with an X.

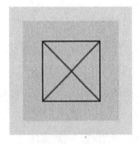

Code 10: A quite square smiley face.

Code 11: An angled square with one corner out of the window.

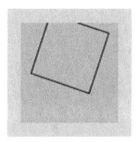

Code 12: Nothing, or rather, a white square. The rectangle covers everything. Without it, it is a circle with a horizontal line through it; the points are outside the window.

Code 13: A triangle; the points lie on its contour, the ellipse has a diameter of 0.

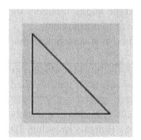

Chapter End Exercises

0. The Wagon and the Castle

   Write a program that produces a 320x200 pixel display window. Draw a black and white 2D view of a wagon (or of a castle) made from a few building blocks onto the screen (Figure 2.6). Use the graphical shapes *Processing* offers (for instance, `rect()`, `ellipse()` and `triangle()`).

1. The Sausage at the Beach

   Draw a sausage with mustard, a parasol on a beach, or a fruit with a mustache. Try out and use the functions `stroke()`, `fill()`, `strokeWeight()` and `background()`.

2. The Album Cover

   Draw your favorite music album cover. Use at least four different of *Processing*'s drawing functions (one of them `bezier()`). Do not invest too much time to make a super-accurate drawing, but experiment with different drawing functions.

FIGURE 2.6   A wagon made up of building blocks

3. The Radiator Mascot

Draw a sleek, futuristic, animal-shaped radiator mascot/hood ornament[16]. Use only Bézier curves.

4. An Interactive Background

Draw a window with a background that changes colour on mouse move.

Notes

1. I use the term command to refer to a function call such as `line(20, 70, 80, 20)` or `size(200, 100)` – the term function refers to the definition of a function, which we will see soon. When somebody asks, 'Where is that function?', he/she wants to know where the function is defined, not where it is invoked.

2. *Processing*'s Integrated Development Environment (IDE) looks like a text editor and is very basic (see the section 'The *Processing* IDE' in Chapter 23).

3. The line is drawn at the same spot if one simply swaps them.

4. For more info on functions, see Chapter 14.

5. It is possible that several functions have the same name if their parameters (type and/or number) are different; this is called overloading. For instance, `fill()` takes one, two, three or four arguments.

6. *Python* is a notable exception; in *Python*, line breaks instead of semicolons are used as statement terminators, and indention instead of brackets.

7. Many programming languages offer a similar structure. For instance, in *Arduino*, the function which runs once on program start is also called `setup()`, and the function that runs repeatedly after that is called `loop()`. The structure can, of course, also be created by the programmer.

8. The window size can only be set once and at the beginning of the program; it is also possible (but slightly more tricky) to have a resizable window, and *Processing* can also run in fullscreen. Roughly speaking, 2D (sprite-based) games typically have a fixed resolution which is scaled up to fullscreen (i.e. the larger the screen, the blockier the display); 3D (vector-based) games typically fully utilise the combined capabilities of the graphics card and screen (i.e. the larger the screen, the more detailed the display).

9. Assuming `strokeWidth` is 1.

10. Pixel screens start to draw the image at the top-left; and nobody knows why they do it like this. Probably because of the Western convention of writing left-to-right and top-to-bottom.

11. Solutions to in-text exercises are given at the end of the chapters.

12. *Processing* offers three more 2D primitive shapes: An arc, a polygon and another curve (see the *Processing* web site at www.processing.org for more info). Two additional graphical functions popped up in *Processing* 3.5 revision 266 (January 2019): A `circle()` and a `square()` function, both of which work as expected (no doubt, they were introduced for convenience; one can as easily use the `ellipse()` and `rect()` functions).

13. The `text()` function takes as arguments a text string and a window location in pixels (see Chapter 20).

14. More details on colour are in Chapter 19.

15. The reason the range of each component goes from 0 to 255 is that values up to 255 can be represented efficiently (i.e. without wasting space) internally as one byte (or 8 bits); a triple of 255 values each also gives a reasonable number of colours (28x28x28=256x256x256=16.777.216).

16. Demonstrate the principle, but do not invest too much time to make a super-accurate drawing.

3

Console Output and Comments

`print()` and `println()`

The `print()` and `println()` functions both output text to the console. Because it is often quite unclear what exactly happens when a program runs, the `print()` and `println()` functions are frequently used within programs to monitor ongoing processes ('if in doubt, print it out'), i.e. to:

- Confirm an event[1]
- Check data (e.g. display the contents of variables)[2]

The `print()` function outputs text given as an argument in quotation marks (see the example below); the `println()` function does the same and starts a new line (in this order).

Text is 'printed' (written) to the console, neither to the drawing window nor to an actual printer. The console is usually the command line. But few people use the command line anymore (actually, quite a few do). So the little black window below the code area in the *Processing* environment stands in as console[3]:

```
print("Hello Console");
```

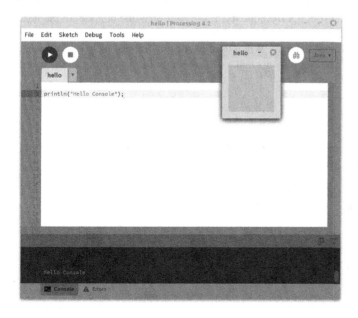

DOI: 10.1201/9781003345916-3

Note that the console is to be used (almost) exclusively for debug output. For communication with the user or player, the screen or window is to be used, because the console might not be, depending on the local setup, visible or attended to, and output to it is also very slow.

Comments

Comments are brief texts in a program that are not executed or even read by the computer.

One might wonder, why anybody would bother to write down stuff that is apparently ignored. There are at least six ways (or reasons) to use comments:

- As programme headers;
- To explain what is going on in a piece of code;
- As pseudo code;
- To temporarily disable parts of the code;
- To mark locations in the code that need work and
- As a resource when debugging.

Headers

This is an example of a Program header. The program header is the *first thing* in a program; all programs should have headers:

```
/*
Program Title: "My Own Private Little Elephant"
Program Description: Elephant with two trunks jumps across the screen
By Blue Spider, [date]
Comments: Would be nice if the elephant would turn around upon reaching the edge
*/
```

Explanation

Comments explain the idea behind code (but not the code itself, i.e. not every line of code) to the next (human) person reading it (who might be the person who wrote the code; it is surprising how completely one can forget what one wrote oneself not long ago). When used to recall what was or to explain what is (or should be) going on in a piece of code, comments make code more usable for editing and revision (and finding bugs).[4]

Pseudo Code

Comments can also be used to design and sketch out how a program should go about a task before one actually writes things out in code. For instance:

```
//Load the hiscore list from harddisk
//Display the top-10 entries
//Wait for fire button
```

Often, this technique improves the design because it lets one think about what one wants the program *to do*, rather than *how* to say it, or *what* to say; it makes the task appear manageable because it breaks down a problem into several small steps; and one can save work because one sees more clearly if things make sense.

Disabling Code

Another way to use comments is to temporarily disable stuff, i.e. *to comment something out*, e.g.

```
size(480, 240);
//noStroke();

background(0, 0, 0);

fill(255, 0, 0);
ellipse(240, 240, 480, 480);
```

or

```
/* size(480, 240);
noStroke();

background(0, 0, 0); */

fill(255, 0, 0);
ellipse(240, 240, 480, 480);
```

Marking Locations

During development comments are often used to mark places that need work, e.g.

```
background(12, 50, 220);  //TODO: Check if colour fits
```

Debugging

When a program behaves unexpectedly, reading the comments in the code, which describe what it should be doing, and comparing that with the actual code, what it is doing, might be helpful in finding bugs.

There are two types of comments in *Processing*. A single-line comment is denoted by two slashes (//), a multi-line comment is framed by /* and */.[5]

In a single-line comment, everything after the // to the end of the line is seen as a comment. The comment can start anywhere in a line.

This line demos a comment, but one that is not very interesting or necessary in real (programming) life:

```
size(200, 400);  //set the size of the display window to 200 by 400 pixels
```

In real life, things look more like this (Code 1; note that there is not really much to say in the program):

Code 1

```
/* Rainbox
 This programm draws a nice rainbow in a rectangular window
 Written by Rainbow Mouse
*/

size(480, 240);
noStroke();

background(0, 0, 0);

fill(255, 0, 0);  //red
ellipse(240, 240, 480, 480);

fill(255, 128, 0);  //orange
ellipse(240, 240, 400, 400);
```

```
fill(255, 255, 0);  //yellow
ellipse(240, 240, 320, 320);

fill(0, 255, 0);  //green
ellipse(240, 240, 240, 240);

fill(0, 0, 255);  //indigo
ellipse(240, 240, 160, 160);

fill(255, 0, 255);  //violet
ellipse(240, 240, 80, 80);
```

Comments should be used as part of good programming practice, but also, or probably mainly, because they are extremely useful.[6]

Chapter End Exercise

0. Printing to the Console

    Print some text to the console. Use *Processing*'s functions print() and println(). Demonstrate the difference between the two functions. Do you know what the console is?

Notes

1. For instance, with an *if* (see e.g. Code 1 in Chapter 6) or in a loop (Code 1 in Chapter 5).
2. See Code 5 in Chapter 4.
3. For more info on how to use the console, see the section, 'The *Processing* IDE' in Chapter 23.
4. Usually, adding comments to one's code is simply part of a job's contract, so other people can maintain and change the code.
5. /* */-style comments were introduced in *PL/I* (IBM 1964) and subsequently adopted in many other languages (Wikipedia 2017). //-comments might originate in *C++*.
6. See the section, 'Adaptability' in Chapter 24.

4

Variables and Data Types

Outline

- What are Variables?
- Data Types
- Issues with Variables
- Declaring and Assigning Variables

What Are Variables?

Variables play a fundamental role in programming. Usually, very few literal (e.g. numerical) values are found in code (as in the examples up to this point).

Variables:

- Are used to store data;
- Can be declared, then assigned, then used;
- Different values are passed through[1] and
- Are of a specific type, which is, depending on the programming language, assigned statically or dynamically; *Processing* uses static types (which is the standard for *C*-based languages).

Exercise: Which of the above is demonstrated in Code 1?

Code 1

```
size(200, 100);

int x = 10;
int y = 20;

line(x, y, 50, 60);
stroke(5);
point(x, y);
point(x + 5, y - 2);

x = x + 100;
y = 80;
point(x, y);
```

DOI: 10.1201/9781003345916-4

Magic Numbers

Code 2 draws lines from the same point (50, 60) outwards. If no variables would be used, the same numbers would have to be used several times. If the program was to change, all the numbers would need to be changed manually; with variables, the change is easy and fast.

Hard-coding values into a program is to be avoided. If there are still literal values used, they are known as Magic Numbers. A well-written program uses only a few or even none.

Code 2

```
int x = 50;
int y = 60;

line(x, y, 70, 20);
line(x, y, 60, 80);
line(x, y, 20, 70);
```

An interactive version of the above example is Code 3.

Code 3

```
void setup()
{ }

void draw()
{
  background(255);
  line(mouseX, mouseY, 70, 20);
  line(mouseX, mouseY, 60, 80);
  line(mouseX, mouseY, 20, 70);

  point(60, 10);
  point(85, 20);
}
```

Data Types

There are different kinds of variables, some hold numbers in different formats, some text, etc. These different kinds are called *data types*.

These are some of the most popular (primitive[2]) data types, roughly sorted by frequency of use:

Name: Integer
Data Type: int
Use: Holds a whole number (0, 12, 236, -5, etc.)

```
int level = 10;
```

Name: Floating point number
Data Type: float
Use: Holds a number with a decimal point (0, 0.12, 66.33, -11.45)

```
float scaleFactor = -1.2;
```

Name: Double precision number
Data Type: double
Use: Holds a large number with a decimal point (0, 7.4, -476503, 833.03765)[3]

```
double moneyExchangeRate = 17.7461593861;
```

The *Processing* data type `double` is imported from *Java*, and not used by any *Processing* functions. Variables of data type int, `float` and `double` may be positive, negative or zero.

Name: Boolean value
Data Type: boolean
Use: Holds either a true or false value

```
boolean jetPackCollected = true;
```

Name: String[4]
Data Type: String
Use: Holds a text

```
String welcomeMessage = "Hello";
```

Name: Character
Data Type: char
Use: Holds a single character (in ASCII code, see Chapter 26)

```
char upButton = 'w';
char myFavoriteLetter = 65;  //this is an 'A'
```

Name: Color
Data Type: color
Use: Holds four 8-bit values (red, green, blue, alpha/transparency)

```
color transGrey = color(42, 100);
color brightGreen = color(20, 222, 2);
```

Name: Byte
Data Type: byte
Use: Holds a whole number between –127 and 128 (0, 17, 86, -26, etc.)

```
byte monsterEnergy = 80;
```

TABLE 4.1

Popular Primitive Data Types in *Processing* Sorted by Size[10]

Data Type	Stored as	Value Range
boolean	1 bit	False or true
byte	8 bits	−128 to 127
char	16 bits	One character (e.g. letter, digit, symbol) in Unicode format[6]
int	32 bits	−2147483648 to 2147483647
float	32 bits	−3.40282347E+38 to 3.40282347E+38 (written in *scientific notation*, i.e. −3.40282347 x 10^{38} to 3.40282347 x 10^{38})[7]
color	32 bits	8 bits (256 values) of each red, green, blue and alpha
double	64 bits	−2.22507438585072014E+308 to 1.7976931348623157E+308 (i.e. 2.22507438585072014 × 10^{-308} to 1.7976931348623157 × 10^{308})[8]
long	64 bits	−9223372036854775808 to 9223372036854775807
String	[9]	Several characters

Name: Long

Data Type: long

Use: Holds a whole number with up to 19 digits (0, -9018949274, 863957385437, etc.)

```
long atoms = 74903857486;
```

Data types use different amounts of memory and can store different amounts of data.

One aims to use the appropriate data type for the job at hand, i.e.to go with the minimal (e.g. smallest and fastest) solution that uses the least resources (Table 4.1).[5] The data type should be able to store all the values that the variable needs to hold. For example, if the values to store are whole numbers between 0 and 3 (number of players, number of lives, number of weapons a player can carry, number of seasons) then a `byte` can be used, and an `int` would be unnecessary. If there are going to be only whole numbers one can use an `int`, and there is no need for a `float` (e.g. number of repetitions of a loop).

If a value is put into a variable that does not fit, *Processing* tells us (*C* wouldn't).

Why Data Types?

At first sight, data types might make little sense – why can't we use just one data type and put everything in it?[11] Can't the computer figure out which type something is? There are several reasons for having data types.

One reason is, the computer needs to know how a value is intended to be read and used. Which type is 65? The value means different things when used as an `int` (then it is a number) and a `char` (then it is a letter, an 'A'; Code 4). Operations (such as '+') are different when performed on different data types (on an `int` (addition) or on a `String` (concatenation)).

Code 4

```
int myInt = 65;
println(myInt);   //outputs 65

char myChar = 65;
println(myChar);   //outputs A
```

Another reason is performance; why use up memory (and potentially compromise running speed) for strings when one only stores bytes?[12]

A well-known saying among old-school computer people is: 'A well-typed program can't go wrong'. In other words, if the programmer makes sure that a program's values are well-behaved (i.e. they fit the type and the size of the variables) the risk of bugs is greatly reduced.

Issues with Variables

There are many instances of errors in programs (and some in games) caused by variables not being able to hold values as intended by the programmer.

In the original *Railroad Tycoon* (MicroProse, 1990) the player's money is held by an int.[13] If he/she gets into more than US$32 million in debt, the value swings around and becomes positive.

Famously, Gandhi is the most peaceful leader in *Civilization* (MicroProse, 1991), and he rarely attacks another civilisation. That is, until his civilisation adopts democracy and develops the atom bomb. This surprising change in behaviour is reportedly caused by a bug.

> 'Each leader in the game [has] an "aggression" rating, and Gandhi – to best reflect his real-world persona – [is] given the lowest score possible, a 1, so low that he'd rarely if ever go out of his way to declare war on someone.
>
> Only, there was a problem. When a player adopted democracy in Civilization, their aggression would be automatically reduced by 2. [...] if Gandhi went democratic his aggression wouldn't go to −1, it looped back around to the ludicrously high figure of 255[14], making him as aggressive as a civilization could possibly be'. (Plunkett 2014)[15,16]

Problems with data types are not a thing of the distant past. Recent games are not immune, either. In the process of increasing the HPs of a minion with *Divine Spirit* in *Hearthstone* (Blizzard, 2014), rounding errors happen (Hearthstone Science 2015). The source code of the game is, of course, unaccessible, but Hearthstone Science speculates that the issue could be caused by the conversion of the int value to float. This causes a loss of precision, because 'after 16,777,216 (or 2^{24}) [...] IEEE single precision floats can no longer hold integer values accurately beyond that point' (ibid.).[17]

Declaring and Assigning Variables

Variable declarations introduce the computer to a new variable. A declaration states the data type of the variable and the name of the variable:

```
int playerScore;
boolean active;
float speed;
```

A variable of type integer, one of type boolean and one of type float are declared. The variables are named playerScore, active and speed. No values are assigned yet.[18]

Values are assigned to variables that were declared before:

```
playerScore = 100;
active = true;
speed = 7.5;
```

Values in variables can be overwritten:

```
playerScore = 200;
playerScore = 80;
playerScore = 160;
```

The value of `playerScore` is now 160.
Often, one declares a variable and assigns a value in one step:

```
int a = 100;
boolean b = true;
float f = 7.5;
```

More than one variable of a type can be declared (no values are assigned):

```
int playerStartLives, playerCurrentLives, rounds;
```

It is also possible to declare multiple variables and assign values to them in one go:

```
int playerStartLives = 3, playerCurrentLives = 0, rounds = 12;
```

Declaring (and assigning) multiple variables in one line is rarely used.
Variables can be assigned values of other variables:

```
playerCurrentLives = playerStartLives;
```

Value of `playerCurrentLives` is now 3;

Naming Conventions

By convention, variables use lower-case names, similar to functions, such as `pos` and `speed`. When the name is made up of several words, the first letter of the second and following words is often capitalised (e.g. `rocketSpeed`, `directionBullet`).

Variables names should be meaningful (Figure 4.1). That is, they should relate to what the variable is used for. The variable to hold the horizontal player position in a *Space Invaders*-style game could be named:

- `x`
- `posX`
- `hor`
- `posHorizontal`
- `playerPosX`
- `playerPositionHorizontalX`

FIGURE 4.1   A well-chosen, expressive variable name

Of these, x and hor are probably saying too little, while the use of both x and horizontal in a variable name is redundant. Very long variable names are also unpopular because it takes time to type them in, and they get in the way of reading the code. I would use posX or playerPosX.[19]

Some people prefer to indicate the variable type in the variable name by prefixing the name with a single lower-case letter referring to its type:

```
int iPosX;
float fTemperature;
```

That way, one is always aware of what kind of variable one uses, and one might avoid or spot bugs. Reserved terms (such as int, if, String, null, width) must not be used as variable names.

Built-in Variables in *Processing*

Several keywords (i.e. system variables) are defined by *Processing* automatically and can be used right away, for instance, width and height:

```
println("The size of the drawing window is " + width + " by " + height +
" pixels");
```

Other interesting built-in variables are mouseX and mouseY (experiment with Code 5). They are updated automatically and reflect always the current state of the system.

Code 5

```
void setup()
{ }
void draw()
{
  println(mouseX);
}
```

Solution

Code 1: The example demonstrates that variables store data; that variables are declared, values are assigned and used; that variables hold different values (one after the other); and that variables are of specific types (here, only int is used).

Chapter End Exercises

0. Recycling Variables

   Demonstrate how to use and re-use variables: Declare three or four variables, assign values, and use the variables to draw an ellipse. Then assign new values to the same variables, and use them to draw a rectangle. Again, assign new values and draw two lines.

1. Drawing Triangles

   Draw a triangle in one screen location, using literal values (e.g. corner points 30/10, 50/50 and 10/50). Then add variables for an x and y offset to the literal values, so the triangle can be drawn at different screen locations by only changing the offset values.

2. Scaling with the Window

   Draw some shapes on the screen that scale with the window size (use *Processing*'s variables width and height). Run the program with different values in size() to test if it works.

Notes

1. That is, the variable holds one value at a time; if the value is overwritten, only the new value is accessible.
2. There are also other kinds of data types such as `Strings`, vectors, arrays, pointers and stacks; some of which also exist in *Processing*.
3. Accuracy is high but not infinite; try this:

```
double piInDouble = 3.141592653589793;
println("Genuine value: 3.141592653589793");
println("double:        " + piInDouble);    //output: 3.1415927410125732.
```

4. See the footnote in Table 4.1.
5. One is in trouble if one gets it wrong though; see the game examples in the section 'Issues with Variables' (in this chapter).
6. *Processing* uses UTF-8 (since release 0134).
7. In IEEE 754 representation, 4-byte floats are usually only precise to 6–9 digits [LearnCpp 2016]; try this: `float f = 0.3 + 0.6; println(f);` [Regan 2012] – output: 0.90000004. Or this: `float g=100 / 0.001` – output: 99999.99.
8. cs.fit.edu/~ryan/java/language/java-data.html (Sep 3, 2022)
9. The data type `String` (note the capitalisation) is actually a class, not a primitive data type. But for the moment we can use it as if it was one.
10. Data types may vary between different programming languages, and even between implementations of the same language (e.g. *C*).
11. There are languages which use dynamic (instead of static, as *Processing* and *C*, etc.) typing, e.g. *Javascript* and *Python*; that is, data types are determined depending on the contents of variables at run time.
12. One variable does not make much difference, but very often, computers store hundreds or thousands of variables.
13. A 2 byte (=16 bits) `int` can have 2^{16}=65536 different values. If the `int` is signed, the value range is from −32768 to 32767.
14. The aggressiveness of *Civilization*'s leaders is apparently stored in an unsigned `char` (size 1 byte or 8 bits, i.e. it can have 2^8=256 different values).
15. The existence of the bug is disputed. In his autobiography (Meier 2020), *Civilization*'s game designer Sid Meier rejects it, and claims the bug 'never happened at all' (qtd. in Maher 2020; cf. Viegas 2020). Meier explains that Gandhi's aggression rating remains constant throughout the game, and lies at a comparable level to other political figures (thanks to Max for pointing this out; see also Walker 2020). In several subsequent releases of the game, Gandhi was intentionally given a propensity for developing and using nuclear bombs, inspired by the popularity of the bug meme.
16. A similar glitch happened in *Overwatch* (Blizzard 2016), competitive season 2; Korean player IzA managed to lose 'hundreds of matches' and hit rank 0, at which point the game awarded him the maximum skill level 5000 (Grayson 2016). I believe it unlikely that this was caused by a similar programming oversight of data types, though.
17. Thanks to Thomas for bringing this to my attention.
18. Usually, programming languages do not assign initial default values when variables are declared. *Processing* might be so nice to indicate when a variable is about to be accessed without having been assigned a value, but many programming languages are not. Of course, one should only use a variable after having assigned it a value.
19. Usually, even a relatively simple game such as *Space Invaders* would use classes. Within a class Player, `posX` would be perfectly sufficient. If no classes are used, `playerPosX` might be more informative.

5

Iteration with the while *Loop*

Outline

- The *while* loop
- Nested Iteration

Up to now we had to type in everything the computer should do. If it should draw three circles we would type in the code for a circle three times. This is going to change with loops

Computers are good at repeating trivial operations very often and very fast with little variation. Many programs do, in fact, nothing else (e.g. an image filter may go through all the pixels in an image and apply a very similar operation to all of them). To have a program repeat something, a structure called a *loop* is used. What is repeated is done 'in the loop', and each run of the loop is called an 'iteration'. Loops are one of the most powerful structures used in programming, and are available in many (if not all) programming languages.

There are two main reasons why people like to use loops: Short code is not so much work to type in; and short code is easy to maintain, modify and debug.[1]

The idea of a loop is to repeat something until a condition is (no longer) met. For instance, the loop is increasing the value of a variable, and if that variable reaches a certain value, the loop exits; or a loop is running as long as nobody presses a mouse button. When a loop is done, program execution resumes.

The two most popular structures for repeating things are the *while* loop and the *for* loop.

The *while* Loop

The *while* loop[2] goes like this (demo'ed in Code 1 using console output[3]):

Code 1

```
int i = 0;
while (i < 10)
{
  println(i);
  i = i + 2;
}
```

Output:

```
0
2
4
6
8
```

DOI: 10.1201/9781003345916-5

Code 2 produces (simple) graphics with a *while* loop:

Code 2

```
int i = 10;

while (i < 80)
{
  line(20, i, 120, i);
  i = i + 10;
}
```

Let's assume we have written a long program with lots of repetitive code, such as the following. The program with 12 lines of code (Code 3) can be re-written in 5 lines using a *while* loop (Code 4):

Code 3

```
size(600, 100);

ellipse(50, 50, 25, 25);
ellipse(100, 50, 25, 25);
ellipse(150, 50, 25, 25);
ellipse(200, 50, 25, 25);
ellipse(250, 50, 25, 25);
ellipse(300, 50, 25, 25);
ellipse(350, 50, 25, 25);
ellipse(400, 50, 25, 25);
ellipse(450, 50, 25, 25);
ellipse(500, 50, 25, 25);
ellipse(550, 50, 25, 25);
```

Code 4

```
size(600, 100);

int i = 50;
while (i < 600)
{
  ellipse(i, 50, 25, 25);
  i = i + 50;
}
```

Now let's look at how *while* loops are made:

```
init⁴;
while (condition)
{
  statements;
  iterate⁵;
}
```

Another example of a while loop (Code 5); check how it matches the structure above:

Code 5
```
int i = 20;
while (i < 150)
{
  line(i, 20, i, 180);
  println("Drawn a vertical line at x position " + i);
  i = i + 10;
}
//rest of the program...
```

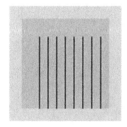

How does a *while* loop work? The test checks if a *condition* is met (we will see how this checking works in a minute). If the condition is true, everything between the curly braces { } is executed line by line. Then the condition is checked again, and so forth. When the condition is checked and found to be not or no longer true, the loop exits, that is, the program continues after the { } without running the statements inside.[6]

Exercise: Let's look at two more examples (Code 6 and Code 7).

Code 6
```
int i = 20;
while (i < 10)
{
  println("I wonder what happens");
  i = i + 10;
}
//rest of the program...
```

Code 7

```
int i = 10;

while (i < 200)
{
  println("i is now " + i);

  i = i + 1000;   //will this make the loop exit?
  i = i - 1000;   //only if the condition test sees it
  i = i + 10;
}

//rest of the program...
```

Nested Iteration

Having a loop iterate over one variable (as in Code 4 to Code 6) is fine. But what if we want to make a regular, two-dimensional pattern, such as a pattern of 10 by 10 dots? We can already formulate a loop that makes a horizontal line of dots (x goes from 10 to 90, the y position of each dot is 20) in Code 8.

Code 8

```
int x = 10;

while (x < 100)
{
  point(x, 20);
  x = x + 10;
}
```

And we can formulate a loop that makes a vertical line of dots (x is constantly 20):

Code 9

```
int y = 10;

while (y < 100)
{
  point(20, y);
  y = y + 10;
}
```

One can put these two loops in a single program one after the other and have it draw first a horizontal and then a vertical line of single dots. But when one *nests* the two loops within each other, one gets a two-dimensional pattern! Nested loops are executed from the inside out: The inner loop is fully run, then the outer loop; the inner loop runs, and so on (Code 10).

Code 10

```
int y = 10;
while (y < 100)
{
  int x = 10;
  while (x < 100)
  {
    point(x, y);
    x = x + 10;
  }
  y = y + 10;
}
```

One horizontal (dotted) line is drawn (in the inner structure). y is increased (in the outer structure). Then another dotted line is drawn… After 81 steps and dots (9 inner loops done 9 times), the program is finished.

Here are two other, more fancy examples. Fancy because they do not only draw the same shape all over the place, but they also change the size of the shape (Code 11f.) and its colour (Code 14; highlighted).

Code 11

```
background(100, 190, 220);

stroke(0);

int y = 10;
while (y < height)
{
  strokeWeight(y * 0.1);

  int x = 0;
  while (x < width)
  {
    point(x, y);
    x = x + 6;
  }
  y = y + 6;
}
```

Code 12

```
background(0, 180, 20);

int x = 0;
int y = 0;

while (y < height)
{
  x = 0;
  while (x < width)
  {
    strokeWeight(1 + (x * 0.1));
    point(x, y);
    x++;
  }
  y += 10;
}
```

Code 13 demos a one-dimensional (mono-chromatic) colour transition (from black to almost scanned grey).

Code 13

```
size(320, 240);
noStroke();

int posY = 0;
int step = 24;

while (posY < height)
{
  fill(posY);  //use vertical position also to set the colour (or shade of grey)
  rect(0, posY, width, step);
  posY += step;
}
```

In Code 14, both x and y values are used to set the colour of the points (with a call to the stroke() function), resulting in a two-dimensional colour gradient.

Code 14

```
size(256, 256);

int y = 0;
while (y < height)
{
  int x = 0;
  while (x < width)
  {
    stroke(x, y, 0);
    point(x, y);
    x = x + 1;
  }

  y = y + 1;
}
```

Solutions

Code 6: The loop never runs because the condition is never true.

Code 7: It runs normally, 19 times; adding 1000 to the variable and subtracting 100 from the variable in the loop has no effect.

Chapter End Exercises

0. Drawing with Loops

   Draw the same shape such as a square to the screen multiple times. The distances between the shapes should be identical (e.g. 10 pixels). Use a while loop.

1. The Movies

   Make a program that allows the user to enact a scene from a movie; for instance, to move a spaceship across a sparkling, starry background. Use a while loop to draw 100 stars at random positions. The documentation of the random() function can be found at processing.org/reference/random_.html (or see the section 'Randomness' in Chapter 12). Use the mouse pointer position as input for the spaceship position.

Notes

1. Of course, it is also true that it can be quite difficult to come up with a loop that does exactly what one wants, and modifying that loop for a slightly different application might be far from easy. But generally speaking, repeating (e.g. copying and pasting) any code in a program with only minute changes is to be avoided.

2. The *for* loop is introduced and compared to the *while* loop in Chapter 12.
3. One difference between the output in the console and output on the screen is that the console is only one-way; one cannot print anywhere on it, but only in-sequence, and one cannot access items already written. Screen output is malleable and can be changed and accessed at any point.
4. Optional; the *while* loop can also run until e.g. a mouse button is pressed. Then there is no initialisation and no iteration.
5. See the previous footnote.
6. In the example above we create (initialize) a new variable to be used with the loop. But the loop could also use an existing variable. Either way, after the loop exits, the variable i has a different value than before because it was modified.

6

Conditionals (if, if/else, if/else if)

Outline

- Conditionals
- Nested Conditionals

We have seen the while loop above, and repetition certainly is one of the things computers are good at; but they shouldn't simply do the exact same thing over and over, so here we look at how computers can make decisions

Conditionals

Conditionals are used when the program needs to make a decision about which lines of code to run.

Specific actions only take place when set out conditions are met:

if (condition) { statements }

One might say, an *if* statement such as the above is similar to a *while* loop, only the statements are executed only once.

Like variables (Chapter 4) and loops (Chapters 5 and 12), conditionals are another essential, very powerful structure in programming.

if Conditional Statements

The most popular conditional statement is the *if* statement (Code 1ff.).

The player's space ship is only drawn, if there are lives left (Code 1).

Code 1

```
int playerLives = 3;
if (playerLives > 0)
{
  rect(42, 80, 16, 10);
  triangle(50, 70, 60, 90, 40, 90);
}
```

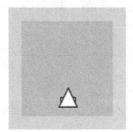

A slightly modified interactive version of Code 1 is shown in Code 2. Move the mouse pointer across the window to see the effect.

Code 2
```
void setup()
{ }
void draw()
{
  int playerLives = 3;

  background(0);
  stroke(0, 240, 0);
  fill(0, 180, 0);

  if (playerLives > 0)
  {
      triangle(mouseX, 70, (mouseX + 10), 90, (mouseX - 10), 90);
  }
}
```

A more mundane example that demonstrates the use of an *if* statement is Code 3.

Code 3
```
float temperature = 28.6;
if (temperature > 25)  //if temperature is greater than 25
{
    ellipse(50, 50, 36, 36);  //draw sun
}
```

Example Code 4 combines a *while* loop with an *if* statement to decide whether or not to draw lines. Note the double ==, which is a test of equivalence, in contrast to an assignment of a value which uses only a single = (e.g. int y = 10; compare the footnote in Table 7.1 in Chapter 7).

Code 4

```
int y = 10;
while (y < 90)
{
  line(10, y, 90, y);
  y = y + 3;
  if (y == 40) { y = y + 3; }  //do not draw a line at y == 40
}
```

Code 5 is more or less the same code, but this time changing the fill halfway through:

Code 5

```
int y = 0;
while (y < 100)
{
  rect(45, y, 10, 10);
  y = y + 20;
  if (y == 40) { fill(100, 190, 220); }
}
```

How to Stop Iteration in Mid-Air

Sometimes it is useful to stop a loop before it is finished, for instance, if a mouse button has been pressed, or something has been drawn. It is possible to break out of a loop using a condition check and the break command (Code 6).

Code 6

```
ellipse(50, 50, 15, 15);
strokeWeight(5);
```

```
while (true)   //this loop never stops by itself
{
  int x = int(random(100));   //get a random number 0 to 99¹
  point(x, 50);

  if (x == 50) { break; }       /* stop loop and continue outside
                                   if point has been drawn at 50, 50 */
}
//program execution continues here...
```

Code 6 demonstrates how to use `break`. But it is factually not necessary in this case. The same result can be achieved differently (and more elegantly; Code 7).

Code 7

```
strokeWeight(5);

int x = 0;
while (x != 50)        //run loop while no point has been drawn at 50, 50
{
  x = int(random(100));
  point(x, 50);
}
//program execution continues here…
```

if else Conditional Statements

One can not say what should happen if a condition is met, but also what should happen if not:

> if (condition) { statements }
> else { other statements }

If the condition is true, then the *if* clause is executed; otherwise, the *else* clause is executed.
One of the two possibilities will always happen; either one or the other (not both, and not neither).
Code 8 is revised from Code 4; instead of a simple *if* statement, an *if/else* statement is employed to decide which colour to use.

Code 8

```
int y = 10;

while (y < 90)
{
  if (y < 50) { stroke(0, 0, 240); }
  else { stroke(120, 170, 80); }

  line(10, y, 90, y);

  y = y + 3;
}
```

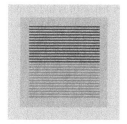

Note that Code 8 demonstrates the *if/else* statement, but otherwise, it is only a less elegant version of Code 5. The code is not as elegant, because, factually, there is only one colour change happening in the program, but the code sets and resets the colour unnecessarily every time a line is drawn.

In Code 9, the line colour is changed in a more interesting pattern. Lines are drawn in white shade if y can be divided by 4,[2] and in grey shade otherwise.

Code 9

```
background(0);
strokeWeight(2);
int y = 10;

while (y < 90)
{
  if (y % 4 == 0) { stroke(240, 220, 0); }
  else { stroke(20, 220, 10); }
  line(10, y, 90, y);
  y = y + 3;
}
```

A player's energy bar is drawn at the top of the window in Code 10.

Code 10

```
int playerEnergy = 80;
int positionX = 1;

while (positionX < playerEnergy)
{
  rect(positionX, 2, 7, 7);
  positionX = positionX + 10;
}
```

A more fancy version with an *if/else* statement is Code 11: The energy the player has (80) is indicated by (8) grey shaded rectangles, and the energy the player has lost, by dark shaded rectangles. The (few) changes from Code 10 are highlighted.

Code 11

```
int playerEnergy = 80;
int positionX = 1;

while (positionX < 100)
{
  if (positionX < playerEnergy) { fill(0, 140, 0); }
  else { fill(140, 0, 0); }

  rect(positionX, 2, 7, 7);

  positionX = positionX + 10;
}
```

else if Conditional Statements

It is also possible to check if one condition is true, and if it is not, to check if another condition is true.

    if (first condition) { statements }
    else if (second condition) { other statements }

If the first condition is true the *if* clause is executed, and program execution moves on. If the first condition is not true, the second condition is checked; if it is true, the *else if* clause is executed, and program execution moves on. If neither is true, nothing is executed, and program execution moves on.

An everyday example might be: *if* hungry, eat, *else if* tired, sleep. Either the *if* clause is executed, or the *else if* clause, or neither; so one can eat *or* sleep (but not both at the same time), or do nothing (Code 12).

Code 12

```
int lives = 1;  //try modify the number of lives
strokeWeight(3);
fill(255, 220, 0);

if (lives <= 0) {  //if no lives left
    ellipse(50, 50, 90, 90);
    line(20, 30, 40, 50);
    line(20, 50, 40, 30);
    line(60, 50, 80, 30);
    line(80, 50, 60, 30);
    line(20, 70, 80, 70);
}
```

```
else if (lives == 1 ) {   //if exactly one life left
    ellipse(50, 50, 90, 90);
    ellipse(30, 40, 20, 20);
    line(60, 50, 80, 30);
    line(80, 50, 60, 30);
    line(20, 70, 80, 70);
}
```

Exercise: What happens if `lives == 0`? What happens if `lives == 2`?

An *else* clause can also be added to an *else if* statement. For example: *if* hungry, eat, *else if* tired, sleep; *else*, go dancing. One (and only one) of the three things will then always happen.

Code 12 only displays the smiley face to signal the number of lives remaining, if there are 0 lives or 1 life left. Code 12 can be fitted with an *else* clause, as shown in Code 13, which is chosen if none of the other clauses are chosen (e.g. `lives = 5`):

Code 13

```
. . .
else {   //executes in any other case
    ellipse(50, 50, 90, 90);
    ellipse(30, 40, 20, 20);
    ellipse(70, 40, 20, 20);
    line(20, 70, 80, 70);
}
```

Revising the interactive example from above (Code 2), Code 14 demonstrates another *else if* statement.

Code 14

```
void setup()
{
  size(300, 200);
}
```

```
void draw()
{
  noStroke();
  fill(0);
  rect(0, 0, 100, 100);   //space
  fill(240, 240, 205);
  rect(100, 0, 100, 100);   //air
  fill(40, 80, 255);
  rect(200, 0, 100, 100);   //water
  strokeWeight(2);
  noFill();

  if (mouseX < 100)   //draw ufo
  {
      stroke(0, 220, 20);
      fill(0, 220, 20);
      ellipse(mouseX, 50, 24, 24);
      fill(0);
      quad(mouseX - 24, 50 - 6, mouseX - 24, 50 + 6, mouseX, 50 + 12, mouseX,
      50 - 12);
  }

  else if (mouseX < 200)   //draw plane
  {
      stroke(0);
      fill(0);
      ellipse(mouseX + 8, 50, 12, 12);
      fill(255);
      triangle(mouseX - 25, 50, mouseX + 25, 50, mouseX + 13, 50 + 10);
  }
  else   //draw submarine
  {
      stroke(120);
      rect(mouseX -25, 50 - 4, 50, 18, 12);
      fill(120);
      rect(mouseX - 9, 50 - 10, 12, 6);
  }
}
```

Exercise: What would happen, and why, if the *else if* statement looked like this?

```
if (mouseY < 200) { ... }  //draw ufo
else if (mouseY < 100) { ... }  //draw plane
else { ... }  //draw submarine
```

Nested Conditionals

if statements can be nested, one in the other. Both statements are independent, that is, each of them checks conditions independently, but of course, the inner (nested) *if* is only reached if the outer *if* is evaluated true.

Code 15 checks first if any mouse button is pressed; if it is, it uses a nested *if* to check if it is the left or the right mouse button.

Code 15

```
int x = 50;
void setup()
{ }
void draw()
{
  background(0);
  fill(255, 255, 0);
  if (mousePressed)   //³
  {
      if (mouseButton == LEFT)
      {
          x = x - 1;
      }
      else if (mouseButton == RIGHT)
      {
          x = x + 1;
      }
  }
  ellipse(x, 50, 20, 20);
}
```

Solutions

Code 12: What happens if `lives == 0`? What happens if `lives == 2`?

Nothing; both conditions are checked in turn (first the first one, then the second one), but neither is met if `lives` is either 2 or 3.

Code 14: What would happen, and why, if the *else if* statement looked like this?

Only the UFO or the submarine are drawn; never the plane; because all `mouseY` values less than 200 trigger the *if* statement and the ufo is drawn; the *else if* and the *else* statements are then not run (or even evaluated). Values greater than or equal to 200 trigger the *else* statement and the submarine is drawn, as in the original example.

Chapter End Exercises

0. Create an interactive program that draws an animal's face with open or closed eyes. Use *Processing*'s mousePressed variable to decide whether to draw the eyes open or closed.

1. Checking the Calendar

   Write a program that prints the current date to the console, formatted as, for instance, month day, year. *Processing* returns the current day of the month with the day() function, the current month with the month() function, and the current year with the year() function (see Chapter 21). In addition, the program checks for several conditions and prints out appropriate messages to the console if they apply (with if) and if they do not apply (with else): Is it getting close to Christmas (i.e. is it December)? Is it Autumn (i.e. in the Northern Hemisphere, is it September, October or November)? Is it the first half of the month? Is it the first of May? Is it your birthday?

2. The Week in Code

   Use a loop to draw seven rectangles to the screen, to represent the days of the week, and use an if clause to colour one of them red to indicate Sunday. Potential extra feature: Use the text() function to number or label the rectangles.[4]

3. Here's for the Weekend

   Modify the code of the previous exercise to also indicate Saturday with a (different) colour. Potential extra feature: Draw a calendar sheet for a whole month with colour codings for Saturday and Sunday.

Notes

1. Note that the order of the arguments is important for random():

```
println(random(0, 100));
println(random(-100, 100));
println(random(0, -100) + " Unexpected result, it is always 0.0");
println(random(-100, 0));
println(random(-10, -100) + " Unexpected result, it is always -10.0");
println(random(-100, -10));
```

   This (unexpected) behaviour is either a bug or a feature; it is consistent across various versions of *Processing* (it can be observed at least in versions 1.5.1, 3.5.4, 4.0b1, 4.0.1 and 4.2).

2. The modulo operator (%) calculates the remainder of a division; e.g. 10% 4 == 2 (10 / 4 is 2, remainder 2); 12% 4 == 0 (12 / 4 is 3, remainder 0).

3. This generates user input to demo a nested conditional, but is no ideal way to integrate mouse input into programs (as a general rule, an event-based paradigm is to be preferred, using the mousePressed() function rather than the mousePressed variable). More on this soon.

4. The documentation of the text() function can be found at processing.org/reference/text_.html (or see Chapter 20).

7

Relational Expressions (e.g. <, >) and Logical Operators (e.g. &&, ||)

Relational Expressions

Relational expressions describe how one value compares to another. Relational expressions are used in the condition check of e.g. *while* loops and *if* statements (see the examples above, e.g. Code 11 in Chapter 6).

There are three or four different kinds of relational expressions and some combinations. Two values can be equal to each other, they can be different from each other, or one value is greater (or less) than the other (Table 7.1). Note that some comparisons only make sense with certain data types such as numbers.

Which of the following statements (in Code 1) are true?

Code 1

```
if (5 == 10) { print("5 is equal to 10"); }
if (5 != 10) { print("5 is unequal to 10"); }
if (5 > 10) { print("5 is greater than 10"); }
if (5 < 10) { print("5 is less than 10"); }
if (5 >= 10) { print("5 is greater than or equal to 10"); }
if (5 <= 10) { print("5 is less than or equal to 10"); }
```

Logical Operators

In structures such as *while* loops and *if* statements, more than one relational expression can be combined by using *logical operators* (Code 2ff).

DOI: 10.1201/9781003345916-7

TABLE 7.1

Relational Expressions

Operator	Meaning
==	Equal[1]
!=	Unequal
>	Greater than
<	Less than
>=	Greater than or equal
<=	Less than or equal

Code 2

```
if ((width > 100) && (height > 100))
{
    println("Window is larger than default size");
}
```

Code 3

```
if ((width > 100) || (height > 100))
{
    println("Either window width or height is (or both are) larger than
    default size");
}
```

Code 4

```
boolean rocketBoost = false;
if (!rocketBoost)  //[2]
{
    println("Rocket is off");
}
```

There are three logical operators: AND (&&), OR (||) and NOT (!) (Table 7.2).

For the logical operator AND to be true, each part of the expression must be true; the first part which is not true makes the whole expression false (Code 2).

For the operator OR to be true, only one part of the expression must be true (they can also all be true, it is not an exclusive OR (which is called XOR); Code 3).

NOT negates something into the opposite (Code 4).

TABLE 7.2

Logical Operators

Operator	Meaning
&&	AND
||	OR
!	NOT

Which of the following statements (in Code 5) are true?

Code 5

```
if ((true) && (true)) { print ("true AND true"); }
if ((true) && (false)) { print ("true AND false"); }
if ((false) && (false)) { print ("false AND false"); }

if ((true) || (true)) { print ("true OR true"); }
if ((true) || (false)) { print ("true OR false"); }
if ((false) || (false)) { print ("false OR false"); }

if (true) { print ("true"); }
if (!true) { print ("NOT true"); }
```

AND (&&) and OR (||)

Several conditions can be connected with the logical operators AND (in code: &&) and OR (||).

Code 15 (in Chapter 6) used a nested *if* to check if the left or the right mouse button is pressed; now the code can rewritten with the logical AND operator (Code 6) – resulting in the same interactive behaviour.[3]

Code 6

```
int x = 50;
void setup()
{ }

void draw()
{
  background(0);
  fill(255, 255, 0);
  if ((mousePressed) && (mouseButton == LEFT))
  {
      x = x - 1;
  }
  else if ((mousePressed) && (mouseButton == RIGHT))
  {
      x = x + 1;
  }
  ellipse(x, 50, 20, 20);
}
```

Code 2 in Chapter 5 shows how two *while* loops can be nested (i.e. put into each other). Drawing little circles instead of dots, and using the *AND* and the *OR* logical operators, one can draw the Danish flag, from top to bottom (Code 7, the lines that do the colouring are highlighted).

Code 7

```
int y = 25;
while (y < 80)
{
  int x = 15;
  while (x < 90)
  {
    if ((y >= 40) && (y <= 60))  //white middle part
    {
        fill(255);  //white
    }
    else  //red-white-red top and bottom parts
    {
        if ((x < 30) || (x > 50))
        {
            fill(255, 0, 0);  //red
        }
        else
        {
            fill(255);  //white
        }
    }
    ellipse(x, y, 8, 8);
    x = x + 10;
  }
  y = y + 10;
}
```

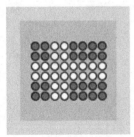

Code 8 shows a different version of the Danish flag. Again, the conditionals using logical operators *AND* and *OR* are highlighted in colour. Note that there are many Magic Numbers in the code, that should be exchanged for variables (e.g. the size of the squares).

Other Scandinavian flags can be drawn with only small changes to either Code 7 or Code 8.[4]

Code 8

```
size(400, 280);
noStroke();
background(255);

int y = 0;
while (y < height)
{
  int x = 0;
  while (x < width)
  {
    if ((y >= 110) && (y < 170))  //'row' of the cross
```

```
    {
        fill(255);   //white
    }
    else
    {
        if ((x < 90) || (x >= 150))   //'column' of the cross
        {
            fill(255, 0, 0);   //red
        }
        else
        {
            fill(255);   //white
        }
    }
    rect(x, y, 5, 5);
    x = x + 10;
  }
  y = y + 10;
}
```

How can Code 8 be changed to draw the Swedish flag? How can the code be changed to draw thicker lines (i.e. a thicker cross)?

For the following three (non-functional) example code snippets (Code 9ff.) assume that there is a 2D shooting game with a space ship (Figure 7.1). This is how code can look in real life.

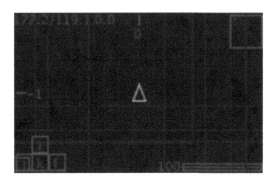

FIGURE 7.1   Action game screenshot

Code 9

```
//checks if the bullet is outside the window; if it is, it is removed (using
a custom-made function, however that works internally)
if ((fBulletX<0) || (fBulletY<0) || (fBulletX>width) || (fBulletY>height))
{ vRemove(); }
```

Code 10

```
//checks if a point (bullet) is inside a rectangular box
if ((fBulletX<fBoxTopLeftX) || (fBulletX>(fBoxTopLeftX+iBoxSizeX)) ||
    (fBulletY<fBoxTopLeftY) || (fBulletY>(fBoxTopLeftY+iBoxSizeY)))
{ ellipse(fBulletX, fBulletY, 3, 3); }
else
{ point(fBulletX, fBulletY); }
```

Code 11

```
//draws the bullet in different colour, depending on (rough) distance from
ship
if ((abs(fShipX-fBulletX)<100) && (abs(fShipY-fBulletY)<100))
{ fill(200, 100, 50); }
else
{ noFill(); }
ellipse(fBulletX, fBulletY, 3, 3);
```

NOT (!)

The *NOT* (!) logical operator inverts a condition.

Code 12 is a bit of a scary example using the *NOT* operator (highlighted); try it out and click with the mouse pointer inside the window:

Code 12

```
void setup()
{ }
void draw()
{
  background(0, 0, 0);
  if (!(mousePressed == true))
  {
      noStroke();
      fill(245, 205, 0);
      ellipse(25, 35, 20, 20);
      ellipse(75, 35, 20, 20);
      fill(0);
      ellipse(25, 33, 6, 14);
      ellipse(75, 33, 6, 14);
      stroke(255, 210);
      strokeWeight(6);
      line(20, 28, 20, 32);
      strokeWeight(10);
      stroke(0);
      line(10, 21, 40, 31);
      line(60, 31, 90, 22);
  }
}
```

Of course, one could also formulate the *if* statement without using the NOT operator – how?

The *NOT* operator does not look too useful, but it is needed as part of boolean logic, and sometimes it just makes more sense to ask for the opposite of something.

Solutions

Code 1: Which of the following statements are true?

```
if (5 != 10) { print("5 is unequal to 10"); }
if (5 < 10) { print("5 is less than 10"); }
if (5 <= 10) { print("5 is less than or equal to 10"); }
```

Code 5: Which of the following statements are true?

```
if ((true) && (true)) { print("true AND true"); }
if ((true) || (true)) { print("true OR true"); }
if ((true) || (false)) { print("true OR false"); }
if (true) { print("true"); }
```

Code 8: How can the code be changed to draw the Swedish flag? How can the code be changed to draw thicker lines (i.e. a thicker cross)?

```
size(400, 280);
noStroke();
background(255);

int y = 0;
while (y < height)
{
  int x = 0;
  while (x < width)
  {
    if ((y >= 80) && (y <= 200))  //'row' of the cross
    {
        fill(255, 255, 0);  //yellow
    }
    else
    {
        if ((x < 60) || (x > 180))  //'column' of the cross
        {
            fill(0, 0, 255);  //blue
        }
        else
        {
            fill(255, 255, 0);  //yellow
        }
    }
```

```
      rect(x, y, 5, 5);
      x = x + 10;
  }
  y = y + 10;
}
```

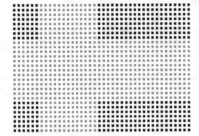

Code 12: Formulating the *if* statement without using the NOT operator:

```
void setup()
{ }
void draw()
{
  background(0, 0, 0);

  if (mousePressed == false)
  {
      noStroke();
      fill(245, 205, 0);
      ellipse(25, 35, 20, 20);
      ellipse(75, 35, 20, 20);
      fill(0);
      ellipse(25, 33, 6, 14);
      ellipse(75, 33, 6, 14);
      stroke(255, 210);
      strokeWeight(6);
      line(20, 28, 20, 32);
      strokeWeight(10);
      stroke(0);
      line(10, 21, 40, 31);
      line(60, 31, 90, 22);
  }
}
```

Notes

1. `==` ('is equivalent to') is different to `=` which assigns a value to a variable. This is a rather common cause of bugs!
2. Some alternative ways to say the same thing are: `if (rocketBoost == false)` and `if (!(rocketBoost == true))` and even `if (rocketBoost == !true)` and `if (rocketBoost != true)`.
3. The balance between nested conditionals and the use of logical operators in a code is often pragmatic. One might be more intuitive or clear to see, or one yields shorter code than the other.
4. Also, one can aspire to remove the Magic Numbers from the codes that make them hard to adapt.

8

Math and Arithmetic

Math and Graphics

Computers can calculate. While it is possible to let the computer add two numbers such as 27 and 41 in a program, it is not very exciting. But for numerous applications, some math is needed, and a prominent one is graphics. Computer graphics is heavily based on math, so let us experiment with some (simple) graphics (Code 1)!

Code 1

```
int x = 10;
int y = 20;

rect(x, y, 60, 40);
rect(x + 20, y + 10, 60, 40);
```

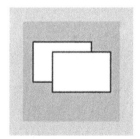

Code 1 (above) draws two rectangles, one is located (i.e. its top-left corner) at position (10, 20), the other is located at (30, 30), i.e. 20 pixels to the right, and 10 pixels down from the first one. To achieve this displacement, addition is used.

Code 2 (below) draws three rectangles, again at slightly different positions, but this time with fillings that go from almost opaque for the dark rectangle to quite transparent for the light shaded one. This change of transparency is done using division.

DOI: 10.1201/9781003345916-8

Code 2

```
int x = 10;
int y = 20;
int opacity = 255;

fill(20, 140, 255, opacity);
rect(x, y, 60, 40);

fill(20, 255, 140, opacity / 2);
rect(x + 10, y + 10, 60, 40);

fill(255, 255, 140, opacity / 4);
rect(x + 20, y + 20, 60, 40);
```

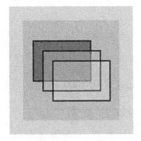

In the examples above (Code 1 and Code 2), the values of the variables were not changed. Throughout the programs, x and y (and `opacity` in Code 2) kept the values they were assigned right at the start. But, we know that variables can be assigned new values at any time. Code 3 demonstrates this.

Code 3

```
int x = 10;
int y = 5;

rect(x, y, 20, 40);

x = 40;
rect(x, y, 20, 40);

x = 70;
y = 50;
rect(x, y, 20, 40);
```

The top-left rectangle is drawn first at position (10, 5), then the middle one is drawn at (40, 5), then the bottom-right one, at (70, 50). x and y were changed; x twice (from 10 to 40, and then to 70), y once (from 5 to 50).

The next example (Code 4) shows how the result of a calculation can be put into a variable. The right side of the = is evaluated first, then the result is put into the variable on the left.

Code 4

```
int x = 20;
int y = 10;

rect(x, y, 20, 40);

x = x + 10;
y = y + 20;
rect(x, y, 20, 40);

x = x + 10;
y = y + 20;
rect(x, y, 20, 40);
```

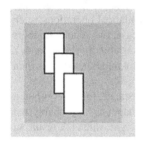

All kinds of calculations can be done, the most popular being, presumably, addition (+), subtraction (-), multiplication (*) and division (/). All four are demonstrated in Code 5.

Code 5

```
int x = 5;
int y = 10;
int red = 255;

fill(red, 128, 24);
rect(x, y, 20, 80);

x = x * 8;
red = red - 120;
fill(red, 128, 124);
rect(x, y, 20, 80);

x = x + 35;
red = red / 2;
fill(red, 128, 24);
rect(x, y, 20, 80);
```

Data Types, Variables and Assignments

When using variables, it is essential to match the container and content. This is relevant in two ways: Things need to be formally correct (i.e. syntactically) and to make sense in an application (i.e. semantically).

For the computer, variables as well as literal values have types. The type is obvious in the case of variables; the declaration clearly states which type a variable is (and variables never change their type). But literal values also have data types; whole numbers such as 3 and 4 are interpreted by *Processing* as integers, numbers such as 3.0 and 4.0 as floats.[1]

Formally, the computer checks[2] if the types of both sides of the assignment operator (=) match each other. This is often obvious when assigning literal values. Int values are assigned to int variables (e.g. int a = 5), floats to float variables (float b = 10.0), etc. It is also possible to put int values into float variables (float c = 5). It becomes less obvious when using mathematical operations, such as int x = 10 + 90 (ok) and int y = 100 * 0.1 (problem). In the first case, two whole numbers are added, resulting in another whole number, and this is put into an integer variable; in the second, a whole number is multiplied by a floating point number, resulting in a floating point number, which is then attempted to put into an integer variable, which does not work.[3]

A second issue is that the values saved must make sense in the program. For instance, for the computer, an assignment such as float e = 10/3 is perfectly fine. But what actually happens, is probably not what the programmer meant to happen: An int value (10) is divided by another int value (3), resulting in another int value (3, *not* 3.333...) which is put into a float variable (Code 6).

Code 6

```
float e = 10 / 3;
println(e);
```

Output:

```
3.0
```

This happens because literal values such as 10 and 3 also have types (both of them int, in this case). *Processing* attempts to preserve accuracy; combining two int values results in another int (Code 6); combining one int and one float value results in a float (Code 7); combining two float values results in another float (Code 8).

Code 7

```
float f = 10 / 3.0;
println(f);
```

Output:

```
3.3333333
```

Code 8

```
float g = 10.0/3.0;
println(g);
```

Output:

```
3.3333333
```

Note that the examples above are somewhat artificial. In an actual program, one is more likely to see something like this:

```
int a = 5;
float b = 4;
//more program code...
int c = a / b;
```

Generally speaking, beware of very small and very large numbers in programs. If the variables are pushed to their limits, inaccuracies through rounding or errors through exceeding the data types' value ranges may occur. For instance, when doing several subsequent multiplications and divisions, do not first do all the multiplications, and then all the divisions – this could lead to a very large number that is rounded heavily and may even exceed the value range of the variable. It is usually better to balance values somewhere around 0 where there are no or few accuracy issues.

Another strategy is, when handling, for instance, very small numbers such as 0.000005, not to store this number, but to store 5 in an integer and multiply it by 10^{-5} when used.

A special case is 0: Division by zero usually causes a program to crash. In *Processing*, the result is Infinity when floats are used (Code 9; but still something that will likely cause a program to behave erratically or to fail, when a number was expected), and a crash when ints are used (Code 10). Because the program is syntactically correct, and the values are only present at run time, the issue cannot be detected by *Processing* in advance. This can also happen when users enter data of an unexpected type into a program, for instance, letters instead of digits into a dialog box.

Code 9

```
float s = 100;
float t = 0;
float error = s / t;   //this results in 'Infinity'
println(error);
```

Output:

```
Infinity
```

Code 10

```
int s = 100;
int t = 0;
int error = s / t;   //this throws an ArithmeticException: / by zero
println(error);
```

Output:

```
- (none)
```

Multiplication by 0 is no problem. The result is 0, of course.
Division by a very small number results in an often unexpectedly large number (Code 11).

Code 11

```
float u = 100 / 0.01;
point(u, 50);
println(u);
```

Output:

```
10000.0
```

When using ints, very small values might be turned into 0, and graphics might not be visible on screen. A number of mathematical functions (such as `sin()`) return values (`floats`) that are mostly less than 1 (-1 to 1 in the case of `sin()`). These are usually scaled up when used to draw something onto the screen.

Order of Operations

Occasionally, programming overlaps with school or real-life math. But often it does not, and one cannot depend on it. *Processing*, for instance, similar to many other modern languages, honours the multiplication-before-addition convention from math ($2 + 6 * 3 = 2 + 18 = 20$ and not `2 + 6 * 3 = 8 * 3 = 24`), but other programming languages or implementations (e.g. *C*) might not. Always use parentheses, if only to make things easy to read: `2 + (6 * 3) = 2 + 18 = 20` or `(2 + 6) * 3 = 8 * 3 = 24`.

Notes

1. Different languages have different conventions; for instance, in *C#*, a literal float value is written as `3.0f`, a double as `4.0d`.
2. A compiler translates the somewhat human-readable program code into machine-readable gibberish that can be executed by the computer.
3. Although 100*0.1 is, in fact, 10, and would fit an `int` variable fine.

9

Short Cuts

Since some expressions in programming are rather common and often repeated, certain shortcuts, sometimes referred to as 'syntactic sugar', are often used. For example, to add 1 to a variable x, instead of the long x = x + 1, one can write x++.[1] A similar shortcut also works for subtraction (Code 1).

Code 1

```
int x = 10;
println(x);
x++;  //instead of x = x + 1;
println(x);

int y = 10;
println(y);
y--;  //instead of y = y - 1;
println(y);
```

Output:

```
10
11
10
9
```

Instead of writing x = x + 10 one can write x += 10; in the same way, subtraction, multiplication and division can be written (Code 2).

Code 2

```
int x = 10;
println(x);
x += 5;  //instead of x = x + 5;
println(x);

int y = 10;
println(y);
y -= 5;  //instead of y = y - 5;
println(y);

int a = 5;
println(a);
a *= 10;  //instead of a = a * 10;
println(a);

int b = 100;
println(b);
b /= 5;  //instead of b = b / 5;
println(b);
```

DOI: 10.1201/9781003345916-9

Output:

```
10
15

10
5

5
50

100
20
```

In most situations, the expressions x += 1 and x++ are equivalent. But to be accurate, there is a difference between suffix (i++) and prefix (++i) operators. In println(i++), the expression is first evaluated (i.e. i is printed), then the value is changed, i.e. for the following statements (Code 3); in println(++i), the value is first changed, then the expression is evaluated (i is incremented by one and then printed; (Code 4). In real (programming) life, ++i is hardly ever used.

Code 3

```
int i = 10;
println(i++);
```

Output:

```
10
```

Code 4

```
int i = 10;
println(++i);
```

Output:

```
11
```

Numbers can be negated using minus (−; Code 5).

Code 5

```
int r = 5;
r =- r;
println(r);
```

Output:

```
-5
```

Note

1. Now it is also obvious how *C++* got its name.

10

Type Conversions (Casting and Rounding)

Outline

- Type Casting
- Rounding

*In an ideal (programming) world, type
conversions are not necessary, because
programs are written so well that they
are not needed - but seriously, avoid
them when possible*

There are a number of reasons to convert variables or values from one data type to another. One reason is that variables of a certain type have been defined in a program and one wants to use them to save values (and not to change their data type); another reason is that functions (such as the random() function; see the section 'Randomness' in Chapter 12) return values of a certain type (in this case a float), but one might want to use the return value as a different type (e.g. an int to access a value in an array, see Chapter 13). A third reason is function arguments; a function such as size() only accepts (two) ints and one has to supply them.[1,2]

Type conversions may introduce a loss of accuracy because a value that is limited by one data type is put into another data type and limited by that; the result is a value limited by both types. Usually, a well-written program, in which the variable types align with the values to be stored, does not require many type conversions.

There are at least two ways to convert a variable from one type to another. One can simply *type cast* it or employ more involved strategies such as rounding.

Type Casting

Type casting is changing the data type of a value or variable temporarily; it is fast and usually involves a loss of accuracy. For instance, type casting a float value into an int simply truncates everything after the decimal point. But sometimes, rough casts are just what is needed (e.g. for debug output).

Two popular ways of type casting are the *C-style cast* and the *functional cast*. Both perform the same service.

The *C*-style type cast looks like this:

(desired data type)value

In code:

```
float myFloat = 17.78;
int a = (int)myFloat;
```

The functional type cast looks like a function call (the desired data type is the function name, the value to be cast the argument):

  desired data type(value)

That is in code:

```
float myFloat = 17.78;
int a = int(myFloat);
```

Note that in both cases the variable `myFloat` is still a `float` (variables never change their data type after being declared), and still contains the value `17.78`. The type cast only truncates the value `17.78` at the decimal point to turn it into an `int` value that can be assigned to an `int` variable.

In principle, all data types can be typed (`int`, `float`, `String`, `boolean`, etc.), but *Processing* might not be equally happy with the results (e.g. it does not know how to cast from `String` to `int`) and not all castings are very useful (e.g. from `long` to `int`).

Often, one needs an `int` but has a `float`. Sometimes that is fine; but often (though not always[3]), one wants to preserve as much accuracy as possible[4].

Rounding

A conversion strategy that attempts to preserve as much accuracy as possible (depending on conventions employed) is rounding. But rounding takes time and should of course be avoided when not required.

Processing has a rounding function that implements the usual mathematical rounding convention (up from .5, down otherwise); it accepts one `float` as argument and returns an `int` (Code 1)[5].

Code 1

```
float f = 10.5;
int i = round(f);
println(i);

f = 10.4;
i = round(f);
println(i);

i = round(10.237);
println(i);
```

  Output:

```
11

10

10
```

Notes

1. The `line()` and `rect()` etc. functions actually do accept floats, although it does not make much sense to draw a point at ⟨7.4, 10.8⟩. Recent *Processing* versions such as 4.2 appear to simply cast values into ints, while earlier versions such as 1.5.1 round them in some undocumented way (up from .75, it seems, for `rect()`).
2. Another reason might be to save memory or harddisk space, or network bandwidth.

3. For example, the seconds of a digital stopwatch should only switch from 0 to 1 when the milliseconds pass 1000; not when they pass 500. A random number between 0 and the screen width (e.g. 100) should be cast, not rounded, to get a coordinate within the window (e.g. `0` to `99`).

4. Usually, for instance, rounding the coordinates to `ints` is the last thing done before something is displayed on screen.

5. In Code 1, one can also see an example of a function that *returns a value*, which happens quite often, in fact. In a game, functions might return values such as the current level, the player's score and the top score in the highscore list.

11

Formatting Code

To make code as human-readable as possible, conventions have been established to facilitate a consistent format. Three aspects are usually meant when talking about the formatting of source code: *Spacing* (`fill(255, _ 0, _ 0)`; `if _ (...)`), use of *parenthesis* (`( )`) and placement of *braces* (`{ }`), and *indention* (by tab or spaces).

Code 1 shows one standard format; the *Processing* IDE applies it, if one lets it auto format one's code[1]:

Code 1

```
int value = 20;

if (value > 50) {
    fill(255, 0, 0);
    rect(20, 20, 60, 60);
}
else {
    fill(255);
    ellipse(50, 50, 60, 60);
}
```

Code 2 shows an alternative way to format one's code, using a slightly more relaxed spacing (with opening braces on new lines).

Code 2

```
int value = 20;

if (value > 50)
{
    fill(255, 0, 0);
    rect(20, 20, 60, 60);
}
else
{
    fill(255);
    ellipse(50, 50, 60, 60);
}
```

Another alternative, a more compressed format is shown in Code 3.

Code 3

```
int x=50;
if (x>100) { line(20, 20, 80, 80); }
else { line(20, 80, 80, 20); }
```

And that's it. These are the options for how to format code.[2]

DOI: 10.1201/9781003345916-11

Notes

1. The default *Processing* IDE offers an 'Auto Format' function in the 'Edit' menu, one can use to clean up the messy formatting of code automatically (`Apple-T` or `Ctrl-T`).
2. Companies often have specific house rules, how they want their code formatted, see the section, 'Coding Rules in Professional Life' in Chapter 24.

12

Iteration with the for *Loop*

The *for* Loop

We saw and used an example of a loop already: The *while* loop. Now let's compare it to another very popular loop, the *for* loop. We compare them using a bunch of examples with points and lines.

The *for* loop is probably the second-most popular loop in programming. It repeats something a specific number of times.

Let's look at how a *while* loop draws a column of dots on the screen, and then how a *for* loop does the same thing. The *while* loop is shown in Code 1.

Code 1

```
int i = 0;
while (i < 100)
{
  point(10, i);
  i += 10;
}
```

An equivalent *for* loop is shown in Code 2.

Code 2

```
for (int i = 0; i < 100; i += 10)
{
  point(10, i);
}
```

The two loops are equivalent in function and similar in syntax; and, surprisingly enough, the programs produce identical graphics.

DOI: 10.1201/9781003345916-12

It turns out that the computer actually only knows one type of loop. All *while* loops can be formulated as *for* loops and *vice versa*. Note that all elements (the initialisation (int i = 0), the condition check (i < 100) and the iteration (i += 10)) are present in both programs.[1] Both loops use the same parts, only in a different arrangement.

Both loops do pretty much the same thing. It is a question of convenience or convention which one to use in a given situation. Generally speaking, *for* loops are used to repeat something a specific number of times (e.g. initializing each item in an array, see next Chapter 13); *while* loops are used to repeat something until a condition has changed, however, long it takes (e.g. start drawing a line of rectangles across the screen, and stop drawing them when the screen border is reached, however, large the screen is; see e.g. Code 3, Code 7 and Code 8).

This is the formal structure of a *for* loop:

```
for (init; condition; iterate)
{
   statements;
}
```

An example is given in Code 3.

Code 3

```
for (int i = 10; i < 50; i += 6)
{
  rect(i, i, 40, 20);
  println(i);
}
```

What happens in Code 3 is, the *for* loop starts by initialising int variable i to 10. The condition if i is less than 50 is checked, then the loop is run, that is, the statements between the { } are executed one after the other. A rectangle is drawn at pos (i, i), that is, at (10, 10) with a size of 40x20 pixels; and i is printed to the console. After the last statement within the loop is evaluated, the iteration (increasing i by 6) is performed. The condition is checked, and if true (which it is, because i is now 16), the loop runs again, and so forth.

The last rectangle is drawn at (46, 46). i is then increased to 52, and the condition is not met, and the loop is not run again.

Very rarely one wants to iterate a *for* loop without (further) executing the contents of it. Code 4 shows an example.

Code 4

```
for (int i = 10; i < 50; i += 6)
{
   if (i == 28) { continue; }  //the 4th rect is not drawn

   rect(i, i, 40, 20);
   println(i);
}
```

If one wants to stop a *for* loop altogether, and continue program execution after it, break works (Code 5), as it does in *while* loops (see Code 6 in Chapter 6). Usually, there is a more elegant solution for *for* loops than using break.

Code 5

```
for (int i = 10; i < 50; i += 6)
{
    if (i==28) { break; }  //the 4th rect is not drawn, and the loop is left
    rect(i, i, 40, 20);
    println(i);
}
```

Now let's use loops a bit. Let's say, this is what we want to have:

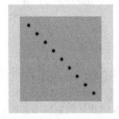

How to get there?

Since there are only nine dots, it is not inconceivable to place each dot by hand. Code 6 is such a solution; it displays what we want to have:

Code 6

```
background(255, 221, 12);
strokeWeight(4);

point(10, 10);
point(20, 20);
point(30, 30);
point(40, 40);
point(50, 50);
point(60, 60);
point(70, 70);
point(80, 80);
point(90, 90);
```

But Code 6 is obviously not very elegant. Formulate a solution with a *for* loop!

A solution with a *while* loop is Code 7.

Code 7

```
background(255, 221, 12);
strokeWeight(4);

int i = 10;
while (i < 100)
{
  point(i, i);
  i += 10;
}
```

For and *while* Loop Applications

Now we have already a fair number of tools on the table, and we can experiment with some applications of (*for* and *while*) loops!

Recall that Magic Numbers are literal values written out in the code (see the section 'Magic Numbers' in Chapter 4).[2] Ideally, these are replaced with variables. If at all, literal values are only at the very top of the code, where variables are set, and the values are easy to find and conveniently to change, not placed (hidden) in the rest of the code.

So while Code 7 works, it is not very general or re-usable. A more adaptable solution is Code 8 which automatically adapts to the window size.

Code 8

```
background(255, 221, 12);
strokeWeight(4);

int i = (int)(width * 0.1);
while (i < width)
{
  point(i, i);
  i += (int)(width * 0.1);
}
```

Code 8 ignores the height of the window. Code 9 (using a *while* loop with the AND (&&) logical operator) takes into account both the width and height of the window and scales the distance between the dots accordingly.

Code 9

```
size(200, 300);
background(255, 221, 12);
strokeWeight(4);
```

```
int i = (int)(width * 0.1);
int j = (int)(height * 0.1);
while ((i < width) && (j < height))
{
  point(i, j);
  i += (int)(width * 0.1);
  j += (int)(height * 0.1);
}
```

Code 10 draws a horizontal line of 50 dots across the window.

Code 10

```
background(66, 221, 12);

int numberPoints = 50;
int pixelSpace = 100;

int i = 0;
while (i < pixelSpace)
{
  point(i, height / 2);
  i += (pixelSpace / numberPoints);
}
```

Using variables instead of Magic Numbers makes it easy to change values, and to try out what works best, e.g. in Code 10.

Grids

Let's now draw a grid.[3] Write a program that displays 20 vertical lines and 10 horizontal lines in a window of 200 by 200 pixels!

For instance, with a *for* loop:

Code 11

```
size(200, 200);
strokeWeight(3);
stroke(23, 222, 122);
background(128, 90, 102);

for (int i = 5; i < width; i += 10)
{
    line(i, 0, i, height);
}
```

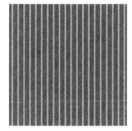

Note that the horizontal lines are still missing.

In real-world programming practice, one often creates a first program version that uses Magic Numbers, which are then iteratively removed: The changes of the code to the previous version are shown in red:

Code 12

```
int numberCols = 20;

size(200, 200);
strokeWeight(3);
stroke(23, 222, 122);
background(128, 90, 102);

for (int i = 0; i < width; i += (width / numberCols))
{
    line(i, 0, i, height);
}
```

Now we add half as many horizontal rows as there are vertical ones (Code 13)!

Code 13

```
int numberCols = 20;
int numberRows = 10;   //or: int numberRows = (numberCols / 2);

size(200, 200);
strokeWeight(3);
stroke(23, 222, 122);
background(128, 90, 102);

for (int i = 0; i < width; i += (width / numberCols))
{
    line(i, 0, i, height);
}
for (int i = 0; i < height; i += (height / numberRows))
{
    line(0, i, width, i);
}
```

And now without using the `line()` function but only using the `point()` function (Code 14). We can then also draw dotted lines and change (e.g. randomise) the colour for each dot (not yet added to the code).

Code 14

```
int numberCols = 20;
int numberRows = 10;

size(200, 200);
strokeWeight(3);
stroke(23, 222, 122);
background(128, 90, 102);

for (int i = 0; i < width; i += (width / numberCols))
{
   for (int j = 0; j < height; j++)
   {
      point(i, j);
   }
}
for (int i = 0; i < height; i += (height / numberRows))
{
   for (int j = 0; j < width; j++)
   {
      point(j, i);
   }
}
```

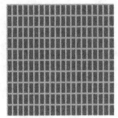

Fades

Fades are cool and can be realised fairly easy with loops. Let's check out Code 15 which shows a transparency fade.

Code 15

```
size(256, 128);
background(133, 145, 140);
strokeWeight(6);

for (int i = 10; i < width; i += 10)
{
   stroke(255, 120, 10, i);
   line(i, 10, i, 118);
}
```

Code 16 shows two fades: A horizontal transparency fade and a vertical colour fade (or transition). It uses two nested *for* loops and fewer Magic Numbers.

Code 16

```
size(256, 128);
background(133, 145, 140);
strokeWeight(6);

for (int i = 10; i < width; i += 10)
{
   for (int j = 10; j < height; j += 10)
   {
      stroke(255, j * 2, 10, i);
      point(i, j);
   }
}
```

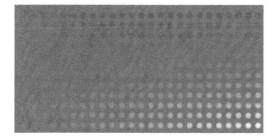

Randomness

Random numbers are very useful. Graphics, audio, levels, etc. – everything can be made less predictable by introducing some random chance (Code 17).

Code 17

```
background(80, 190, 240);
strokeWeight(3);
stroke(243, 18, 140, 128);

for (int i = 10; i < (width - 10); i+=10)
{
   for (int j = 10; j < (height - 10); j+=10)
   {
      rect((i + random(-2, 2)), (j + random(-2, 2)), 10, 10);
   }
}
```

The random function in *Processing* is called random(). It takes one or two floats as arguments. The one-argument version generates a random number between 0 and the given float[4]; the two-argument version generates a random number between the given floats[5] (Code 18). In both cases, the random number is a float.

Code 18

```
background(80, 190, 240);
strokeWeight(3);
stroke(243, 18, 140, 128);

for (int i = 10; i < (width - 10); i += 10)
{
    for (int j = 10; j < (height - 10); j += 10)
    {
        rect(i, j, (10 + (random(-i, i) * 0.1)), (10 + (random(-j, j) * 0.1)));
    }
}
```

With random, one can go arbitrarily crazy (Code 19).

Code 19

```
size(500, 300);
background(80, 190, 240);
strokeWeight(3);

for (int i = 10; i < (width - 40); i += 10)
{
    for (int j = 10; j < (height - 40); j += 10)
    {
        fill(random(140), 220, random(255), (150 + random(100)));
        stroke(80, (40 + random(120)), 0, (50 + random(150)));
        rect((i + random(-2, 2)), (j + random(-2, 2)),
            (10 + (random(-i, i) * 0.1)), (10 + (random(-j, j) * 0.1)));
    }
}
```

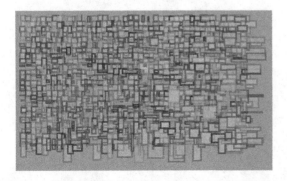

Solution

But Code 6 is obviously not very elegant. Formulate a solution with a *for* loop!

```
background(255, 221, 12);
strokeWeight(4);
for (int i = 10; i < 100; i += 10)
{
    point(i, i);
}
```

Chapter End Exercises

0. Drawing with Loops Again: The *for* Loop

   Modify the code from exercise 1 in Chapter 5 to use a `for` loop instead of the `while` loop.

1. Adjacent Points

   Generate a grid (i.e. several crossing horizontal and vertical lines) made up of adjacent points (i.e. points that touch each other) and not by using the `line()` function. I repeat: Produce adjacent points but do not use the `line()` function.

2. The Tartan

   Draw a pattern very vaguely resembling a Scottish tartan by using two nested `for` loops. The colours and transparency can be randomised. All of *Processing*'s drawing functions such as lines and rectangles can be used.

3. The Tartan is Back

   Modify the code of the previous exercise. Still, draw the same graphics but use `while` loops instead of `for` loops.

Notes

1. The only tangible difference between the two programs is, that variable i's scope is limited to the for loop, while it is accessible also outside the while loop. We will return to the question of the visibility (or 'scope') of variables when we talk about functions.
2. It is seen as desirable to separate a program from its data. A first step is to avoid Magic Numbers, that is, literal values mixed up with code. One should use variables instead. A further step is to use data files, such as text files, that hold data such as highscore tables or level layouts. An extreme case are game engines, that work with whatever material the user inputs.
3. This is also an example how a program is typically developed step-by-step or iteratively. Programming is not about complex things – it is about how to combine basic structures in clever ways. The parts are not interesting but rather the ways one combines them. Complex behaviour may emerge.
4. That is, from (and including) 0 and up to (but excluding) the given `float`.
5. That is, from (and including) the first `float` and up to (but excluding) the second.

13

Arrays

Outline

- Declaration, Creation and Assignment of Values
- Access

Arrays are a step up from using heaps
of named variables; they are super useful
to handle a large number of values, and
they are not rocket science

An array is something like a variable that can hold multiple values, which are numbered for access (they are indexed; Figure 13.1). All the values are of the same type (such as int, float or String).

While it is conceivable to write programs without using arrays, it is often convenient to access values by index (i.e. in an array) instead of name (i.e. using individual variables). Arrays are usually used in tandem with loops; for instance, all array items are read and output to the console, or used to draw rectangles at specific positions on the screen.

For example, one wants to store the number of inhabitants of New Zealand from 1950 to 1995 in 5-year steps. The numbers are (World Population Review 2016):

Year	1950	1955	1960	1965	1970	1975	1980	1985	1990	1995
Number	1908001	2136000	2371999	2628002	2819548	3082883	3146770	3268192	3397534	3674886

An array to store these numbers would be of type int, would hold 10 values (numbered from 0 to 9[1]), and would look like this:

Item	0	1	2	3	4	5	6	7	8	9
Number	1908001	2136000	2371999	2628002	2819548	3082883	3146770	3268192	3397534	3674886

One can access (e.g. read) the first element of this array at position 0, the second element at position 1, and so forth; the last (i.e. tenth) element is at position 9.

Arrays are used when the values stored cannot (easily) be (re-) created in other ways.[2] For instance, names of players, population numbers and screen coordinates of swarming alien space ships. A program might keep track of the temperature of every minute in the last 24 hours. One could store all these individual values in different variables, but the program would be a disaster – nobody wants to handle 1440 variable names. In these cases, arrays are very useful.[3]

The size of an array is set when it is created and does not change afterwards.[4] That makes it possible for the computer to find a spot in memory where the array fits; ideally, this is a continuous piece of memory, so all array items are ordered consecutively in memory; when iterating through an array, the computer can then get quickly and easily from one item to the next. An array cannot be resized (specifically, enlarged), because the memory around it can be taken up by other data.

DOI: 10.1201/9781003345916-13

FIGURE 13.1 Array with 10 indexed (and empty) items

Declaration, Creation and Assignment of Values

We know now that an array is a collection of objects of a single data type. The twist is that the individual objects are not *named* but *numbered*.

An array declaration consists of a *type specifier* (e.g. int), an *identifier* (e.g. inhabitantsNZ) and a *dimension* (e.g. 10):

```
int[] inhabitantsNZ = new int[10];
```

This creates ten spaces in computer memory where one can store ints.[5]

The thermometer program sketched in the "Outline" might store the temperature of every minute during the last 24 hours in an array with 1440 items (60 minutes * 24 hours). This could be the array definition:

```
float[] pastTemperatures = new float[1440];
```

A program to store the number of inhabitants of New Zealand from 1950 to 1995 might look like Code 1.

Code 1

```
int[] inhabitantsNZ = new int[10];

//storing the values:
inhabitantsNZ[0] = 1908001;
inhabitantsNZ[1] = 2136000;
inhabitantsNZ[2] = 2371999;
inhabitantsNZ[3] = 2628002;
inhabitantsNZ[4] = 2819548;
inhabitantsNZ[5] = 3082883;
inhabitantsNZ[6] = 3146770;
inhabitantsNZ[7] = 3268192;
inhabitantsNZ[8] = 3397534;
inhabitantsNZ[9] = 3674886;
```

There are three (syntactic) ways to define arrays: One is to have a separate declaration, creation and assignment of values:

```
int[] inhabitantsNZ;  //declaration

inhabitantsNZ = new int[10];  //creation

inhabitantsNZ[0] = 1908001;  //assignment (there would be 9 more assignments
similar to this one)
```

The second possibility is to combine the declaration and the creation, and write them in one line (as in Code 1):

```
int[] inhabitantsNZ = new int[10];

inhabitantsNZ[0] = 1908001;  //assignment (there would be 9 more assignments
similar to this one)
```

The third possibility is to define an array *implicitly*, that is, not to say how many values one wants to store, but just to give the type and the literal values:

```
int[] inhabitantsNZ = {1908001, 2136000, 2371999, 2628002, 2819548, 3082883,
3146770, 3268192, 3397534, 3674886};
```

This last version looks practical, but in reality, one often does not have the values up front when one creates the array. One knows usually only how many values to expect.

Access

After one has declared and created an array, and assigned values to it, one can access (e.g. read) them.
   Code 2 extends Code 1 with a *for* loop that goes through the array and prints each item.

Code 2

```
int[] inhabitantsNZ = {1908001, 2136000, 2371999, 2628002, 2819548, 3082883,
3146770, 3268192, 3397534, 3674886};

for (int i = 0; i < 10; i++)
{
   println(inhabitantsNZ[i]);
}
```

One can also imagine an array used to draw rectangles onto the screen (Code 3).

Code 3

```
int[] rectPosY = {10, 35, 50, 80};

for (int i = 0; i < 4; i++)
{
   rect(20, rectPosY[i], 25, 10);
}
```

One has to be careful with the boundaries of the array. One can only access items that lie within the array. In Code 3, one can access items 0, 1, 2 and 3 but not e.g. -1 or 4 or 20.[6]
   Processing offers a variable named length that contains the size of an array which can conveniently be used, for instance, in a *for* loop (Code 4). But one should always know the sizes of one's arrays.

Code 4

```
int[] rectPosY = {10, 35, 50, 80};

for (int i = 0; i < rectPosY.length; i++)
{
   rect(20, rectPosY[i], 25, 10);
}
```

Not underrunning or overrunning one's arrays appears to be quite trivial, but in real life, things may become slightly tricky (Code 5).

Code 5

```
int[] rectPos = {20, 10, 60, 40, 10, 80};
for (int i = 0; i < 5; i += 2)
{
    rect(rectPos[i], rectPos[i + 1], 25, 10);
}
```

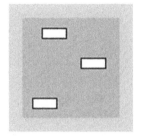

Note how the array is used to store both, the x and the y positions of the rectangles, and how the *for* loop is iterated by 2 each round; because of this, the *for* loop condition has to check if i is still less than 5 (and not less than 6, which would produce an ArrayIndexOutOfBoundsException in line rect(rectPos[i], rectPos[i + 1], 25, 10);.

What happens in Code 6?

Code 6

```
int[] data = new int[20];
for (int i = 0; i < data.length; i++)
{
    data[i] = 0;
}
```

And what happens here (Code 7)?

Code 7

```
int[] data = new int[20];
for (int i = 0; i < data.length; i++)
{
    data[i] = i;
}
```

Arrays can store all data types, e.g. boolean (true/false) values. In the next example (Code 8), the values from the array are used to draw something like a piano keyboard or a bar code. An array is used because the values cannot easily be mathematically calculated but are somewhat arbitrary.

Code 8

```
boolean[] data = {true, true, false, false, true, true, true, false};
for (int i = 0; i < data.length; i++)
{
    if (data[i] == true) { fill(255); } else { fill(0); }
    rect(10 + (i * 10), 10, 10, 80);
}
```

Or the contents of an int array can be read as grey values and used to colour a series of rectangles (Code 9).

Code 9

```
int[] data = {1, 7, 5, 3, 6, 3, 8, 9, 0, 2, 4, 6, 2, 7, 5, 4};
for (int i = 0; i < data.length; i++)
{
    fill(data[i] * 20);
    rect(10 + (i * 5), 10, 5, 80);
}
```

Arrays can also be multi-dimensional. Note the nested { }. Code 10 shows how to arrange bricks for a level in a ball-and-paddle game such as *BreakOut*. The array only needs to hold the info if a brick is on or off, so a boolean array is used. All bricks are on at the start of the level, and then get switched off when they are hit by the ball. In the code example, only the initial condition with all bricks on is demo'ed (ball, paddle and interaction are omitted).

Code 10

```
size(320, 240);
background(0);
noStroke();
```

```
boolean[][] bricks =  {{true, true, true, true},
                       {true, false, false, true},
                       {true, false, false, true}};

for (int j = 0; j < 3; j++)
{
    for (int i = 0; i < 4; i++)
    {
        if (bricks[j][i] == true)  //swapping i and j, so the array in the code
        looks like what is shown on screen
        {
            fill(((4 - i) * 317) % 255, (j * 211) % 255, ((33 + j) * 111) % 255);
            //just some funky colours
            rect((i * 70) + 25, (j * 36) + 25, 60, 25, 4);  //+ 25 is offset from
            screen borders
        }
    }
}
```

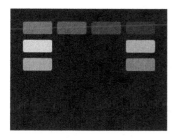

Code 11 shows a 2D array that holds grey values.

Code 11

```
int[][] data = {{175, 255, 191, 191,  32,  16,  96, 255},
                {191, 175, 128,  16,  32,  80, 143, 255},
                { 32,  48, 112, 175,  48,  96, 239, 255},
                {  0,   0, 112, 255, 239, 255, 255, 255},
                {  0,   0,  32, 255, 255, 255, 255, 255},
                {  0,   0,   0, 175, 255, 239, 207, 239},
                {  0,   0,   0,  64, 143,  48,  64, 175},
                {  0,   0,   0,   0,   0,  16,  80,  96}};

for (int j = 0; j < data.length; j++)
{
    for (int i = 0; i < data[j].length; i++)
    {
        fill(data[j][i]);
        rect(10 + (i * 10), 10 + (j * 10), 10, 10);
    }
}
```

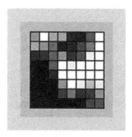

If one wants to use colour, arrays can also hold colour values (e.g. `color[]` `data` = {color(100, 120, 40), color(20, 200, 140)}) or the values of an array can be used to index colours, e.g. in a second array (Code 12).

Code 12

```
//Mario by Mediocre Lobster 2017

size(480,480);

//picture data in 2D array
int[][] picture = {{1,1,1,3,3,3,3,1,1,1,1,1},
                   {1,1,3,3,3,3,3,3,3,3,1,1},
                   {1,1,0,0,0,0,4,4,1,1,1,1},
                   {1,0,4,4,0,4,4,0,4,4,4,1},
                   {1,0,4,4,0,0,4,4,0,4,4,4},
                   {0,0,0,4,4,4,4,0,0,0,0,1},
                   {1,1,1,4,4,4,4,4,4,4,1,1},
                   {1,1,7,7,7,7,7,7,1,1,1,1},
                   {1,7,7,7,7,3,3,7,7,1,1,1},
                   {1,7,7,7,3,3,4,3,3,1,1,1},
                   {1,7,7,7,3,3,3,3,3,3,1,1},
                   {1,7,7,4,4,4,3,3,3,3,1,1},
                   {1,7,7,7,4,4,3,3,3,1,1,1}};

//index colours
color[] colors = new color[8];
colors[0] = color(0,0,0);        //black
colors[1] = color(128,128,128);  //grey
colors[2] = color(255,255,255);  //white
colors[3] = color(255,0,0);      //red
colors[4] = color(255,255,0);    //yellow
colors[5] = color(0,255,0);      //green
colors[6] = color(0,255,255);    //cyan
colors[7] = color(0,0,255);      //blue

int scale=40;

//use int values in the picture array to colour rectangles
for(int y = 0; y < picture.length; y++){
 for(int x = 0; x < picture[y].length; x++){
  int colorIntData = picture[y][x];  //retrieve colour index from 2D array
  fill(colors[colorIntData]);  //look up index in colour array and use for fill
  rect(scale * x, scale * y, scale, scale);
 }
}
```

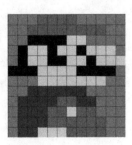

One probably does not want to enter images by hand into arrays; but structurally, there is little difference between an image file in memory, and an array in memory, and one can do almost the same things with both.

Code 13 presents another example, using the New Zealand numbers[7] to draw a basic chart.

Code 13

```
size(500, 200);

strokeWeight(10);
strokeCap(SQUARE);

int[] inhabitantsNZ={1908001, 2136000, 2371999, 2628002, 2819548, 3082883,
3146770, 3268192, 3397534, 3674886};

int scaleX = (width / 10);  //divided by 10 because there are 10 numbers in
the array, one could also write width/inhabitantsNZ.length

float scaleY = (height / 4000000.0);  //4000000 is a bit larger than the
maximum number of people, and it should be float

for (int i = 0; i < 10; i++)
{
    stroke(i * 15);  //colour transition from black to grey
    line((scaleX * 0.5) + (i * scaleX), height, (scaleX * 0.5) + (i*scaleX),
    (height-(inhabitantsNZ[i] * scaleY)));
}
```

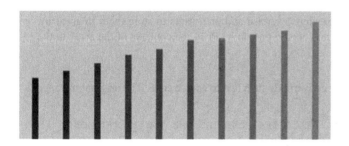

The variable scaleX is only an int (and not a float) because I know that it will be sufficient to hold the value (i.e. a whole number: width (500) divided by 10). scaleY is a float because it needs to hold a (very small) number with a decimal point. height is only used because one needs to invert the y dimension; otherwise, the lines would be drawn from the top down.

Solutions

What happens in Code 6?

Every item (0 to 19) in the int array is set to 0 (Figure 13.2); this is usually the first thing to do after creating an array. *Processing* may do this automatically, but other languages may not.

What happens in Code 7?

The items are numbered from 0 to 19. That is, item 0 contains 0, item 1 contains 1, etc. (Figure 13.3).

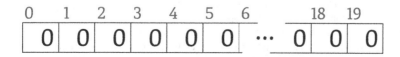

FIGURE 13.2 Contents of array (Code 6)

FIGURE 13.3 Contents of array (Code 7)

Chapter End Exercises

0. Arrays and Loops

   Make an array which contains the numbers 7, 21, 16, 42, -101 and 27. Print the contents of the array to the console; use a loop to access each array item (i.e. do not simply use println(arrayname)). Which loop is usually used with arrays? Why?

1. More and Different Arrays

   Make an array which contains the numbers 82.6, 10.7, -70.1, 28.2, -14.5 and 92.5. Print the contents of the array to the console. What is the difference between the code of this exercise and the previous one? If there is no difference except for different numbers something is not quite right. Which data types can be put into arrays?

2. Fitting Floats into Ints

   If one has the numbers from the previous exercise and one wants to store them in an array, but can only use an integer array,[8] how would one do it? Print the contents of the array to the console to check if it works.

3. The Morse Code Translator

   Write a program that automatically converts English text to Morse code. The original message is a string:

   ```
   String sourceMessage = "ABC HELLO TEST ONE TWO ONE TWO IS THIS ON";
   ```

   The program uses two arrays to store the English alphabet and the Morse translation for each letter:

   ```
   alphabet = new char[] {' ', 'A', 'B', 'C', ...};  //only space and
   capital letters A-Z
   morseCode = new String[] {" ", ".-", "-...", "-..-", ...};  //first item
   is space
   ```

   The coded message should be assembled in a String translatedMessage, and this string should be printed to the console when the whole message is translated. Use two nested for loops to go through sourceMessage letter by letter, and to find each letter's Morse translation. Use the charAt() method to access one letter in a String, e.g. print(sourceMessage. charAt(0)). Potential extra features: Solve this exercise without using the alphabet array; write a program to translate strings in Morse code to English.

Notes

1. Everything in computing is numbered starting at 0 (not at 1).
2. For instance, if one wanted to access the number sequence 100, 200, 300, 400, 500, 600, 700, 800, 900, one would not use an array but e.g. a *for* loop.
3. And can be accessed with loops, in contrast to 1440 individually named variables.
4. In established languages such as *C* and *C++* (and even in *Java*), arrays have a fixed size. *Processing* (and *C#*) are some of the few languages in which arrays can apparently be resized. Of course, actual resizing does not happen; under the hood, and hidden from the programmer, a new array of the desired size is

created, the values from the old array are copied into it, and the reference to the old array is replaced with the reference to the new one. In *Processing*, the size of arrays can be increased (with the append() and expand() functions), and decreased (with the shorten() function).) A properly thought-out program should not need to resize its arrays. If this functionality is really required, one can use the ArrayList class (see Chapter 34).

5. Note that arrays are given a length when they are created, and that the length of an array never changes. The program needs to tell the computer how many values of which type are to be saved, then the computer can find a spot in memory to save the array. If one wants an array to hold items such as *BreakOut* bricks or bullets, that might be removed from a game, the usual strategy is to use a Boolean variable to track if something is on or off (i.e. if the brick or the bullet still exists). There is also a more convenient kind of array, called ArrayList in *Processing*, that has variable length, that is, items can be added and deleted (recent versions of C contain support for *variable length arrays* (VLAs); C++ does not know VLAs, but offers instead the *vector*). This is, however, relatively complex (and time-intensive) for the computer to handle.

6. In *Python*, an array position of -1 is valid (if the array has at least one item) and would count backwards from the end of the array, thus refer to the last array item.

7. And the elusive (and rarely used) strokeCap() function.

8. For instance, for reasons of speed or space; although in *Processing*, both ints and floats have a size of 32 bits. The *Arduino* serial port can only read/write bytes, not e.g. floats, so some conversion needs to be done.

14

Functions

Outline

- setup() and draw() Functions
- Eye and Math Examples
- Passing Arguments
- Return Values
- Variable Scope

In this chapter, we talk
about functions: how to use
them and to create your own

Functions collect, encapsulate and provide often-used functionality in a program; e.g. drawing rectangles or eyeballs. The use of functions simplifies programming (because one can offload tedious detail work to functions) and shortens code (because code does not get repeated in a program). Creating functions also supports breaking down a complex programming task into (more) manageable chunks. Functions are essential to achieve an efficient, modular code structure.

An essential part of the design process is making one's own tools for a specific task. Not just to apply or (re-) use generic tools that somebody else has (pre-) made. Same thing with programming. We have already used standard functions such as line(),

background(), println().

Code 1 is a program we already discussed (Code 2 in Chapter 8); where are the functions?

Code 1

```
int x = 10;
int y = 20;
int opacity = 255;

fill(20, 140, 255, opacity);
rect(x, y, 60, 40);

fill(20, 255, 140, opacity / 2);
rect(x + 10, y + 10, 60, 40);

fill(255, 255, 140, opacity / 4);
rect(x + 20, y + 20, 60, 40);
```

DOI: 10.1201/9781003345916-14

So far we have only seen function calls but no function definitions. Function definitions consist of ordinary code which is grouped in a structure.

What are functions? Functions:

- Contain code that is (re-) used often (i.e. more than once)
- Use arguments to define action (data that goes into the function)
- Can return values (data that comes out of a function)
- Are invoked (*called*)

Some functions are provided by the language (or a library) but most of them are defined by the programmer.

```
println("Print this");

drawMonster(100, 200, 80);

iCalculateNumberBonusItems(1, 2, 100);
```

setup() and draw() Functions

There are two special functions that are almost always present in *Processing* programs[1]: setup() and draw().[2]

These are actually function definitions. Function definitions say what happens when the functions are called. setup() and draw() are called automatically by *Processing*: setup() once as soon as the program is started, and draw() repeatedly after that (Code 2).

Code 2

```
void setup()
{
    //is called once at the start of the program,
    //e.g. to initialise and load everything one wants to use later
}
void draw()
{
    //is called repeatedly as long as the program is running,
    //e.g. to move something across the screen, interaction
}
```

In a program that contains functions, little happens in the global scope of the program (i.e. outside of all functions).[3] Almost everything goes into setup(), draw() and one's own functions.

Eye and Math Examples

Functions should be used when code is used several times in a program. For instance, to draw several (more or less) identical items onto the screen (such as aliens, stars, platforms or eyes).

Let's assume we have a program (Code 3) that draws an eye at position (50, 40). Nothing new so far.

Code 3

```
background(12, 146, 0);

fill(255);
ellipse(50, 40, 20, 26);

fill(0);
ellipse(50, 40, 6, 8);
```

We could now duplicate the code to draw two eyes, but this is, of course, something to avoid for modular, trim code. Time to introduce functions![4]

First, let us make a function (highlighted) that does exactly the same thing as the code above (Code 4).

Code 4

```
void setup()
{
    background(12, 146, 0);
    drawEye();
}

void drawEye()
{
    fill(255);
    ellipse(50, 40, 20, 26);

    fill(0);
    ellipse(50, 40, 6, 8);
}
```

The custom-made function `drawEye()` is called in `setup()`, and it draws an eye at position (50, 40). It can do nothing else. If it is called several times (e.g. by several calls `drawEye()` in `setup()`), it draws several eyes, but all of them at the same position.

The keyword `void` in front of the function name means the function does not return a value (see the section 'Return Values' later in this chapter for a function that does). The function name is `drawEye`; and the function does not accept any arguments (the ( ) are empty).

The structure of a function definition is:

```
returnDataType functionName(dataType parameterName, ...)
{
    statements
}
```

Code 5 shows how one can use a function with a parameter (of type `int`) to draw an eye at position (50, 40). Formally, the call is not different from, e.g. invoking *Processing*'s `rect()` function.[5]

Code 5

```
void setup()
{
    background(12, 146, 0);

    drawEye(50);
}

//function takes an x coordinate to draw an eye
void drawEye(int x)
{
    fill(255);
    ellipse(x, 40, 20, 26);
```

```
    fill(0);
    ellipse(x, 40, 6, 8);
}
```

Now we can use the argument to draw two eyes in different (horizontal) positions (Code 6). Again, there is no difference to the function calls we have used already, invoking, e.g. the `rect()` and the `ellipse()` functions. Only here, our own function is called (twice, first with 20 as an argument, then with 80; two eyes are drawn, one at a time, at (20, 40) and at (80, 40)).

Code 6

```
void setup()
{
    background(12, 146, 0);

    drawEye(20);
    drawEye(80);
}

void drawEye(int x)
{
    fill(255);
    ellipse(x, 40, 20, 26);

    fill(0);
    ellipse(x, 40, 6, 8);
}
```

And that is how it is done. Never duplicate code again! Now we can draw cool things, and not just lines and rectangles.

Modify the function definition from Code 6 to have two parameters, to draw anywhere on the screen! Demonstrate that it works.

The author prefers this arrangement of code inside a program: First `setup()`, then all the custom functions in alphabetical order, and `draw()` at the end. It is similar to *C*, where all functions must be defined before they can be used. However, one arranges things, one should not put `setup()` and `draw()` in the middle somewhere where they are hard to find.

Passing Arguments

Very often, one wants to give a function some data to work with, when calling it. We have done this already, for instance, when drawing rectangles with the `rect()` function. The data the function is to use is typically given within the brackets ( ) after the function name, when calling a function[6]:

```
rect(10, 20, 40, 60);
```

This is called *passing arguments*. When passing arguments to functions, there are three technical rules:

- One must pass the same number of arguments as defined in the function definition.
- Arguments must be of the same type as declared within the function definition. An integer argument must be passed into an integer parameter, a floating point into a floating point and so on.
- The order matters in which arguments are passed (even if using different types; e.g. *Processing*'s text() function, Code 1 in Chapter 20).

The value one passes as an argument to a function can be a literal value (20, 5, 4.3, etc.), a variable (x, y, ticksElepsed, etc.), the result of an expression (4 * x/2 or 8% 3) or the return value of another function call (e.g. println(random(0,10))).[7]

Parameters act as local variables to a function and are only accessible within that function (see the section 'Variable Scope' later in this chapter).

A call would look like this; arguments are 12 and 6:

```
float f = fAverage(12, 6);   //find the average of 12 and 6, assign result to f
```

The so-called overloading of functions is possible: Functions can have the same name when their parameters are different (type, number, order). For instance, the fill() functions takes from one to four arguments. For a function call, the computer then picks the function that fits the call.

```
fill(0);   //the function called fill that takes one argument is invoked
fill(255, 0, 0);   //the function called fill that takes three arguments is
invoked
```

Return Values

When a function returns data (rather than e.g. draws on the screen) it has a *return type* that is not void. We have seen already the round() function that takes a float number and returns an int.

The type of data returned is the first thing in the function definition; it is found left of the function name. The definition of the fAverage() function shows that it will return a float (if it is called):

```
float fAverage(float num1, float num2)
{
    float av = (num1 + num2) / 2;
    return av;
}
```

It's a good habit to always add a comment just above a function definition that explains in a few words what the function receives, does and returns. Except for the most trivial functions, this is useful and good practice

A full program example is given in Code 7; the calcAverage() function is given an array of values,[8] and the function returns their average as a float. This value is then put into a variable and printed to the console.

Code 7

```
int[] playerTimes = {406, 506, 629, 764, 1243};

void setup()
{
    float averageTime = calcAverage(playerTimes);
    println(averageTime);
}
```

```
//the function is given an array of values, it calculates the average, and
returns it
float calcAverage(int[] times)
{
    float addedTimes = 0;
    for (int i = 0; i < times.length; i++) { addedTimes += times[i]; }
    return (addedTimes / times.length);
}
```

Here are some example function calls:

```
float f = fAverage(12, 6);   //find the average of 12 and 6, assign result to f
```

The return value goes into f (the function fAverage() is defined above).

This is a call to the drawEye() function defined in Code 5, which has a return type of void and therefore does not return anything:

```
drawEye(65);   //returns no data (return type is void), just draws on the screen
```

This is a call to a function which we don't know. Presumably, it loads a file from harddisk and returns true on success.

```
boolean success = loadHiscores();   //returns a boolean, depending on the
success of the operation (the highscore file could e.g. be missing)
```

This code uses a function call as part of a condition check:

```
if (isPlayerFlying() == true) { /* draw blue backgound */ }   //function's
return value is used at once in an if statement
```

This code uses the return values from two function calls as arguments in a call to another function:

```
ellipse(getPlayerPosX(), getPlayerPosY(), 50, 80);   //functions' return values
are used in a call to another function
```

Variable Scope

The *scope* of a variable is the area of the program in which it is available, or *visible*. The scope of a variable is determined by the location it is declared.

A variable can (only) be used:

- From the point of its declaration onwards (Code 8; once a variable is declared, it cannot be 'undeclared');
- Within the structure it is declared in; such structures are, for instance, a loop (Code 9), a function (Code 10) and a class (e.g. Code 1 in Chapter 25) and
- In sub-structures of the structure it is declared in; for instance, a variable declared at the top of a function is available within all loops in the function.

Code 8

```
int i = 10;
while (i < 90)
{
    rect(i, 20, 7, 60);
    i += 10;
}
println(i);   //i is still visible here
```

Code 9

```
for (int i = 10; i < 90; i += 10)
{
    rect(i, 20, 7, 60);
}

println("i is not declared outside the loop");
```

Code 10

```
void setup()
{
    face();
}

void face()
{
    int x = 50;
    int y = 50;
    ellipse(x, y - 25, 200, 100);
    ellipse(x - 25, y - 25, 10, 10);
    ellipse(x + 25, y - 25, 10, 10);
    println("Face drawn at " + x + "/" + y);
}
```

Intuitively, one would probably aim to make the scope of a variable as wide as possible, encompassing the whole program, i.e. to make it *global* (Code 11). But actually, one usually tries the opposite, to structure the program clearly, to make it easy to read and modular.

Code 11

```
int x = 50;   //global variables, avoid when possible
int y = 50;

void setup()
{
    face();
}

void face()
{
    ellipse(x, (y - 25), 200, 100);
    ellipse((x - 25), y - 25, 10, 10);
    ellipse((x + 25), y - 25, 10, 10);
    println("Face drawn at " + x + "/" + y);
}
```

Ideally, values are passed around the program at well-defined points by arguments (Code 12) and return values (Code 7), rather than by the (mis-) use of global variables as transport vessels.

Code 12

```
void setup()
{
    face(50, 50);
}

void face(int x, int y)
{
    ellipse(x, (y - 25), 200, 100);
    ellipse((x - 25), (y - 25), 10, 10);
    ellipse((x + 25), (y - 25), 10, 10);
    println("Face drawn at " + x + "/" + y);
}
```

By design, *Processing* (and *Java*) promote the passing of arguments 'by value' (and not 'by reference'). That means that in most cases passing arguments to functions (and methods) is a one-way street: The value is taken, copied and given to the function; whatever the function then does with this value stays within the function, and does not influence the state of things without it (Code 13). This applies to all basic datatypes (and to strings as well).

Code 13

```
void setup()
{
    int testValue = 0;
    println("Initially, the value is " + testValue);  //value is 0
    modifyInt(testValue);
    println("But outside of the function, the value is unchanged; it still is
    " + testValue);  //value is still 0
}

//modifies the int value that is passed to the function
void modifyInt(int value)
{
    value = 1;
    println("Within a function the (passed) value can be changed, it is now "
    + value);  //value is 1
}
```

Output:

```
Initially, the value is 0

Within a function the (passed) value can be changed, it is now 1

But outside of the function, the value is unchanged; it still is 0
```

If the function should return something to the caller, a return value is used (see the section 'Return Values' earlier in this chapter).

When objects (such as arrays (Chapter 13) and programmer-made class objects (Chapter 25) or PVectors (Chapter 33)) are passed to functions, a pointer is given, so that changes that happen in a function modify the original object (Code 14).[9]

Code 14

```
void setup()
{
    int[] testArray = {0, 1, 2, 3, 4};
    printArray(testArray);  //here the array contains 0, 1, 2, 3, 4 which is
    unsurprising
    modifyArray(testArray);
    printArray(testArray);  //but here the array contains 7, 7, 7, 7, 7
    because the function modified it
}

//sets all items of the given array to 7, and this modifies the contents of
the array in the calling variable scope
void modifyArray(int[] array)
{
    for (int i = 0; i < array.length; i++) { array[i] = 7; }
}

void printArray(int[] array)
{
    print("Array contents:");
    for (int i = 0; i < array.length; i++) { print(" " + array[i]); }
    println();
}
```

Output:

```
Array contents: 0 1 2 3 4
Array contents: 7 7 7 7 7
```

To modify an object in the caller's scope can be very practical, for instance, to get more than one value back from a function (Code 15, a (very rudimentary) software version of Norman White's *Four-Letter Word Generator*, 1974).[10]

Code 15

```
char[] fourLetterWord = new char[4];

void setup()
{ }

void createFourLetterWord(char[] word)
{
  for (int i = 0; i < word.length; i++)
  {
    word[i] = char(int(random(65, 91)));   //modifies contents of given array
  }
}

void draw()
{
  createFourLetterWord(fourLetterWord);   //note, no return value used
  for (int i = 0; i < fourLetterWord.length; i++) { print(fourLetterWord[i]); }
  println();
}
```

Solutions

Code 1 is a program we already discussed (Code 2 in Chapter 8); where are the functions?

The functions in Code 1 are fill() and rect(), each called three times. x, y and opacity are variables.

Modify the function definition from Code 6 to have two parameters, to draw anywhere on the screen! Demonstrate that it works.

```
void setup()
{
    background(12, 146, 0);

    drawEye(20, 20);
    drawEye(80, 60);
}

void drawEye(int x, int y)
{
    fill(255);
    ellipse(x, y, 20, 26);

    fill(0);
    ellipse(x, y, 6, 8);
}
```

Chapter End Exercises

0. Welcome to my Kitchen

   Make a function to draw a modern house or a kitchen appliance to the screen. Modify the function to accept one `int` argument to control the horizontal position of the object to draw.

1. More Features

   Modify the implementation of the function in the previous exercise to accept more arguments: Another `int` value to control the object's vertical position, several drawing attributes (such as object size, colours and line thickness), and a `boolean` to indicate e.g. if a house has a door, or if the appliance is a fridge or an oven.

2. Doing it a Hundred Times Over

   Modify the code of the previous exercise. Use a loop to call the function several times (the function can be given randomised values for the screen positions and the other values).

3. My Very Own Speech Bubble Function

   Make your own function to draw comic-style text bubbles (Figure 14.1). The function takes as parameters the `String` to be printed and the screen coordinates. It outputs the text inside a bubble or rectangle, and draws a little graphics of a head or similar under it. The size of the bubble is (roughly) determined by the length of the `String`.

4. Moving the Machine

   Make a function that draws a 2D view of a machine such as a printing press. The machine has one moving part that moves vertically or horizontally. Use the `sin()` or `cos()` function (see Chapter 15) together with the `millis()` function (see Chapter 27) to make it move.

5. The Indie Band Name Generator

   Write a program that prints out randomly generated indie band names. The program has two custom-made functions:

   One function that returns a `String` such as 'Beany Twins' when called. There are no arguments. The function works with a call such as `println(createBandName())`. For this exercise, a band name is taken to consist of one adjective (e.g. 'Sweet', 'Bland', 'Snappy', 'Mediocre', 'Purple', 'Wooden'), and a noun (e.g. 'Melons', 'Lobsters', 'Pigeons', 'Zebras', 'Detour', 'Elevators', 'Nova'. The function uses two `String` arrays to store the adjectives and nouns, randomly assembles a `String` from them in the form 'Adjective Noun' and returns it.

   A second function takes one `int` argument which controls how many band names are printed to the console. The function has no return value. The function call to print out five names is: `printBandNames(5)`. Do not duplicate code from the `createBandName()` function; but call it from within the `printBandNames()` function. Use a loop.

FIGURE 14.1 Example output of a comic text bubble function

The expected program structure is (return values and parameters are omitted here):

```
setup()
{
    ...
    printBandNames();
}

createBandName()
{
    ...
}

printBandNames()
{
    ...
    println(createBandName());
    ...
}

draw()
{ }
```

Implement the program and test the result.

Potential extra feature: Load the two arrays from two text files (see the section 'Loading and Saving Data' in Chapter 20).

6. The Haiku Generator

Write a program that creates a random haiku and outputs it to the console. Use several `String` arrays that contain verbs, nouns and adjectives. Then assemble the haiku word-by-word by using the random function to pick which words to use.[11]

Notes

1. Except very basic ones, e.g. many of the examples we use.
2. To use functions in *Processing*, one has to use at least the `setup()` function. The `draw()` function is optional but needed to keep programs running e.g. for interaction through `mousePressed()` (see the section 'Mouse Events in *Processing*' in Chapter 26).
3. Such as declaring and assigning (global) variables, creating (global) instances of classes, and importing libraries.
4. This is another example of iterative code development. Iterative means that the next idea, approach or implementation improves over the previous. And usually, one can get to the second iteration only by way of having done the first. This is a common process.
5. The correct lingo is, *arguments* are passed to functions which have *parameters*. The notion of *arguments* is used when talking about invoking functions (i.e. from the outside); *parameters* exist only within function definitions.
6. Passing data to functions as arguments is a very clean way to move around data in a program. But it is not impossible that a function gets the data it should work with in other ways, e.g. from global variables. But this is generally to be avoided, because it is then hard to see when and where the data is used in the program, and by which functions; and it functions are also modular when they are prepared to work with the data that is passed to them, instead of only working on specific global data (see the section 'Variable Scope' in this chapter). If functions are to return data, that is also possible (see the section 'Return Values' in this chapter).
7. All passing of arguments into functions (and methods) happens 'by value' in *Processing* (as it does in *Java*), not 'by reference': Values of primitive datatypes (including `String`s) are copied when passed to functions; whatever functions do with these values, the original value is not changed. For objects (such as arrays, `PVector`s and programmer-made class objects), pointers are passed to functions, that allow these objects to be modified in the called function, but nothing is passed by true reference (like it is possible, e.g. in *C*). More info is in the section 'Variable Scope' in this chapter.

8. Note that the code receives the array as a parameter, and does not simply grab the global variable; this is the clean way to do it, because the path of the data can be traced in the code.
9. Note that this pointer is not a reference as it could be, e.g. in *C*. In *Processing*, the pointer allows the modification of the object that it points to, but the pointer itself cannot be changed (as could be a reference).
10. See Norman White's web site at www.normill.ca (September 28, 2022).
11. For info on haikus and inspiration see e.g. examples.yourdictionary.com/examples-of-haiku-poems.html, www.creative-writing-now.com/how-to-write-a-haiku.html, www.poetrysoup.com/poems/haiku, or www. haiku-poetry.org/famous-haiku.html.

15

Movement

One way to understand movement is as displacement over time. In Figure 15.1, a sphere (a balloon?) is moving up and right, that is, it moves a little bit in each frame. The whole display is redrawn in each frame to create the illusion of continuous movement.

Movement can happen automatic, i.e. controlled by the computer or it can be controlled by the user/player. We start here with automatic movement, which is technically actually not much different from interactive movement.[1,2]

Let's make a (short) toy train move across the window. A function (drawTrain()) is used to draw the train at a certain point (i.e. x and y coordinates are given as arguments). First of all, the train is drawn, but nothing moves (Code 1).

Code 1

```
void setup()
{
    drawTrain(10, 20);
}
//function takes a screen location in pixels to draw a train waggon
void drawTrain(int x, int y)
{
    fill(222, 22, 0);
    rect(x, y, 20, 10);
    fill(0);
    ellipse(x + 2, y + 12, 4, 4);
    ellipse(x + 7, y + 12, 4, 4);
    ellipse(x + 13, y + 12, 4, 4);
    ellipse(x + 18, y + 12, 4, 4);
}

void draw()
{ }
```

Now let's move the train by introducing a (global) variable that holds the horizontal (x) position of the train, and then modifying this variable each time the draw() function is called. We also erase the background every time the train is drawn, otherwise it leaves a trail of ex-graphics behind. The same drawTrain() function is employed that was used in Code 1 and is abbreviated in this code snippet (Code 2).

DOI: 10.1201/9781003345916-15

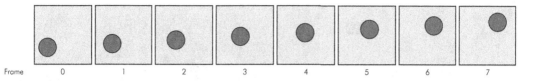

FIGURE 15.1 Movement as displacement over time

Code 2

```
int trainX = 0;

void setup()
{ }
//function takes a screen location in pixels to draw a train waggon
void drawTrain(int x, int y)
{ rect(x, y, 20, 10); println("Get the function's body from Code 1"); }

void draw()
{
    background(255, 235, 0);  //erases the background every round
    drawTrain(trainX, 20);
    trainX++;  //move the train right one pixel
}
```

We can even have two trains running with different speeds (Code 3).

Code 3

```
int firstTrainX = 0;
int secondTrainX = 0;

void setup()
{
    size(600, 100);
}
//function takes a screen location in pixels to draw a train waggon
void drawTrain(int x, int y)
{ rect(x, y, 20, 10); println("Get the function's body from Code 1"); }

void draw()
{
    background(255, 235, 0);  //erases the background every round

    drawTrain(firstTrainX, 20);  //each train is drawn at its new position
    firstTrainX++;  //here the first train is moved (right one pixel)

    drawTrain(secondTrainX, 80);
    secondTrainX += 2;
}
```

If we wanted many more trains, named variables such as firstTrainX and secondTrainX become somewhat unmanageable. Using an array and a loop is a much better solution. The trains start at x positions 0, 10 and 20, and move with the same speed (Code 4).

Code 4
```
int[] trainsX = {0, 10, 20};   //usage of array instead of named variables
void setup()
{
    size(600, 100);
}
//function takes a screen location in pixels to draw a train waggon
void drawTrain(int x, int y)
{ rect(x, y, 20, 10); println("Get the function's body from Code 1"); }
void draw()
{
    background(255, 235, 0);   //erases the background every round
    for (int i = 0; i < trainsX.length; i++)
    {
        drawTrain(trainsX[i], 10 + (i * 25));   //train i is drawn at new position
        trainsX[i]++;   //train i is moved (right one pixel)
    }
}
```

We could, of course, have the trains run with different speeds (the use of i to change the position would do this (trainsX[i] += i); or one could introduce a second array that holds the different speeds for the three trains).

The examples above only moved things horizontally (in x direction). We can also make a little cannon shoot a little cannonball across the screen using x and y coordinates (Code 5).

Code 5
```
float ballX = 0;
float ballY = 0;
float velocityX = 1.2;
float velocityY = -2;

void setup()
{
    stroke(255);
    ballY = height;   //height is only available now
}
```

```
void draw()
{
    fill(0, 12, 240, 50);
    rect(0, 0, width, height);   //clear background with semi-trans colour

    strokeWeight(14);
    strokeCap(SQUARE);   //³
    line(0, height, 12, height-20);   //draw cannon

    fill(255);
    strokeWeight(1);
    ellipse(ballX, ballY, 10, 10);   //draw ball

    ballX = ballX + velocityX;   //move ball
    ballY = ballY + velocityY;
}
```

The first two lines in draw()

```
fill(0, 12, 240, 50);
rect(0, 0, width, height);
```

are just a (graphically) fancy way to clear the background for a redraw. background() can't be used because it does not have an opacity parameter.[4]

And now we can add something like gravity (also changed is the initial velocityY value to -10; Code 6).

Code 6

```
float ballX = 0;
float ballY = 0;
float velocityX = 1.2;
float velocityY = -10;
float gravity = 0.3;

void setup()
{
    noStroke();
    ballY = height;   //height is only available now
}

void draw()
{
    fill(0, 12, 240, 50);   //clear background with semi-trans colour
    rect(0, 0, width, height);

    fill(255);
    ellipse(ballX, ballY, 10, 10);   //draw ball

    ballX = ballX + velocityX;   //move ball
    ballY = ballY + velocityY;
    velocityY += gravity;   //add gravity
}
```

One can imagine a game *à la Burrito Bison* (JuicyBeast 2011), with a launcher at the bottom-left corner of the playing field, and some items to hit or collect. So far, collision detection is not performed (neither with the window borders nor with the coins; Code 7).[5]

Code 7

```
float ballX = 0;
float ballY = 0;
float velocityX = 3.2;
float velocityY = -10;
float gravity = 0.3;

void setup()
{
    size(320, 200);
    noStroke();
    textAlign(CENTER, CENTER);
    ballY = height;   //height is only available now
}

void drawCoin(int x, int y)
{
  fill(230, 210, 20);
  ellipse(x, y, 20, 20);
  fill(110, 40, 10);
  text(x%9, x, y);   //just to put some number on the coin6
}

void draw()
{
    fill(0, 12, 240, 50);   //clear background with semi-trans colour
    rect(0, 0, width, height);
    fill(255);

    drawCoin(160, 100);
    drawCoin(220, 60);
    drawCoin(300, 160);

    fill(255);
    ellipse(ballX, ballY, 10, 10);

    ballX = ballX + velocityX;
    ballY = ballY + velocityY;

    velocityY += gravity;
}
```

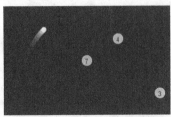

Now let's look at two other ways to move stuff: Random movement and movement controlled by sine and cosine.

In some cases random movement can be desirable, e.g. for generating patterns; in many cases, though, a combination of directed movement and randomness is more attractive and easier to engage with (Code 8).

Code 8

```
float minimumVelocityY = 1;

float snowflake1PosX = 0;   //we will soon see how to use a class
float snowflake1PosY = 0;   //to handle multiple and fairly identical objects

float snowflake2PosX = 0;   //[7]
float snowflake2PosY = 0;

float snowflake3PosX = 0;
float snowflake3PosY = 0;

void setup()
{
    size(300, 200);

    snowflake1PosX = width * 0.25;
    snowflake1PosY = -10;

    snowflake2PosX = width * 0.5;
    snowflake2PosY = -10;

    snowflake3PosX = width * 0.75;
    snowflake3PosY = -10;
}

void draw()
{
    background(0);

    ellipse(snowflake1PosX, snowflake1PosY, 20, 20);
    snowflake1PosX = snowflake1PosX + random(-2, 2);
    snowflake1PosY = snowflake1PosY + minimumVelocityY + random(1);
    if (snowflake1PosY > height + 10) { snowflake1PosY = -10; }

    ellipse(snowflake2PosX, snowflake2PosY, 20, 20);
    snowflake2PosX = snowflake2PosX + random(-2, 2);
    snowflake2PosY = snowflake2PosY + minimumVelocityY + random(1);
    if (snowflake2PosY > height + 10) { snowflake2PosY = -10; }

    ellipse(snowflake3PosX, snowflake3PosY, 20, 20);
    snowflake3PosX = snowflake3PosX + random(-2, 2);
    snowflake3PosY = snowflake3PosY + minimumVelocityY + random(1);
    if (snowflake3PosY > height + 10) { snowflake3PosY = -10; }
}
```

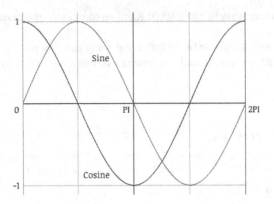

FIGURE 15.2 Sine and cosine waves between 0 and 2PI

The `sin()` and `cos()` functions are popular for moving objects because the values they return describe a circular or wave-like movement. For things that move back and forth or up and down, this is ideal. The values returned by sine functions lie between -1 and 1, and repeat every 2PI. `sin()` and `cos()` return identical values, but are offset by PI/2 (Figure 15.2).

The values can, for example, be used to draw ellipses (Code 9) or spirals (Code 10). The essential code in the loop is highlighted, the rest is just centring the output in the window and scaling it up. The y coordinates are inverted because, on screens, the coordinate origin is located at the top left (instead of following math's convention which is bottom left).

Code 9

```
int centrePointX = int(width * 0.5);
int centrePointY = int(height * 0.5);

float scaleX = (width * 0.5);
float scaleY = (height * 0.5);

for (int i = 0; i < 360; i++)
{
    float radiansI = radians(i);   //8

    point(centrePointX + (cos(radiansI) * scaleX), centrePointY -
    (sin(radiansI) * scaleY));
}
```

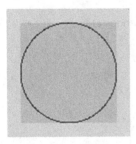

Code 10

```
int centrePointX = int(width * 0.5);
int centrePointY = int(height * 0.5);
```

```
float scaleX = (width * 0.001);
float scaleY = (height * 0.001);

for (int i = 0; i < 720; i++)
{
    float radiansI = radians(i);
    strokeWeight(1 + int(i * 0.05));

    point(centrePointX + (cos(radiansI) * scaleX * i), centrePointY -
    (sin(radiansI) * scaleY * i));
}
```

Letting the *for* loop run as long as i < 720 makes the spiral go around twice.

Many 2D sideview shooting games use a sine function (highlight) to move, for instance, aliens across the screen and towards the player's space ship (Code 11, space ship omitted). Instead of duplicating code with many variables three times for three aliens, we should really be using arrays to store the alien positions, and loops to initialise, access and update them (Code 12 and Code 13).

Code 11

```
float VelocityX = -2;

float alien1PosX = 0;  //we will soon see how to use a class
float alien1PosY = 0;  //to handle multiple and fairly identical objects

float alien2PosX = 0;
float alien2PosY = 0;

float alien3PosX = 0;
float alien3PosY = 0;
void setup() {
    size(300, 200);

    alien1PosX = width + 10;
    alien2PosX = width + 10 + 45;
    alien3PosX = width + 10 + 90;
}

void draw() {
    background(0);

    //first alien:
    ellipse(alien1PosX, alien1PosY, 20, 20);
    alien1PosX = alien1PosX + VelocityX;
    alien1PosY = (height * 0.5) - (sin(alien1PosX * 0.02) * 50);
    if (alien1PosX < -10) { alien1PosX = (width + 10); }

    //second alien:
    ellipse(alien2PosX, alien2PosY, 20, 20);
    alien2PosX = alien2PosX + VelocityX;
    alien2PosY = (height * 0.5) - (sin(alien2PosX * 0.02) * 50);
    if (alien2PosX < -10) { alien2PosX = (width + 10); }
```

```
    //third alien:
    ellipse(alien3PosX, alien3PosY, 20, 20);
    alien3PosX = alien3PosX + VelocityX;
    alien3PosY = (height * 0.5) - (sin(alien3PosX * 0.02) * 50);
    if (alien3PosX < -10) { alien3PosX = (width + 10); }
}
```

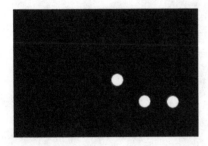

Code 11 can (and should be improved). Code 12 uses arrays instead of named variables and one *for* loop to access the arrays and draw the aliens. Note how compact the code gets!

Code 12

```
float VelocityX = -2;

float[] alienPosX = {0, 0, 0};   //usage of array instead of six variables
float[] alienPosY = {0, 0, 0};   //but implicit declaration -
void setup() {
    size(300, 200);

    alienPosX[0] = width + 10;   //and this should not be done by hand, either
    alienPosX[1] = width + 10 + 45;
    alienPosX[2] = width + 10 + 90;
}
void draw() {
    background(0);

    for (int i = 0; i < alienPosX.length; i++) {
        ellipse(alienPosX[i], alienPosY[i], 20, 20);
        alienPosX[i] = alienPosX[i] + VelocityX;
        alienPosY[i] = (height * 0.5) - (sin(alienPosX[i] * 0.02) * 50);

        if (alienPosX[i] < -10) { alienPosX[i] = (width + 10); }
    }
}
```

Code 12 is alright as a transitional version, but it still is not super elegant or easy to extend. Particularly, the global implicit array declaration at the top and the assignments in setup() only work well with few items – imagine 100 aliens or more attacking! The next version (Code 13) should use a loop in these places, too.

Code 13 uses *for* loops everywhere; this program is much shorter than Code 11, and more versatile than Code 12.

Code 13

```
float VelocityX = -2;
int numOfAliens = 3;

float[] alienXCoords = new float[numOfAliens];
float[] alienYCoords = new float[numOfAliens];
```

```
void setup()
{
    size(300, 200);

    //initialise X coords
    for (int i = 0; i < numOfAliens; i++) {
        alienXCoords[i] = (width + 10) + (i * 45);
    }

    //initialise Y coords
    for (int i = 0; i < numOfAliens; i++) {
        alienYCoords[i] = 0;
    }
}
void draw()
{
    background(0);
    for (int i = 0; i < numOfAliens; i++) {
        ellipse(alienXCoords[i], alienYCoords[i], 20, 20);
        alienXCoords[i] = alienXCoords[i] + VelocityX;
        alienYCoords[i] = (height * 0.5) - (sin(alienXCoords[i] * 0.02) * 50);
        if (alienXCoords[i] < -10) { alienXCoords[i] = (width + 10); }
    }
}
```

The next improvement will be an alien *class* (see Chapter 25), that we can use to create alien objects. Each object can then store and update its own position.

Chapter End Exercise

0. The Line Demo

    Make a line move around within a window.[9] The endpoints of the line move independently of each other and diagonally, and bounce off the window edges (do not use any sine function; the endpoints should not just repeat the same simple motion over and over).

Notes

1. One essential aspect of motion the examples ignore, is real time: The programs run fast on fast computers, and slow on slow ones, something definitely to be avoided in anything that moves or is animated. In a real world setting, the programs would be fitted with a so-called *time fix* which takes into account real (elapsing) time (i.e. use the `millis()` function). We'll get there in no time (in Chapters 27 and 28)!

2. The difference is, roughly, that in interactively controlled movement, the user/player switches it on (e.g. pressing a cursor key sets a `boolean` variable to `true`), and then it happens just like automatic movement. For info on real-time controls, see Chapter 26.

3. Info on the `strokeCap()` function follows in Chapter 17.

4. And first defining a colour with transparency and then passing it on to `background()` (color c = color(0, 12, 240, 50); background(c);) does not produce any transparency.

5. For info on collision detection, see Chapters 16 and 32.

6. Info on the `text()` function follows in Chapter 20.

7. If one finds the variable names too long and cumbersome to type, one can of course also use shorter names, such as `sf2PosX`. However, it might not be immediately apparent to a reader of the code what `sf` stands for.

8. `sin()` and `cos()` take radians (not angles) as parameters, so a function is called to convert angles to radians.
9. Use a window or fullscreen mode (documentation at processing.org/reference/fullScreen_.html). During development it is usually more convenient to use a window to be able to see the code, any console output, and the graphical output at the same time.

16

Basic Collision Detection

Spaceships crash into aliens, balls bounce off paddles and users click on buttons – these are all instances of collision detection, and that's what we do here

In a myriad of cases a program needs to find out how two (or more) objects are positioned in relation to each other. Is the mouse pointer hovering over the bear? Is the rabbit hit by the bullet? Is the car still on the road? Has Starkiller left the spacecraft?

Collision detection can be highly sophisticated. But in many cases, doing an approximate rectangle (bounding box) check is good enough to prototype (Figure 16.1, left), before employing more accurate (and complex and slow) methods (Figure 16.1, right).[1]

Even in a finished game, a quick bounding box check is fine to establish that there is no collision, which will probably be the case almost all of the time. If the bounding box method reports a collision (Figure 16.2), other, more involved checks can be done, to find out if, indeed, a collision occurs.

The check if something moves out of the screen borders is a kind of primitive bounding box collision check. Revising example Code 2 from Chapter 15 that moved a train across the window, we can keep the train from disappearing, or rather, reset its position when it reaches (or rather exceeds) the edge of the window (Code 1).

Code 1

```
int trainX = 0;

void setup()
{ }

//function takes a screen location in pixels to draw a train waggon
void drawTrain(int x, int y)
{
  fill(222, 22, 0);
  rect(x, y, 20, 10);
  fill(0);
  ellipse(x + 2, y + 12, 4, 4);
  ellipse(x + 7, y + 12, 4, 4);
  ellipse(x + 13, y + 12, 4, 4);
  ellipse(x + 18, y + 12, 4, 4);
}

void draw()
{
  background(255, 235, 0);  //erases the background every round
  drawTrain(trainX, 20);
  trainX++;  //move the train right one pixel

  if (trainX >= width) { trainX = 0; }
}
```

This is still a quite rudimentary program; it would be nice, for instance, if the train would not materialize in the window, but smoothly move into the window from the left. Another change might be to not have the train move along the same path (or track) every time but to introduce a variable for the y position, and have the train travel different y positions. Or the train could accelerate as it goes, and the speed could be reset when the position is reset. The train could also go back and forth between the left and right window edges.

Code 2 is a revised version of Code 6 from Chapter 15 where a ball was shot into the sky (changes are highlighted, i.e. the two *iflelse if* clauses at the end[2]). It adds collision detection of the ball with the window borders. In this case, both colliding objects can easily be approximated as rectangles without losing accuracy, which simplifies things.[3]

Code 2

```
float ballX = 0;
float ballY = 0;
float velocityX = 1.2;
float velocityY = -10;
float gravity = 0.3;
```

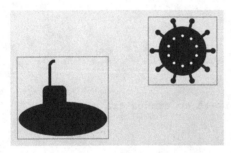

FIGURE 16.1   Bounding box collision check (left) and pixel perfect collision check (right)

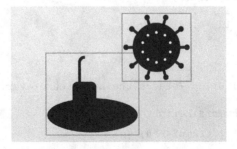

FIGURE 16.2   The bounding box collision check reports a collision where there is none

```
void setup()
{
  noStroke();
  ballY = height;   //height is only available now
}
void draw()
{
  fill(0, 12, 240, 50);   //clear the background with a semi-trans colour
  rect(0, 0, width, height);

  fill(255);
  ellipse(ballX, ballY, 10, 10);

  ballX = ballX + velocityX;
  ballY = ballY + velocityY;
  velocityY += gravity;

  if ((ballX - 5) < 0) { velocityX = -velocityX; ballX = 5; }  //collides
  with left border
  else if ((ballX + 5) >= width) { velocityX = -velocityX; ballX = (width
  - 5); }  //collides with right border⁴

  if ((ballY - 5) < 0) { velocityY = -velocityY; ballY = 5; }  //collides
  with top border
  else if ((ballY + 5) >= height) { velocityY = -velocityY; ballY = (height
  - 5); }  //collides with bottom border
}
```

Code 3 demonstrates collision detection between a square and the window border.

Code 3

```
float boxPosX = 0;
float boxPosY = 0;

int boxWidth = 20;
int boxHeight = 20;

float boxVelocityX = 2.11;
float boxVelocityY = 1.47;

void setup()
{
  size(300, 200);
  stroke(0, 180, 0);
  noFill();
}

void draw()
{
  background(0);

  rect(round(boxPosX), round(boxPosY), boxWidth, boxHeight);

  boxPosX = boxPosX + boxVelocityX;
  boxPosY = boxPosY + boxVelocityY;
```

```
if (boxPosX < 0) { boxVelocityX = -boxVelocityX; boxPosX = 0; }  //collides
with left border
else if ((boxPosX + boxWidth) >= width) { boxVelocityX = -boxVelocityX;
boxPosX = ((width - boxWidth) - 1); }  //collides with right border

if (boxPosY < 0) { boxVelocityY = -boxVelocityY; boxPosY = 0; }  //collides
with top border
else if ((boxPosY + boxHeight) >= height) { boxVelocityY = -boxVelocityY;
boxPosY = ((height - boxHeight) - 1); }  //collides with bottom border
}
```

The ball reflections in Code 3 are robustly but somewhat crudely approximated (the reflection angle is, however, correct; Figure 16.3); and they are possibly good enough for an example or a prototype.

For a finished game in which ball reflections are the main (if not the only) mechanic (e.g. in a *BreakOut*-style game or in a pinball game), they should be calculated mathematically correctly (i.e. the program should find the point of contact between the ball and the wall or paddle, and from there the location of the reflected ball).

Code 4 demonstrates how two objects can collide with each other: The square from the previous example and a paddle controlled by mouse x position.

Code 4

```
float boxPosX = 0;
float boxPosY = 0;
int boxWidth = 20;
int boxHeight = 20;
float boxVelocityX = 3.11;
float boxVelocityY = 2.47;

int paddleWidth = 60;
int paddleHeight = 10;
```

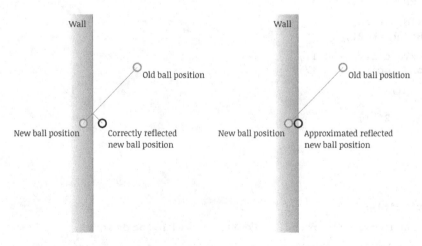

FIGURE 16.3 Approximated (left) and correct (right) ball position after wall reflection

```
void setup()
{
  size(320, 200);
  stroke(0, 180, 0);
  noFill();
}

void draw()
{
  background(0);

  rect(round(boxPosX), round(boxPosY), boxWidth, boxHeight);

  boxPosX = boxPosX + boxVelocityX;
  boxPosY = boxPosY + boxVelocityY;

  if (boxPosX < 0) { boxVelocityX = -boxVelocityX; boxPosX = 0; }  //collides
  with left border
  else if ((boxPosX + boxWidth) >= width) { boxVelocityX = -boxVelocityX;
  boxPosX = ((width - boxWidth) - 1); }  //collides with right border

  if (boxPosY < 0) { boxVelocityY = -boxVelocityY; boxPosY = 0; }  //collides
  with top border
  else if ((boxPosY + boxHeight) >= height) { boxVelocityY = -boxVelocityY;
  boxPosY = ((height - boxHeight) - 1); }  //collides with bottom border

  rect(mouseX, (height - 20), paddleWidth, paddleHeight);
  if (boxPosY + boxHeight >= (height - 20))  //box is lower than the top of
  the paddle in y dimension
  {
      if ((boxPosX < (mouseX + paddleWidth)) &&
         ((boxPosX + boxWidth) >= mouseX))  //and it overlaps with it in x
         dimension
      {
         boxVelocityY = -boxVelocityY;
         boxPosY = ((height-20) - boxHeight);
      }
  }
}
```

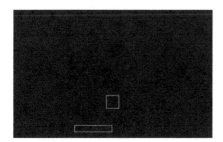

Note that only the top edge of the paddle collides with the square.

Add collision with the sides of the paddle to Code 4!

Bounding box collision is a somewhat rough but quite inexpensive (i.e. fast) method to perform because it uses only a couple of additions and subtractions. An alternative is distance, for instance, between the centre points of two circles. But calculating distance involves extracting a square root, which is among the most expensive (i.e. slow) things to do computationally.[5] The following two code snippets time a bounding box collision check (Code 5) and a distance collision check (Code 6).[6] Both detect if a random point on screen is inside an area (a square for the bounding box method, a circle for the distance method) or not.

Code 5

```
//bounding box

int rectX = 30;
int rectY = 30;
int rectSize = 40;
int repeats = 1000000;

void setup()
{
  frameRate(999999999);  //to defeat the speed limit Processing imposes by
  default7

  rect(rectX, rectY, rectSize, rectSize);

  int startTicks = millis();
  for (int i = 0; i < repeats; i++)
  {
    int x = int(random(1) * width);
    int y = int(random(1) * height);

    if ((x >= rectX) && (x < rectX + rectSize) && (y >= rectY) && (y < rectY +
    rectSize))
    { stroke(0, 255, 0); }
    else
    { stroke(255, 0, 0); }

    point(x, y);  //comment this out for probably more accurate tests
  }
  println(millis() - startTicks);
}
void draw()
{ }
```

Performing one million bounding box checks takes about 1750 ms (on my computer). Ten million checks take just under 17 seconds. Without drawing points, the times appear to vary less between different runs and are thus probably more accurate and representative; then ten million checks take around 600 ms, 100 million around 4.5 seconds.

Code 6

```
//distance

int circleCentreX = 50;
int circleCentreY = 50;
int circleSize = 20;
int repeats = 1000000;
```

```
void setup()
{
  frameRate(999999999);  //to defeat the speed limit Processing imposes by
  default⁸

  ellipse(circleCentreX, circleCentreY, circleSize * 2, circleSize * 2);

  int startTicks = millis();
  for (int i = 0; i < repeats; i++)
  {
    int x = int(random(1) * width);
    int y = int(random(1) * height);

    if (fCalcDistance(x, y, circleCentreX, circleCentreY) < circleSize)
    { stroke(0, 255, 0); }
    else
    { stroke(255, 0, 0); }

    point(x, y);  //comment this out for probably more accurate tests
  }
  println(millis() - startTicks);
}
//calculate and return distance between two given points
float fCalcDistance(float x1, float y1, float x2, float y2)
{
  return sqrt(((x2 - x1) * (x2 - x1)) + ((y2 - y1) * (y2 - y1)));
}

void draw()
{ }
```

Calculating one million distances takes (on my computer) about 1700 ms. Ten million calculations take just under 16 seconds. Without drawing points, ten million checks take around 640 ms, 100 million around 5 seconds.

It appears that this particular comparison shows a minimal speed advantage of the bounding box check over the distance check.

Solution

Add collision with the sides of the paddle to Code 4! Changes are highlighted:

```
float boxPosX = 0;
float boxPosY = 0;
int boxWidth = 20;
int boxHeight = 20;
float boxVelocityX = 3.11;
float boxVelocityY = 2.47;
```

```
int paddleWidth = 60;
int paddleHeight = 10;

void setup()
{
  size(300, 200);
  stroke(0, 180, 0);
  noFill();
}

void draw()
{
  background(0);

  rect(round(boxPosX), round(boxPosY), boxWidth, boxHeight);

  boxPosX = boxPosX + boxVelocityX;
  boxPosY = boxPosY + boxVelocityY;

  if (boxPosX < 0) { boxVelocityX = -boxVelocityX; boxPosX = 0; }  //collides
  with left border
  else if ((boxPosX + boxWidth) >= width) { boxVelocityX = -boxVelocityX;
  boxPosX = ((width - boxWidth) - 1); }  //collides with right border

  if (boxPosY < 0) { boxVelocityY = -boxVelocityY; boxPosY = 0; }  //collides
  with top border
  else if ((boxPosY + boxHeight) >= height) { boxVelocityY = -boxVelocityY;
  boxPosY = ((height - boxHeight) - 1); }  //collides with bottom border

  rect(mouseX, (height - 20), paddleWidth, paddleHeight);
  if (boxPosY + boxHeight >= (height - 20) + 5)  //box is (much) lower than
  the top of the paddle in y dimension
  {
      if ((boxPosX < mouseX) && ((boxPosX + boxWidth) >= mouseX))  //and is
      colliding with the paddle from the left
      {
          boxVelocityX = -boxVelocityX;
          boxPosX = ((mouseX - boxWidth) - 1);
      }
      else if ((boxPosX <= (mouseX + paddleWidth)) &&
              ((boxPosX + boxWidth) > (mouseX + paddleWidth)))  //and is
              colliding with the paddle from the right
      {
          boxVelocityX = -boxVelocityX;
          boxPosX = (mouseX + paddleWidth);
      }
  }
  else if (boxPosY + boxHeight >= (height - 20))  //box is (slightly) lower
  than the top of the paddle in y dimension
  {
      if ((boxPosX < (mouseX + paddleWidth)) &&
          ((boxPosX + boxWidth) >= mouseX))  //and it overlaps with it in x
          dimension
      {
          boxVelocityY = -boxVelocityY;
          boxPosY = ((height-20) - boxHeight);
      }
  }
}
```

Chapter End Exercise

0. The Billiards Simulator

   Make a basic 2D, top-down three-cushion billiards simulator. There is only one ball, the white cue ball. The window is the table, and the ball bounces off the edges. On program start, the cue ball is shot automatically from a starting position in a random direction with a random speed. The speed of the ball remains constant. Textually display the pixel coordinates of the cue ball (e.g. '40/60') on it or just below it. Potential extra features: Place one red ball on the table at a random position; when the red ball is hit by the cue ball, remove it and replace it at a random location; restart the cue ball from the starting position with a random direction and speed; count and display the number of collisions of the cue ball with cushions.

Notes

1. Pixel-perfect collision detection is described in Chapter 32.
2. There are too many Magic Numbers in these code snippets.
3. Ignored is friction, etc.
4. It is checked `<  0` because the window starts at pixel `0` and anything below is out; and it is checked `>= width` because the window ends at pixel `99` and anything equal to or greater than `100` is out.
5. A clever way to avoid doing a square root on one side of an equation, is to square the other side. This is not an exact way to calculate the distance between two points, though, because there are several numbers that evaluate to the same squared number (e.g. 3^2 and -3^2 both evaluate to 9). But it is good enough to compare two distances (see the demo program distancecomparison.zip which is available from the book's web site).
6. For info on elapsed (real) time, see the section 'Elapsed Time' in Chapter 27.
7. This has little effect in this program, because `draw()` does not run (and it appears only the `draw()` function is effected by the `frameRate()` setting (but not the `setup()` function)). For info on how to achieve a consistent game speed despite different hardware speeds, see Chapters 27 and 28.
8. See footnote 7.

17

Drawing Modes and Drawing Lines

Outline

- Drawing Modes
- Drawing Lines

Drawing Modes

By default, rectangles are drawn from their top-left corners with width and height, ellipses from their centre points with x and y diameters. In *Processing*, it is possible to use different reference points. In effect, it is done by changing how the parameters are used – this is for convenience only.

Rects and ellipses have drawing modes. The functions are called `rectMode()` and `ellipseMode()`.

For rectangles the default setting is CORNER, which means, the parameters are read as x, y, width and height. There are three other options available: CORNERS, RADIUS, and CENTER. With the CORNERS setting, the parameters are read as the top-left and bottom-right corners; with the RADIUS setting, the parameters are read as centre point, x radius and y radius; with the CENTER setting, the parameters are read as centre point, x diameter, y diameter (this is the standard setting for ellipses) (Figure 17.1).

The same code is used in all cases: `rect(50, 60, 40, 20)`

For ellipses the default setting is CENTER, which means, the parameters are read as centre point, x diameter, y diameter. There are three other options available: RADIUS, CORNER and CORNERS. With the RADIUS setting, the parameters are read as centre point, x radius, y radius; with the CORNER setting, the parameters are read as the would-be top-left corner, width and height (i.e. the standard setting for rectangles); with the CORNERS setting, the parameters are read as the would-be top-left and bottom-right corners (Figure 17.2).

The same code is used in all cases: `ellipse(50, 60, 40, 20)`

Drawing Lines

We have already seen that lines can drawn in different ways: In colours and shades of grey, opaque and transparent, in various weights (or thicknesses), or not at all. *Processing* has some additional functions to manipulate the drawing of lines.

FIGURE 17.1   Default `rectMode()`, CORNER, CORNERS, RADIUS and CENTER

DOI: 10.1201/9781003345916-17

FIGURE 17.2 Default ellipseMode(), CENTER, RADIUS, CORNER and CORNERS

The strokeCap() function takes one argument, either ROUND, SQUARE, or PROJECT. ROUND is the standard setting and produces rounded line ends. SQUARE makes square ends. PROJECT also makes square ends but adds half a line width to the end of a line (the *Processing* online documentation[1] calls this style 'extended' ends). This function is not really necessary but may simplify code.

Code 1

```
strokeWeight(12);
line(20, 10, 20, 90);
strokeCap(ROUND);
line(40, 10, 40, 90);
strokeCap(SQUARE);
line(60, 10, 60, 90);
strokeCap(PROJECT);
line(80, 10, 80, 90);
```

With the strokeJoin() function, the corner joins of shapes can be set. The standard is MITER which is a square corner; other options are BEVEL for cutoff corners and ROUND for round ones (Code 2).

Code 2

```
size(200, 300);
strokeWeight(10);
quad(100, 145, 50, 170, 100, 270, 150, 170);
strokeJoin(MITER);
quad(100, 105, 50, 130, 100, 230, 150, 130);
strokeJoin(BEVEL);
quad(100, 65, 50, 90, 100, 190, 150, 90);
strokeJoin(ROUND);
quad(100, 25, 50, 50, 100, 150, 150, 50);
```

Note

1. www.processing.org/reference/strokeCap_.html (January 24, 2017).

18

Polygons and Vertex Functions

So far we have only used *Processing*'s shape primitives. They are convenient but also limiting. There is another way to draw shapes, especially suited to be used with structures such as loops and arrays.

A 2D shape made up of straight lines, and with more than two corners,[1] is called a *polygon* in computer graphics lingo. In *Processing*, drawing such a polygon starts with the command beginShape(), followed by the vertices of this shape (given through calls to the vertex() function), and ends with the command endShape(). The polygon is drawn with the current stroke and fill. Being able to draw filled polygons of any shape extends what is possible to draw with primitive shapes (see the section 'Pixel Graphics' in Chapter 2).

The vertex function might or might not appear terribly useful at the moment, but it is an example of a typical programming structure: A bunch of commands that is grouped by begin and end commands. There are a handful of such structures in programming.[2]

Code 1 shows a square drawn this way, and Code 2 shows a more custom-shaped polygon.

Code 1

```
beginShape();

vertex(10, 10);
vertex(90, 10);
vertex(90, 90);
vertex(10, 90);

endShape(CLOSE);
```

Code 2

```
beginShape();

vertex(10, 10);
vertex(50, 35);
vertex(90, 10);
vertex(90, 90);
vertex(65, 90);
vertex(65, 60);
vertex(35, 60);
vertex(35, 90);
vertex(10, 90);

endShape(CLOSE);
```

DOI: 10.1201/9781003345916-18

One can describe simple shapes by providing a number of vertex() commands, but using a loop reduces the typing (Code 3).

Code 3

```
beginShape();
for (int i = 10; i < width; i += 20)
{
  vertex(i, 10);
  vertex(i, 90);
}
endShape(CLOSE);
```

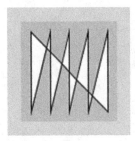

One can instruct beginShape() to interpret the given vertices in a specific way. It has as arguments: POINTS (Code 4), LINES, TRIANGLES, TRIANGLE _ STRIP and QUAD _ STRIP (all Figure 18.1), TRIANGLE _ FAN (Code 5f.) and QUADS (Code 8). endShape() has either no argument or the argument CLOSE to connect the last given vertex to the first, and close the shape. vertex() takes two arguments to designate a location in 2D space, or three arguments to designate one in 3D space.

The selection of these particular shapes may seem arbitrary. But they are efficient for the computer to process and widely used. Virtually all 3D graphics, for instance, are drawn as TRIANGLES (or even as TRIANGLE _ STRIPS).[3]

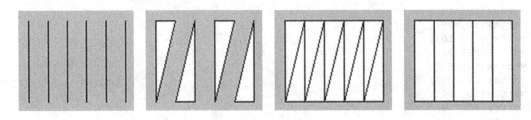

FIGURE 18.1 Code 4 with beginShape() arguments LINES, TRIANGLES, TRIANGLE _ STRIP and QUAD _ STRIP

Code 4

```
size(120, 100);

beginShape(POINTS);

for (int i = 10; i < width; i += 20)
{
  vertex(i, 10);
  vertex(i, 90);
}

endShape();
```

Code 5

```
size(120, 100);

beginShape(TRIANGLE_FAN);

vertex((width + 10), (height * 0.5));

for (int i = 10; i < width; i += 20)
{
  vertex(i, 10);
  vertex(i, 90);
}

endShape();
```

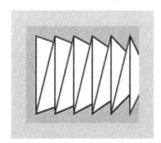

A different example using the TRIANGLE _ FAN is Code 6 (based on Code 9 in Chapter 15).

Code 6

```
int widthHalf = int(width * 0.5);
int heightHalf = int(height * 0.5);

float scaleX = (width * 0.5);
float scaleY = (height * 0.5);
```

```
beginShape(TRIANGLE_FAN);

vertex(widthHalf, heightHalf);

for (int i = 0; i <= 360; i += 36)
{
  float radiansI = radians(i);

  vertex(widthHalf + (cos(radiansI) * scaleX), heightHalf - (sin(radiansI) *
  scaleY));
}

endShape();
```

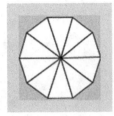

Note that the *for* loop runs as long as i <= 360; otherwise, the last triangle is left incomplete and is not drawn.

Code 7 shows the same program with the QUAD _ STRIP setting and a slightly modified *for* loop.

Code 7

```
int widthHalf = int(width * 0.5);
int heightHalf = int(height * 0.5);

float scaleX = (width * 0.5);
float scaleY = (height * 0.5);

beginShape(QUAD_STRIP);

for (int i = 0; i <= 400; i += 36)
{
  float radiansI = radians(i);

  vertex(widthHalf + (cos(radiansI) * scaleX), heightHalf - (sin(radiansI) *
  scaleY));
}

endShape();
```

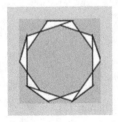

Modify Code 7 to draw any regular n-sided polygon!

Code 8 demonstrates the use of the QUADS mode.

Code 8

```
size(120, 100);

beginShape(QUADS);
for (int i=10; i<width; i+=40)
{
  vertex(i, 10);
  vertex(i, 90);
  vertex(i+20, 90);
  vertex(i+20, 10);
}
endShape();
```

The strokeJoin() function (see the section 'Drawing Lines' in Chapter 17) that sets the style for joining vertices together (i.e. the corner style; MITER, BEVEL or ROUND), works not only with primitive shapes such as quads but also with polygons (Code 9). Default is, as before, MITER.

Code 9

```
size(200, 300);

strokeWeight(10);

beginShape(QUADS);
vertex(100, 145);
vertex(50, 170);
vertex(100, 270);
vertex(150, 170);
endShape();

strokeJoin(MITER);
beginShape(QUADS);
vertex(100, 105);
vertex(50, 130);
vertex(100, 230);
vertex(150, 130);
endShape();

strokeJoin(BEVEL);
beginShape(QUADS);
vertex(100, 65);
vertex(50, 90);
vertex(100, 190);
vertex(150, 90);
endShape();
```

```
strokeJoin(ROUND);
beginShape(QUADS);
vertex(100, 25);
vertex(50, 50);
vertex(100, 150);
vertex(150, 50);
endShape();
```

Solution

Modify Code 7 to draw any regular n-sided polygon. Changes are highlighted.

```
int widthHalf = int(width * 0.5);
int heightHalf = int(height * 0.5);

float scaleX = (width * 0.5);
float scaleY = (height * 0.5);

int numberVertices = 6;

beginShape();
for (int i = 0; i < 360; i += (360 / numberVertices))
{
  float radiansI = radians(i);

  vertex(widthHalf + (cos(radiansI) * scaleX), heightHalf - (sin(radiansI) *
  scaleY));
}
endShape(CLOSE);
```

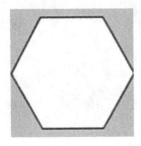

Note that the *for* loop runs only as long as i < 360; thus, to close the shape, the CLOSE argument of the endShape() function is invoked (compare Code 6).

Notes

1. The fancy word for corner is *vertex*, plural *vertices*.
2. Certainly, they were popular in early *OpenGL*.
3. Not that anybody would do 3D graphics with *Processing*.

19

Colour and Transparency

Outline

- Specifying colours
- Colour spaces
- *Processing*'s colour modes
- *Colour components*

Colour is often seen as one of the essential assets in visual design (the others being, for instance, material and form). For the use in programming, colour needs to be coded in some way, and we have already used the widely-known RGB format to code colours. But there exist (and are used) many other colour modes such as CMYK and HSB. Colour modes describe colours through numerical values, and they differ from each other in how they do map (numerical) values to (visible) colours. Colour modes are geared towards and suited for specific, different applications.

Specifying Colours

In *Processing*, greys can be specified as a single parameter, colours in RGB or in RGBA (RGB and alpha/ transparency) format:

```
color dark = color(40);

color brightRed = color(255, 0, 0);

color transparentBlue = color(0, 0, 200, 100);
```

   color is a data type in *Processing*, and color() is a function that takes one to four int (or float) parameters, and returns a color value.

   Code 1 draws coloured ellipses at random locations within the window.

Code 1

```
strokeWeight(2);
background(255, 190, 0);

for (int i = 0; i < 50; i++)
{
  int rand = int(random(255));
  color c = color ((rand * 7) % 255, (rand * 13) % 255, (rand * 17) % 255);
  fill(c);
  ellipse(random(width), random(height), 28, 35);
}
```

DOI: 10.1201/9781003345916-19

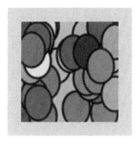

The same code with added constant transparency (highlight; Code 2):

Code 2

```
strokeWeight(2);
background(255, 190, 0);

for (int i = 0; i < 15; i++)
{
  int rand = int(random(255));
  color c = color ((rand * 7) % 255, (rand * 13) % 255, (rand * 17) % 255, 100);
  fill(c);
  ellipse(random(width), random(height), 28, 35);
}
```

Colour Spaces

Colour spaces describe subsets of colours within the visible spectrum. The range of colours that lie within a colour space is called a *gamut*.

Certain devices use certain colour spaces. For example, screens use RGB, and printers use CMYK. Because the colour spaces are not equivalent, and colours need to be converted between devices, they change.[1] When a colour cannot be described in a colour space, it is said to be *out of gamut* (Figure 19.1).

RGB and CMYK are widely used; other popular colour models are HSB and LAB.

RGB

RGB (red, green, blue) is the colour model for (computer, TV) screens and the default colour model in *Processing*. The RGB model is called an *additive* colour model because white is created by having all components at maximum value. A wide range of colours of the visible spectrum can be described in RGB.

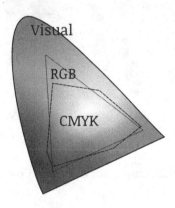

FIGURE 19.1   Visual gamut, RGB colour space and CMYK colour space

In *Processing*, each of the three components are described by an 8-bit (int) value, that is, 0 to 255.

But the RGB model is not God-given. In fact, if it wasn't for the computer and its displays, few people would know about it. It is not very intuitive and basically a technical artefact.

HSB

A colour model that is considerably closer than RGB to how humans see colour is the HSB (hue, saturation, brightness) model. Hue and brightness are obvious, but what is saturation? The saturation of a colour determines how full or fat or sweet a colour looks. Rock band photos and war movies have their saturation regularly reduced substantially; comics and children's TV programs often feature very saturated colours.

Processing can use either the RGB or the HSB model. The command to change the colour model is colorMode().

CMYK

The CMYK (cyan, magenta, yellow, key/black) colour model is used in printing (and high-end DTP). Black is added to produce dark colours, rather than mixing them from CMY alone. While the RGB model relies on red, green and blue light *emitted* from a device (e.g. a screen), colours on paperwork by *absorbing* some of the light that shines on them and reflecting the rest. CMYK is called a *subtractive* colour model because white is created by having all components at minimum value.

LAB

The LAB colour model is conceived to be device-independent. It defines colours as they are perceived by a person with normal vision. LAB's three channels are luminance (brightness), green to red, and blue to yellow. *Photoshop* uses Lab internally to e.g. convert between RGB and CMYK (Weinmann/Lourekas 2012).

Processing's Colour Modes

Processing has two colour modes, RGB and HSB. RGB is enabled by default.

Code 3 uses RGB and Code 4 HSB to display a range of colours.

Code 3

```
size(140, 280);
noStroke();
background(0);

int y=0;

for (int r = 0; r < 256; r += 127)
{
  for (int g = 0; g < 256; g += 127)
  {
    for (int b = 0; b < 256; b += 127)
    {
      if ((y % 2) == 0)   //display only every second time
      {
        fill(r, g, b);
        rect(0, (y * 10), (width * 0.5), 10);
        text(nf(r, 3) + " " + nf(g, 3) + " " + nf(b, 3), (width * 0.5), 10 +
        (y * 10));
      }
      y++;
    }
  }
}
```

Code 4

```
size(140, 255);
noStroke();
colorMode(HSB);
background(0);

for (int h = 0; h < 256; h += 16)
{
  fill(h, 255, 255);
  rect(0, h, (width * 0.5), 10);
  text(nf(h, 3) + " 255 255", (width * 0.5), 10+h);
}
```

Colour Components

We have seen (in the section 'Specifying Colours', earlier in this chapter) how the `color()` function can be used to get values *into* a `color` variable. But how to get values *out of* a `color` variable?

Processing offers seven colour component functions to extract a single component from a given colour. The functions `red()`, `green()`, `blue()`, `hue()`, `saturation()`, `brightness()` and `alpha()` work the same way regardless of the active colour mode (RGB or HSB; Code 5).

Code 5

```
size(250, 200);

noStroke();
color c = color(128, 196, 255, 100);
fill(c);
rect(0, 0, width, height);

fill(0);

text("Red component of color c is "+red(c), 10, 30);
text("Green component of color c is "+green(c), 10, 50);
text("Blue component of color c is "+blue(c), 10, 70);

text("Hue component of color c is "+hue(c), 10, 100);
text("Saturation component of color c is "+saturation(c), 10, 120);
text("Brightness component of color c is "+brightness(c), 10, 140);

text("Alpha component of color c is "+alpha(c), 10, 170);
```

Red component of color c is 128.0
Green component of color c is 196.0
Blue component of color c is 255.0

Hue component of color c is 147.2441
Saturation component of color c is 127.0
Brightness component of color c is 255.0

Alpha component of color c is 100.0

Note

1. Another aspect is that the display technology influences how colours are shown. Some colours in print cannot be shown on screen and vice versa.

20

Text and Fonts, and Loading and Saving Data

Outline

- *Processing*'s text() Function
- Fonts in *Processing*
- Loading and Saving Data

Processing's `text()` Function

Processing's function to output text unto the screen (rather than to the console, Chapter 3) is called text(). The text() function has already been used, for instance, in Code 7 in Chapter 15 and in Code 3 in Chapter 19. It takes as parameters the string to display and two screen coordinates (Code 1).

Code 1

```
text("Hello World", 10, 50);
```

The text() function also handles concatenated (i.e. put together) strings.[1] Such strings can be concatenated from various types of variables, such as strings and ints. The text size can be set with the textSize() function (Code 2).

Code 2

```
size(500, 100);
textSize(18);
text("This string " + "is" + " concatenated", 10, 40);
int a = 100;
String s = "with variables";
text("One can also concatenate strings " + s + ": " + a, 10, 70);
```

This string is concatenated
One can also concatenate strings with variables: 100

DOI: 10.1201/9781003345916-20

		Horizontal alignment		
		LEFT (default)	CENTER	RIGHT
	TOP	Text Output	Text Output	Text Output
Vertical alignment	CENTER	Text Output	Text Output	Text Output
	BOTTOM (default)	Text Output	Text Output	Text Output

FIGURE 20.1 Reference points in horizontal and vertical text alignment

Similar to changing the reference points for rectangles and ellipses (see the section 'Drawing Modes' in Chapter 17), the reference points for outputting text can be altered. The function textAlign() takes one or two arguments. The one-argument version sets the horizontal reference point with regard to text alignment to either LEFT, RIGHT or CENTER. The two-argument version sets the horizontal alignment with the first argument, the vertical alignment (TOP, BOTTOM or CENTER) with the second (Figure 20.1). The default text alignment is LEFT, BOTTOM. Note that the BOTTOM alignment places the reference point not on the baseline of the text but at its lower boundary. Code 1 in Chapter 21 demonstrates the use of the function.

Fonts in *Processing*

There are two ways to use fonts in *Processing*. One can render them at run-time from their vector format or one can use a *Processing* Environment-made bitmapped version.

For the first method (using createFont(); Code 3), the font needs to be available on the system the program runs on, or to be included (as a ttf or otf file) in the sketch's data folder; but this method can output text in any size.

The second method (using loadFont(); Code 5) displays the correct font no matter which fonts are (not) installed on the user's system, but every font and font size needs to be prepared. It looks terrible when the font sizes used are different from the font sizes which were pre-rendered.

Code 3
```
void setup()
{
  size(600, 600);
  fill(0);
  PFont fontRender = createFont("Times-Roman", 48);
  textFont(fontRender);

  for (int i = 0; i < 10; i++)
  {
    text(i+" abcdefghijklmnopqrstuvwxyz0123456789", 10, 50 + (i * 50));
  }
}
```

```
0 abcdefghijklmnopqrstu
1 abcdefghijklmnopqrstu
2 abcdefghijklmnopqrstu
3 abcdefghijklmnopqrstu
4 abcdefghijklmnopqrstu
5 abcdefghijklmnopqrstu
6 abcdefghijklmnopqrstu
7 abcdefghijklmnopqrstu
8 abcdefghijklmnopqrstu
9 abcdefghijklmnopqrstu
```

To establish, which fonts are available on a system, use the `PFont.list()` method, which returns a `String` array (Code 4).

Code 4

```
for (int i = 0; i < PFont.list().length; i++)
{
  println(PFont.list()[i]);
}
```

For the second method (using `loadFont()`; Code 5) a bitmapped version of a font is created and saved in the sketch's `data` folder (select Tools/Create Font...).

Code 5

```
void setup()
{
  size(600, 600);
  fill(0);
  PFont fontBitmapped = loadFont("Times-Roman-48.vlw");
  textFont(fontBitmapped);

  for (int i = 0; i < 10; i++)
  {
    text(i+" abcdefghijklmnopqrstuvwxyz0123456789", 10, 50 + (i * 50));
  }
}
```

```
0 abcdefghijklmnopqrstuvwxyz
1 abcdefghijklmnopqrstuvwxyz
2 abcdefghijklmnopqrstuvwxyz
3 abcdefghijklmnopqrstuvwxyz
4 abcdefghijklmnopqrstuvwxyz
5 abcdefghijklmnopqrstuvwxyz
6 abcdefghijklmnopqrstuvwxyz
7 abcdefghijklmnopqrstuvwxyz
8 abcdefghijklmnopqrstuvwxyz
9 abcdefghijklmnopqrstuvwxyz
```

Loading and Saving Data

Processing, and virtually all other programming languages, can load data from files (i.e. from disk or even from other sources, such as online links (see Code 4 in Chapter 22). Data that is popularly loaded include images (Code 1 in Chapter 22), mouse pointers (Code 3 in Chapter 22), fonts (Code 5), as well as text and graphics files that define tiled levels (Code 1 and Code 2 in Chapter 29).

Here it is explained how to load and save plain text files. *Processing* looks for a file identified by a filename in the current folder. If the file is located in the `data` folder, this needs to be added to the filename, i.e. `data/textfile.txt`. Include the file extension (`txt`, in this case). Note that file extensions are sometimes not visible (i.e. shown) by the operating system on the default setting (but showing file extensions can be switched on). If a program cannot find a file it is supposed to load, it usually crashes (if no exception handling is performed[2]).

Code 6 shows how a program can load a text file from a disk (the program code, in this case) and display it on the screen. It uses *Processing*'s the default font, in size 20. The source code file must be named 'textfileload.pde' for the code to work.

Code 6

```
void setup()
{
  size(640, 480);
  textSize(20);
  background(0);

  String[] stringsFromFile = loadStrings("textfileload.pde");
  int lineSpacing = 24;

  for (int i = 0; i < stringsFromFile.length; i++)
  {
    text(stringsFromFile[i], 16, lineSpacing + (i * lineSpacing));
  }
}
```

Note, the file can be any length, but only about 20 lines fit into the window.

Code 7 displays a text file on screen and saves it to disk (to the data folder). By default (i.e. without specifying a path), *Processing* saves files to the program folder. If a file is to be saved to the data folder, this needs to be specified (as in this example).

Code 7

```
void setup()
{
  size(640, 480);
  textSize(20);
  background(0);

  int lineSpacing = 22;
  int lineNumber = 20;
  String[] stringsToFile = new String[lineNumber];

  for (int i = 0; i < lineNumber; i++)
  {
    stringsToFile[i] = "";  //start with an empty string...
    for (int j = 0; j < 4; j++) { stringsToFile[i] += char(65 +
    int(random(26))); }  //...then add a random four-letter word
  }
```

```
for (int i = 0; i < stringsToFile.length; i++)  //show on screen
{
  text(stringsToFile[i], 16, lineSpacing + (i * lineSpacing));
}
saveStrings("data/textfile.txt", stringsToFile);  //save to disk
}
```

The text file that is saved contains 20 lines, each containing a random four-letter word. Running the program again overwrites the previously created file.

Code 8 demonstrates how a text file can be read, edited by the user,[3] and saved. A text file is automatically loaded on program startup, then the user can add (and delete) characters, and the text file is saved when the enter/return key is pressed. The next time the program is started, the text entered the previous time comes up. A file 'enter.txt' must exist in the data folder for the code to work.

Code 8

```
String enter = "";

void setup()
{
  String[] lines = loadStrings("data/enter.txt");  //the file 'enter.txt' is
  in the data folder
  enter = lines[0];
}

void keyPressed()
{
  if ((key == ENTER) || (key == RETURN))
  {
    String[] lines =  new String[1];
    lines[0] = enter;
    saveStrings("data/enter.txt", lines);
  }
  else if (key == BACKSPACE)
  {
    String enterTemp = "";
    for (int i = 0; i < enter.length() - 1; i++)  //copy all chars except
    the last one
    {
      enterTemp += enter.charAt(i);
    }
```

```
      enter = enterTemp;
  }
  else if (key != CODED) { enter += key; }
}
void draw()
{
  background(50);
  text(enter + "_", 10, 50);
}
```

Note that loadStrings() has an undocumented feature: If a file to load is given without any path info, it appears, loadStrings() first tries to load the file from the data folder (located within the program folder); if the file cannot be found there, it tries to load the file from the program folder.[4] Of course, there is no reason to let *Processing* search around for the file when we know where it is, and we can easily give loadStrings() the path to it. When saving a file, *Processing* cannot do this. saveStrings() only saves the file at the specified location.

Code 8 is not very elaborate. A slightly more powerful and interesting program is available from the book's website.

Chapter End Exercise

0. The Chose-Your-Own-Adventure Book Reader

Implement a program that simulates a text-only chose-your-own-adventure (CYOA) book. The program reads a text file (e.g. '0.txt') and shows it to the player. The player can then decide what to do (e.g. where to go), and the program loads the corresponding file, etc. Each file has a story segment and the possible options.

The output for one segment could look like Table 20.1.

TABLE 20.1

Example Incident

```
The Bear Incident

As you exit the dense bush of the forest and come to a small, open area, you suddenly
hear the unmistakable sound of an approaching bear. What do you do?

Run into the direction you came from (option 0); prepare a magic spell, so you are ready
to cast it, as soon as the bear appears (option 1); climb the tall tree to your left
(option 2); or step into the centre of the opening, calmly draw your sword, and prepare
for the confrontation with the beast (option 3).

Press 0, 1, 2 or 3!
```

Notes

1. To be precise, a `String` can be concatenated and then passed as an argument to the `text()` function. The `text()` function simply accepts a `String`.
2. For brief info on exception handling, see the section 'Crashes at Run Time' in Chapter 23.
3. For info on keyboard interaction, see Chapter 26.
4. Note also that `loadStrings()` can load files from online sources (`loadStrings("https://www.dace.de/index.html")`).

21

Real Time

Processing (as well as other languages) can access the computer's internal clock. *Processing* retrieves the current time data with the six functions second(), minute(), hour(), day(), month(), and year(). Code 1 uses some of these functions (highlight) and displays a digital clock with an appropriate font (the nf() function inserts leading zeros as needed).

Code 1

```
void setup()
{
  size(300, 100);

  PFont q = createFont("Digit", 48);  //use a font available on the computer
  textFont(q);
  textAlign(CENTER, CENTER);
  textSize(72);

  fill(0, 128, 0);
}
void draw()
{
  background(0);

  String nowHour = nf(hour(), 2);  //nf() inserts leading zeros
  String nowMinute = nf(minute(), 2);
  String nowSecond = nf(second(), 2);

  text(nowHour + ":" + nowMinute + ":" + nowSecond, (width * 0.5), (height *
  0.5));
}
```

The clock works ok. But ideally, it would only be redrawn when actually there is something to redraw, i.e. when there was indeed a change. Modify Code 1 so that the window is only redrawn after the seconds have changed!

DOI: 10.1201/9781003345916-21

Solution

Modify Code 1 so that the window is only redrawn after the seconds have changed!

```
int oldSecond = -1;  //set to -1 to draw at the start in any case¹
void setup()
{
  size(300, 100);

  PFont q = createFont("Digit", 48);
  textFont(q);
  textAlign(CENTER, CENTER);
  textSize(72);

  fill(0, 128, 0);
}

void draw()
{
  if (oldSecond != second())  //did a change occur?
  {
    oldSecond = second();  //then save value for next comparison

    background(0);  //and redraw everything

    String nowHour=nf(hour(), 2);  //nf() inserts 2 leading zeros
    String nowMinute=nf(minute(), 2);
    String nowSecond=nf(second(), 2);

    text(nowHour + ":" + nowMinute + ":" + nowSecond, (width * 0.5), (height
    * 0.5));
  }
}
```

Chapter End Exercises

0. The Stop Watch

   Make a stopwatch with a (numerical) display of the elapsed time and three separate buttons that can be clicked with the mouse to start, stop and reset the watch (the action should be triggered on-button-press, not on-release). Do not use second(), minute(), hour() or frameRate(). Use classes and objects.

1. The Flip Watch

   Make a digital flip clock that shows the time numerically in 24-hour format (hhmmss). The clock has five functions beyond showing the current time: Toggle alarm function on/off (i.e. does the clock sound the alarm sound when the alarm time is reached), set an alarm time, sound an alarm (import and use the *Minim* library, see Chapter 37), switch alarm off when it is currently on, and illuminate the clock display for five seconds. All functions are triggered by both mouse and keyboard.

   Potential extra feature: Digit animation (i.e. when one digit is replaced with another).

Note

1. oldSecond is a global variable, visible in the whole program. Try to use as few global variables as possible, otherwise programs get crowded and unclear fast. Use local variables where possible, that is, variables declared inside structures such as loops and functions.

22

Images

A raster (or bitmap) image consists of a number of pixels with colour (and/or transparency) values.[1] Images have a size (in pixels) and a colour depth (in bits).[2] Popular colour depths for digital images are 1 bit (black and white), 8 bits (256 colours), 16 bits (65536 colours) and 24 bits (16777216 colours).

The computer needs to know how to interpret and use the image data; therefore, image formats organise it in specific ways. There are many different (bitmapped) graphics formats. *Processing*[3] can read gif, jpeg (or jpg), png, targa (tga) and tiff (or tif)[4] files (Processing 2016). By default, *Processing* tries to load files from the sketch folder or from the data folder inside the sketch folder.[5]

Each graphics format has different properties; Table 22.1 lists the most essential properties for the five (or four) graphics formats *Processing* can read.

The image() function is called to show an image on screen. The function takes either three or five arguments: The image to use, the top left screen coordinates, and (optionally) the dimensions (width and height) of the (stretched, if necessary) image.

The data type for images is PImage. PImage is a class that has variables (or *fields*) such as width and height (Code 2), and methods such as get() and set().

In *Processing*, images can be loaded from disk (or from online resources), manipulated (e.g. resized, filtered) and displayed on the screen.

TABLE 22.1

Image Format Properties

Name	Graphics Interchage Format (version 89a, 1989)	Joint Photographic Experts Group (1994)	Portable Network Graphics (2004)	Truevision Advanced Raster Graphics Adapter, Truevision Graphics Adapter (version 2, 1989)	Tagged Image File Format (version 6.0, 1992)
File suffix	gif	jpeg or jpg	png	tga	tiff or tif
Maximum colour depth	8 bit	16 bit	24 bit	24 bit	24 bit
Transparency	Yes	No	8 bit alpha	8 bit alpha	No
Compression	Lossless LZW	Lossy	Lossless	Lossless RLE	Lossless (RLE, PackBits, LZW) or lossy (JPEG)
Speciality	Proprietary format, interlaced, animation	-	Interlaced	-	Versatile, several images per file
Typical application	Small online graphics	Offline and online photos	Editing images, drawings, online images	Textures	Editing and exchanging images
Read by *Processing*	Yes	Yes	Yes	Yes	Its own files

DOI: 10.1201/9781003345916-22

▼ 🗀 arrow	2 items
▼ 🗀 data	1 item
🔖 arrow.png	575 bytes
🖼 arrow.pde	138 bytes

FIGURE 22.1 Directory structure and file locations for the arrow example: The program file `arrow.pde` is in the program folder `arrow`; the graphics file `arrow.png` is in the `data` folder within the program folder

Code 1 loads an image from disk (which needs to exist, of course, for the program to run; Figure 22.1) and displays it. The `image()` function is called from within `setup()` (and not from within `draw()`) because we only want to draw it once (and not repeatedly).

Code 1

```
PImage image;

void setup()
{
  image = loadImage("arrow.png");
  image(image, 10, 20);
}

void draw()
{ }
```

The image file `arrow.png` is located in the same folder as the sketch or in the sketch's `data` folder (Figure 22.1).

Code 2 not only shows an image but also demonstrates how to access the `width` and `height` fields of the image.

Code 2

```
PImage sign;

size(700, 900);
background(220, 140, 0);

sign = loadImage("sign.jpg");   //⁶
image(sign, 50, 50);
text("Image size " + sign.width + " x " + sign.height + " pixels", 50,
(height-20));
```

Code 3 demonstrates how an image can be used as a pointer. It replaces the standard mouse pointer with an image loaded from disk.

Code 3

```
PImage arrow;
void setup()
{
  arrow = loadImage("arrow.png");
  cursor(arrow, 0, 0);

  background(10, 190, 70);
}
void draw()
{ }
```

One could use an image instead of the default mouse pointer, of course, also without using *Processing*'s cursor() function (but noCursor() is used). How? Modify Code 3!

Code 4 loads an image from an online resource and displays it. Make sure the file exists for the program to work.

Code 4

```
PImage skyline;
void setup()
{
  size(320, 240);
  strokeWeight(height * 0.4);
  noFill();

  skyline = loadImage("https://upload.wikimedia.org/wikipedia/commons/6/60/
  Pittsburgh_skyline_view.jpg", "jpg");
}
void draw()
{
  background(0);
  image(skyline, ((width - mouseX) - width), ((height - mouseY) - height));

  rect(0, 0, width, height, (height * 0.5));
}
```

Solution

One could use an image instead of the default mouse pointer, of course, also without using *Processing*'s `cursor()` function (but `noCursor()` is used). How? Modify Code 3! Changes are highlighted.

```
PImage arrow;

void setup()
{
  arrow = loadImage("arrow.png");
  noCursor();
}

void draw()
{
  background(10, 190, 70);
  image(arrow, mouseX, mouseY);
}
```

Chapter End Exercises

0. The Art Photo

   Load a photo from a hard disk and display it on screen.[7] Modify the code to display the image twelve times, in a 4x3 arrangement.

   Potential extra feature: Apply a graphical filter to the images. One can do the image filtering oneself (i.e. looping through the images pixel by pixel), or one can use *Processing*'s rudimentary built-in image filters to manipulate `PImage`s (check out the documentation at www.processing.org/reference/PImage_filter_.html).

1. The Dither Filter

   Make a dither function that modifies a greyscale or colour image into a black and white image. The function loads and goes through the image, looks at blocks of e.g. 4x4 pixels, and calculates the average brightness. It then places a black dot corresponding the brightness of the screen (low brightness triggers a large black dot, high brightness no or a small black dot).

Notes

1. Graphics can also be represented in vector formats such as `dxf`, `svg`, `eps`, `ai` (Adobe *Illustrator*) and `cdr` (Corel *Draw!*).
2. The Commodore *64* has a native resolution of 320x200 pixels (plus a border); these can be addressed in different graphic modes. A popular mode is the multicolour mode (160x200 pixels in 16 colours) (www.studiostyle.sk/dmagic/gallery/gfxmodes.htm, grumbel.blogspot.dk/2011/03/c64s-graphical-capabilities.html (March 5, 2016)), the ZX *Spectrum* has a 256x192 resolution with 8 colours (www.c64vsspectrum.com (March 5, 2016)). The *CPC* has three official graphics modes of 160×200 pixels with 16 colours (4 bpp), 320×200 pixels with 4 colours (2 bpp) and 640×200 pixels with 2 colours (1 bpp) (www.cpcwiki.eu/index.php/Video_modes (March 5, 2016)). A typical resolution for a windowing system around 2000 is 1024x768 in 16-bit colour (e.g. a PC with *Windows 95*). My current 2020 M1 *MacBook Air* has a 13" display with a resolution of 2560x1600 pixels in many colours (it is surprisingly difficult to find out, what the exact specs are; various websites report 'millions of colours', 'True Tone technology', and/or 'Wide colour (P3)').
3. Version 4.2; later versions are probably able to read more formats.

4. It appears that 'Processing can only read its own TIFF files' (*Processing* 3 error message, attempting to read a *Photoshop CS6* 13.0 x64-written `tif` file (without compression, interleaved pixel order, and *Mac* byte order)).
5. The sketch folder is where the code of the program (or *sketch*, in *Processing* lingo) is located.
6. Check out where the image file should be located on the hard disk in Figure 22.1.
7. Check out the *Processing* documentation on `image()` to find out how to load an image and display it.

23

The Processing *IDE, Technical Documentation, Debugging and Common Errors*

Outline

- The *Processing* IDE
- Reading Technical Documentation
- The Process of Debugging
- Common Errors

The *Processing* IDE

Integrated Development Environments (IDEs; Figure 23.1) are *front ends* for programming languages. IDEs such as the *Processing* IDE (called the *Processing Development Environment (PDE)* in *Processing* lingo; Figure 1.1), are not identical with the programming language, in the way that *Photoshop is* the program. IDEs are a kind of text editor but usually integrate writing code, compiling and debugging. In principle (and in practice as well; Figure 23.6) code can be created with any simple text editor and then compiled on the command line. But IDEs offer desirable features and are more comfortable to use than a stand-alone text editor with a command-line compiler. The most notable programming-specific function is probably an integrated compiler, to compile (and run) programs from within the IDE.

Here, several relevant and useful features of *Processing*'s IDE are briefly described.

Compiler

The primary feature that the *Processing* IDE offers compared to plain text editors, is an integrated compiler. Compilers which are used from the command line usually only list errors and the files and line numbers where the errors occur. The compiler in the *Processing* IDE not only lists errors[1] but also tries to highlight them in the code and to mark relevant lines and even the specific position on a line.[2] Recent versions of the *Processing* IDE also provide a syntax check in real-time, while the user is (still) typing (similar to spell-checking in word-processing software).[3]

Hotkeys

The hotkey (or *shortcut*) Ctrl-S (or Apple-S) saves the whole project; this is probably the most frequently used hotkey. In most programs (such as editors), only the currently active file is usually saved (e.g. the text in the current editor tab), but the *Processing* IDE saves all tabs or source files. Today, computers crash relatively infrequently in ordinary use, so manic saving behaviours are usually not necessary. But computers still crash, particularly when coding. One should save the project before running particularly wonky code, because the computer might crash or freeze, and the last code changes might then be lost. One can compile and run the program (or *Sketch*, as they are called in official *Processing* lingo) with Ctrl-R (Apple-R). Autoformat of the current tab is triggered with Ctrl-T (Apple-T; see Chapter 11).

DOI: 10.1201/9781003345916-23

FIGURE 23.1 A typical window layout for an IDE is shown by *Eclipse* (left, version 2022-12R): Code on top, the console on the bottom and a view of files, functions or classes, etc. on the left (plus an overview over the current structure on the far right of the window); *VS Code* (right, version 1.76.0, from 2023) shows a similar arrangement (plus a visual minimap of the code on the far right)

Tabs

Tabs refer to different files on the disk. They are useful for separating the program code into manageable chunks. Usually, one tab is used for the main program, and the other tabs for one class each.[4] The advantages of tabs are that one can relatively quickly switch between them and find locations in the code, and one can also easily copy individual files such as classes to other projects. Internally, the compiler treats all tabs as one long file. That means, that any code that is placed in a tab outside of all structures is on the global scope (but one should really collect all global variables at the top of the main program, not at various places in different tabs).

Autocompletion

Autocompletion (or *autocomplete, code completion*) is a feature that automatically completes words the user starts to type. This is not intended primarily for saving the user some typing (this also happens), but to inform the user of code syntax, such as variable names, function names, and the number, type and order of function and method arguments. Without autocompletion, the user needs to either remember these things or to look them up (e.g. in the *Processing* online documentation, see the section 'Reading Technical Documentation' later in this chapter). Remembering the arguments for the most common functions such as `rect()` or `stroke()` might be easy enough, but specifically for obscure or rarely used functions autocompletion is very helpful (Figure 23.2 (left)).[5]

Finding and Downloading Libraries

The *Processing* IDE has a feature for the user to browse, search, download, install and use programming libraries such as *minim* (in the menu under `Sketch/Import Library.../Manage Libraries...`; see Chapter 37; Figure 23.3 (left)). Libraries can also be downloaded manually, but the automatic feature is quite convenient, of course. A great number of libraries are available through the platform, and many of them are of high quality.

Different Programming Modes

IDEs are not tied to particular programming languages and can be used for different languages. The *Processing* IDE can be used in different *modes*. The current mode is shown in the top right corner. By default, the *Java* mode is activated and supports the *Processing* programming language, but it also supports *Java*, of course. Other modes can be installed for languages such as *p5.js*, *Python* and *R*. Very

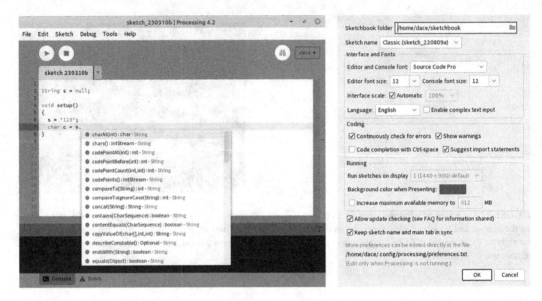

FIGURE 23.2   Autocompletion suggesting class methods (left); and *Processing* IDE preference settings (right)

interesting is the possibility to develop programs for *Android* devices with the 'Processing for Android' mode (Figure 23.3 (right)).

Syntax Highlighting

Syntax highlighting (or *code highlighting*) is a feature of virtually all IDEs (and many editors; Figure 23.6 (left)), to colour-code different syntactical parts of a program. Different parts of the code such as comments, function names, loops, literal `strings` are then visually marked in different colours (see, e.g. Figure 23.4). Different IDEs use different colour schemes (which can usually also be customised by the user).

Debugger

A *debugger* is a specialised tool to support the process of debugging program code. Debuggers are usually integrated with IDEs and offer powerful functions such as stopping program execution at a

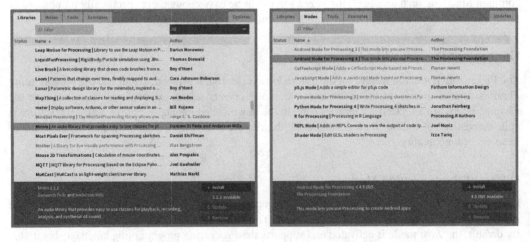

FIGURE 23.3   Adding programming libraries (left) and language support (right) to *Processing* through the IDE's *Contribution Manager*

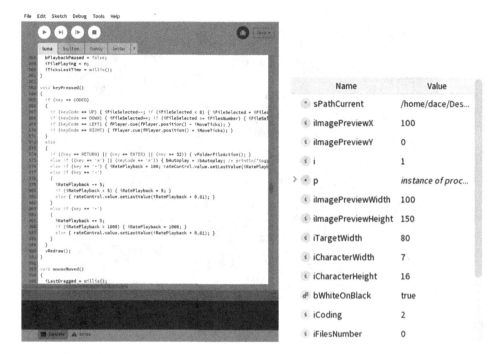

FIGURE 23.4 *Processing IDE* with enabled debugger (note the four buttons; left) and the debugger window showing the contents of variables (right)

particular point in the code, or stepping through the program execution line by line, and allowing the user to see, for instance, the contents of variables (what would otherwise be done with console or screen debug output, see the section 'The Process of Debugging' later in this chapter). A debugger can simplify and streamline the tracking of bugs considerably. *Processing*'s debugger (which was only recently added to the IDE in *Processing 3*) can be activated in the menu under Debug/Enable Debugger (Figure 23.4).

A feature that IDEs regularly have, but which is (yet) omitted from *Processing*'s IDE is to allow the user to *collapse* (or *hide*) and *expand* code structures such as loops or function definitions (Figure 23.1 (right); note that the function fFilelistMake() and the else clause in the function vFolderFileAction() are collapsed and not shown). The idea is that parts of the program that are currently not worked on, do not need to be shown to the user and to take up screen space. Collapsing structures make long program code (virtually) shorter. It does not affect which code is compiled or run, though; collapsing and expanding is merely a visual effect. Of course, many bugs have been spotted because a piece of code was coincidentally visible on screen.

The default *Processing* IDE is rather basic and not very sophisticated. There are very elaborate and (considerably more) powerful IDEs available for many programming languages. Currently popular appear to be, for instance, *Eclipse* and *Visual Studio Code*, and also *NetBeans IDE* (for *C, C++, Java*), *Komodo IDE* (*Python*) and *PyCharm* (*Python*).

Eclipse (Figure 23.1 (left); originally developed by IBM in 2001) is primarily known as a *Java* development environment. Support for a host of other languages can be added through plug-ins (called *bundles*); and *Eclipse* can be made to work with *Processing* as well. *Eclipse* is free.

Visual Studio Code (*VS Code*, Figure 23.1 (right); first released 2015) is a lightweight IDE that runs on *Windows, Mac* and *Linux*. It provides all essential IDE features including version control. Support for languages and additional editor features can be installed via plug-ins (called *extensions*; Figure 23.5). The IDE is popularly used with *C*-based languages and *Python*. A *Processing* extension is available. *VS Code* is free.

Several text editors have developed into capable tools beyond basic text editing, and support programming as well, e.g. *Emacs, Atom* and *Sublime Text*, and also *Vim, Notepad++* (only for *Windows*) and

FIGURE 23.5   Language support can be added to *VS Code* via extensions

BBEdit (formerly called *Text Wrangler*, only for *Mac*), to name a few. Most of these are available for the popular platforms (*Windows*, *Mac* and *Linux*).

Emacs (initially released in 1976 on *Unix*) is an early, programmable, customisable and versatile editor that can be made to do (almost) anything, including to work as an IDE. The editor's behaviour can be scripted in *Lisp*. It supports many languages out of the box, such as *C*, *C++*, *Java*, *JavaScript*, *Python*, *FORTRAN*, *Prolog* and *Ruby*. Support for further languages can be added by installing packages. *Emacs* is a specialised tool, and may have a somewhat steep learning curve; but once mastered, it is extremely powerful and affords the user a level of control that is beyond what most IDEs (or editors) offer. *Emacs* is, of course, free.

Atom (Figure 23.6; released in 2011) is a highly configurable text editor.[6] Heaps of packages with specific features and functions can be browsed and installed. *Atom* is free.

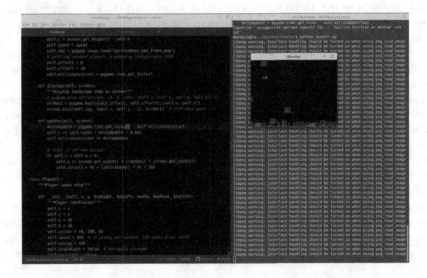

FIGURE 23.6   An alternative to IDEs: A text editor (*Atom*) and a command-line compiler (*Python*)

Sublime Text (initially released in 2008 for *Windows*) is a popular and powerful editor that is (also) intended to be used for programming. It natively supports many programming and scripting languages. Editor features and language support can be added through plugins. *Sublime Text* is shareware and thus not free.

While several IDEs and text editors support *Processing*, or can be made to work with it, for small-scale coding projects, *Processing*'s default IDE is sufficient and gets the job done.[7]

Reading Technical Documentation

There are mainly three types of documentation one needs to read when programming: Language, library and Application Programming Interface (API) documentation. Often, programming involves using somebody else's code, e.g. when using a library. Many programming languages (e.g. *C*) offer only the most basic structures and commands; everything else (e.g. graphic output, fonts, disk i/o, network) is written by the programmer or supplied by libraries. *Processing* is a bit special because it offers many high-level, specialised functions. In any case, there is documentation available on how to use things.

Programming documentation can look quite technical, but that's exactly what we want. The most relevant things to find in the documentation are probably the existence and names of functions and methods, the number and data types and order of arguments, and the return value data types. Usually, in technical documentation, the info is given in a highly efficient manner.

Let's look at *Processing*'s online documentation to get a feel for things. For example, the map() function (Figure 23.7 (left)); look it up in the documentation, i.e. search for map() on processing.org!

Typically, documentation for a function provides (in this or a similar order) the syntax of the function call (i.e. return value and arguments), then the description of the arguments (which are often self-explanatory), a brief explanation of what the function does, and (optionally) a demo program and finally pointers to related content (such as similar functions).[8]

Processing's documentation for map() starts with the description, then gives three example programs, then the syntax and finally the description of the arguments. The (first part of the) description reads:

'Re-maps a number from one range to another.

In the first example above [sic], the number 25 is converted from a value in the range of 0 to 100 into a value that ranges from the left edge of the window (0) to the right edge (width).'

(Processing 2023)

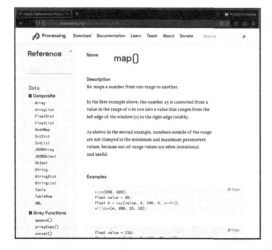

FIGURE 23.7 *Processing*'s online documentation for the map() function and the PImage class

Of the three example programs, only the first one is shown here:

```
'size(200, 200);
float value = 25;
float m = map(value, 0, 100, 0, width);
ellipse(m, 200, 10, 10);' (ibid.)
```

Then the syntax is given:

```
'map(value, start1, stop1, start2, stop2)' (ibid.)
```

Function return type and argument data types are omitted from the call syntax. The argument data types are integrated with the description of how the arguments are interpreted by the function:

```
'value    (float)   the incoming value to be converted
start1   (float)   lower bound of the value's current range
stop1    (float)   upper bound of the value's current range
start2   (float)   lower bound of the value's target range
stop2    (float)   upper bound of the value's target range' (ibid.)
```

The return type is separately given, it is a `float` (ibid.). Two related functions (`norm()` and `lerp()`) are linked to (ibid.).

Let's look up how to load an image from a disk and display it on screen! The author starts with the documentation for the `PImage` class (Figure 23.7 (right)), and follows the links to related content. The info that the author gathers from the documentation for `PImage`, `loadImage()` and `image()`, is, for instance, that images can be loaded (from disk or an online resource) by calling the method `loadImage()` with a `String` as an argument that designates the filename including the path (if any) and the extension (such as png). The `loadImage()` method returns a `PImage`.

To then display the image on screen, one uses the `image()` function that takes as arguments a `PImage` and two `floats` describing the top-left corner coordinates of the screen location (optionally, one could also set the size of the displayed image). If one wants to know the dimensions of the (loaded) image, one can access the fields `PImage.width` and `PImage.height`, both of which return the info as `ints`.

The author can now quickly put together a program such as this:

```
PImage img = loadImage("picture.png");   //image file needs to exist, of course
image(img, 20, 40);
println("Image dimensions are " + img.width + " x " + img.height + " pixels");
```

Now look up how to load and save text files such as a highscore list (this is also covered in the section 'Loading and Saving Data' in Chapter 22)!

The Process of Debugging

In programming things always seem to go wrong before they go right; it is most amazing how buggy a program can be and still run. Now we see what we can do to fix things

Debugging is Part of the Gig

Debugging is part of programming – not anybody's fault. Dealing with programming bugs is actually a skill that people learn together with coding. Certain strategies are most appropriate given different kinds of errors.

Three kinds of errors can happen: The program not doing what was intended, crashes when the program is running, and errors when compiling the code.

The Program Runs but Doesn't Do What I Told It To!

Computers do exactly what they are told. When a program exhibits unexpected behaviour it is, in most cases, because the computer is simply doing *what the program says it should do.* And this is not always identical what the programmer *wanted* it to do.

If the program runs, but does wonky things, the problem lies in the semantics (not in the syntax). This kind of error is often quite tricky to find. What can be done?

Take it step by step – Read through the program one line at a time, imagining (or saying out loud, or writing down) what it does. Strictly assume only that happens what one reads. Is this what is wanted? If it is, maybe one or more of the functions used behave differently than expected (look them up)?[9] If it is not, how is the program result different, and which changes to the code would align the program to the intentions?

Retrace the latest changes – Chances are, if the program was running fine before a change, and it does not after, the change is responsible.

It might also happen that the latest change only exposes a bug that was present in the code for a long time already. Codes are full of bugs. When one finds them one often wonders how they could function at all.

Identifying the part of the code that contains the bug is almost as good as fixing it. One can start a new sketch and only run the suspicious code to see if the bug can still be reproduced.

Make things visible – Display the contents of variables such as the position of objects (on the console or in the window). Draw usually hidden objects such as bounding boxes. Output some text to the console to see which parts (e.g. *if* clauses, loops) of the program run.

Identify the most popular bugs – There are certain bugs that one repeats over and over. For these one can check first.

Do something else, talk to somebody – Take a break, and take a fresh look later. Work on a different part of the program for a while.

Explain the code to somebody else (real or imaginary).

Just continue – Assume it works, fix something else first. Sometimes one discovers a better way, and re-writes the code with the bug anyway.

Don't get stuck and don't stop – See if friends can help. One can also post to an online forum.

Errors at Compile Time

These are the best errors to have. Many errors of this type are simple typos and are easily found and fixed. If this is not the case, things can be more tricky. The compiler tries to help to locate the error but is not always very good at that. As a general rule, the error is in the line where the compiler says it is or *earlier* (never later) in the code. There are error messages that are quite straightforward; some are more obscure (Figure 23.8). Usually, and even if one does not immediately know what a message means, one can figure out what the problem is by checking the code carefully.

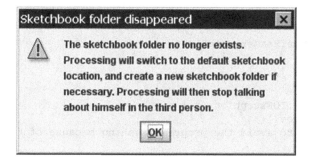

FIGURE 23.8   When a program's files or folder are (re-) moved while *Processing*'s IDE is running, it gets upset

When the *Processing* compiler encounters a problem, it tries to diagnose what goes wrong and outputs a message to the console. It is pretty tricky to estimate what the problem is, and often the message is cryptic. But in time one learns what the compiler tries to say, and one can also look up what things mean (in books or online) – chances are, other people have seen the message already, and wondered (and explained) what it meant.

Crashes at Run Time

At the moment, we are not doing much that can cause a program to crash during execution. But even the most trivial programs can crash! Very often, crashes at run-time are caused by programming bugs, such as missing (image) files, overshooting arrays, or dividing by zero. Programs should be thoroughly tested before they are shared (e.g. by different people, on different systems), and such bugs should be found and fixed, of course. This is not much different than when encountering errors at compile time (see the previous section).

But sometimes it is not a program's fault if something does not pan out. For example, in instances when the program deals with input and output of various kinds. Thus, a program may well encounter an issue not of its own making, when it reads from a file or network address, writes to disk, reserves a resource such as a software MIDI sequencer, or accesses a serial port. There is a mechanism that can (and should) be used when performing operations that *can potentially fail*. The mechanism is called *exception handling*. Exception handling is to be done when dealing with occurrences that lie outside the program's control. In case of a problem, instead of crashing, the program detects that something went wrong (e.g. the file is corrupt and cannot be read, the network is down, the disk is full, the resource or hardware is unavailable) and *raises* or *throws* an exception that is then *caught* and *handled*. A program can work around some errors, for instance, in the case of the full disk, by informing the user that the disk is full and asking him/her to pick a different location to save a file; there are other errors a program can occasionally not recover from (e.g. running out of memory or missing hardware). Often it is quite tricky (and time-consuming and not very rewarding) to anticipate (and test) what might go wrong in a program and find ways to recover, but it should be done for programs that are not just prototypes.

Different kinds of exceptions are handled by different catches. A specific catch statement catches only one specific type of exception (such as `IOException`, `FileNotFoundException`, `EOFException` and `NullPointerException`), so it is possible for the program to react to different kinds of errors. 'Processing will fire the first catch block that matches the exception's class *or* superclass. […] you need to put the most specific type of exceptions first and more general exceptions later. […] As a final catch all, you can simply add a catch (Exception e) as the final catch block. This is the most generic type of exception object, so it should catch most errors' (Odewahn 2011). An exception that is thrown and not caught is called an *unhandled exception*, and it crashes the program.

Code 1 first tries to catch `IOExceptions` and `NullpointerExecptions`, and then all other exceptions that might be thrown in the `try` statement.[10]

Code 1

```
BufferedReader buffReader = createReader("missing-file.txt");
String lineOfFile = null;

try
{
    lineOfFile = buffReader.readLine();
}

catch (IOException e)   //catches only IOExceptions
{
    println("Caught IOException: " + e);
    e.printStackTrace();
    //do something to avoid the program crashing because of the error...
}
```

```
catch (NullPointerException e)   //catches only NullPointerExceptions
{
   println("Caught NullPointerException: " + e);
   e.printStackTrace();
   //do something to avoid the program crashing because of the error...
}
catch (Exception e)   //catches every other Exception
{
   println("Caught other xception: " + e);
   e.printStackTrace();
   //do something to avoid the program crashing because of the error...
}
```

Output

The file 'missing-file.txt' is missing or inaccessible, make sure the URL is valid or that the file has been added to your sketch and is readable.
   Caught NullPointerException: java.lang.NullPointerException: Cannot invoke 'java.io.BufferedReader.readLine()' because 'buffReader' is null.

```
java.lang.NullPointerException: Cannot invoke 'java.io.BufferedReader.
readLine()' because 'buffReader' is null
  at exceptionfile.setup(exceptionfile.java:24)
  at processing.core.PApplet.handleDraw(PApplet.java:2051)
  at processing.awt.PSurfaceAWT$9.callDraw(PSurfaceAWT.java:1388)
  at processing.core.PSurfaceNone$AnimationThread.run(PSurfaceNone.java:356)
```

Common Errors

This section attempts to discuss the most common and frequent programming errors. It lists, describes and explains them and outlines how they can be avoided and fixed. Briefly mentioned are the compiler messages that these errors typically cause, which may not always be straightforward to interpret for a human.[11] The focus here is on low-level errors, such as syntax errors and bugs that make a program crash or to behave in unexpected ways. High-level logic errors are context- and application-dependent and are beyond the scope of this section.[12]

Many errors are simple typos or omissions, most of which are immediately pointed out by the real-time syntax check or the compiler. One learns which mistakes or which kind of mistakes one regularly makes when coding; it is pretty much the same five or so errors, and one can then quickly recognise and rectify these. Even if a compiler error message seems to indicate another type of error and to point in another direction, it might be a good idea to look for any of the regular bugs first before believing the machine and going on a tangent. Also, over time one learns to interpret the compiler's error messages, many of which are rather clear, but some are still quite cryptic.

Here is a list of frequent programming errors, usually with code examples and error messages; it is explained what the problem is, and how it can be fixed.[13]

Missing Statement Terminator

Every statement needs to be terminated with the statement terminator (;). Usually (but not always; see the *for* loop example below that suffers from too liberal use of the statement terminator), that means that there is a semicolon at the end of each line of code; e.g.:

```
size(100, 200)

background(60, 120, 180) rect(40, 60, 120, 80)
```

instead of

```
size(100, 200);
background(60, 120, 180); rect(40, 60, 120, 80);
```

Error messages about missing semicolons are sometimes obscure.

Missing Delimiters

Opening or, more often, closing brackets (( )), braces ({ }) or quotation marks (single or double) are often forgotten. This is usually hard to see, although the IDE highlights opening and closing brackets when the cursor is on them. In the case of missing double quotation marks, one can also spot the problem by the colours the IDE uses to mark literal strings.

```
println("Am I...);
println("missing something here");
```

The error message is 'Syntax Error - Missing ")''', which is somewhat nebulous, and the compiler locates the error (incorrectly) on the following line.[14] In cases when delimiters are involved, the compiler can have a hard time to identify the issue and point to the correct line in the code (or even to the correct file; e.g. in the case of missing (closing) braces of a class definition in a tab).

Missing Return Data Types

All function and method definitions (except class constructors) need to specify a return data type (or void) in their headers. If this is forgotten, the error message is pretty clear: 'Return type for the method is missing'.

```
setup()
{
  size(200, 100);
}
```

This error is fixed, of course, by adding the missing data type (or void, in this case) in front of setup().

Misspelled Function Names in Function Calls and in Function Headers

Typos in the function names of function calls to *Processing*'s (such as printLn()) or programmer-made functions trigger the real-time syntax check and concrete error messages ('The function "printLn()" does not exist'). Correctly spelled function names in calls to *Processing* functions can also be confirmed by checking the colour coding.

Less obvious, because they do not cause syntax errors, are mistyped function names in function headers such as Setup(), Draw(), KeyPressed() or mouseMove():

```
void mouseMove()   //moving the mouse pointer will never call this
{
  //...
}
```

The error is tricky to spot. Usually, when one mistypes function names (either in a function call or a function header), the compiler complains about the *call* going nowhere. In the cases of Setup(), Draw(), KeyPressed() and mouseMove(), there is no function call to trigger an error message, because the functions setup(), draw(), keyPressed() and mouseMoved() are called automatically by *Processing*. One can observe, however, different syntax colour coding in the IDE: The names of programmer-defined functions are of a different colour than the names of *Processing*'s functions. When there are typos in the function names, *Processing* does not recognise the functions as its own, and assumes that they are programmer-made functions.

Wrong Types of Delimiters

Using the wrong type of delimiters (such as in `println('Hello');`) or separators (for `(int i = 0, i < 10, i++) {println(i); }`) causes problems. In the first instance, the error message is 'Invalid character constant', because single quotation marks can only be used for single characters (data type `char`), so having more than one character within single quotation marks makes the compiler angry. Double quotation marks (`"Hello"`) are needed.

In the second instance, the error message is a rather clear 'Syntax Error - Missing ";"'. Factually, two semicolons (`;`) are needed (instead of the two commas).

Assignment (=) vs Check (==)

Mixing up = with == is a classic mistake and a tricky one at that! A single equal sign (=) is an assignment operator, and assigns the value on the right to the variable on the left. A double equal sign (==) checks two given values for equality:

```
int n = 10;
if (n == 10) { println("n is ten!"); }
```

Processing's compiler does not compile code such as:

```
int n = 10;
if (n = 10) { println("n is ten!"); }
```

This is because in *Processing*, integers do not double as booleans as they do in some other languages (such as in *C*). The error message is a corresponding 'Type mismatch: cannot convert from int to boolean'.

There is no message from the compiler, and the code from this example runs:

```
boolean b = false;
if (b = true) { println("b is true!"); }
```

But the real-time syntax check warns: 'Possible accidental assignment in place of a comparison. A condition expression should not be reduced to an assignment'. Most likely, the programmer did not intend an assignment but a check in the *if* condition (i.e. `if (b == true) { println("b is true!"); }`).

Order of Operations

Order of operations errors (e.g. `int n = 2; println(n + n * n);`, output: 6) can be avoided with bracketing, as in real-life math (`println((n + n) * n);`, output: 8).

Data Types and Accuracy

A common oversight is that mathematical operations with two `int`s result in another `int`, and thus lead to a loss of accuracy:

```
void setup()
{
  size(320, 240);
  println(width / height);
  println(float(width) / height);
}
```

Output

```
1
1.3333334
```

Be careful with bracketing, though:

```
size(320, 240);
float fRatio = float(width / height);
println("Window size is " + width + " x " + height + ", fRatio is " + fRatio);
```

The brackets need to be around one of the ints (i.e. for instance, `float fRatio = float(width)/ height;`); but not as shown here, around the result of the whole mathematical operation (i.e. division of one int by another).

Not only variables have data types, but literal values as well. The result of dividing mouse pointer coordinates x by 100 (i.e. `mouseX/100`) might unexpectedly be zero:

```
void draw()
{
  println(mouseX / 100);
}
```

Output

```
0
0
0
...
```

The result is 0 because both `mouseX` and `100` are of type integer, and doing a mathematical operation with two integers results in another integer. If the default window size of 100 by 100 pixels is used, all horizontal mouse pointer coordinates are between 0 and 99, all of which evaluate to 0 when divided by 100.

Characters and Character Codes

Mixing up ASCII (or Unicode) characters with numbers (i.e. character codes) can be problematic:

```
char a = 1;
char b = '2';
int n = 3;
char c = n;  //this is the line on which the compiler spots a problem
```

The error message is 'Type mismatch: cannot convert from int to char', although three lines above the program did apparently exactly this (it should be noted that assigning 1 to a char is syntactically correct, but probably not what the programmer wanted; more likely, he or she forgot the single quotation marks around the digit ('1')). Assigning an integer c to a char (in the example `char c = n;`) does not work *because it is an integer*. When the program assigns 1 to char a, the compiler reads the literal value 1 as a char (i.e. as a character code, not as an int). If one wants to code a char by its ASCII (or Unicode) number, one can do so:

```
char d = 65;  //65 is the code for 'A'
println(d);

int n = 66;  //66 for 'B'
char e = char(n);
println(e);

char f = 'C';  //C should have number 67
println(int(f));
```

Output

```
A
B
67
```

Non-Terminating Loops

Non-terminating *while* and *for* loops are a classic programming bug. In a *while* loop, the condition might never be triggered. If one uses a *while* loop to repeat something a specific number of times,[15] one can easily forget to increment the counter variable at the end of the loop (iCounter++, for instance, in this case):

```
int iCounter = 0;
while (iCounter < 10)
{
  println(iCounter);
}
```

Output

```
0
0
0
...
```

If one creates nested *for* loops, and copies the outer loop to use as the inner loop, one can forget to change the variable names (all or, even more tricky, some of them):

```
int iPixelX = 100;
int iBlockWidth = 14;
int iBlockHeight = 8;
for (int x = iPixelX; x < (iPixelX + iBlockWidth); x++)   //go through in
x direction
{
  for (int y = iPixelX; y < (iPixelX + iBlockWidth); x++)   //go through in
  y direction
  {
    print(x + "/" + y + " ");
  }
}
```

The inner loop ('go through in y direction') never terminates because the end condition (y < (iPixelX + iBlockWidth)) checks y, but the loop increments x (x++).

If one suspects wonky loop behaviour, one can use debug output during the loop and after the loop to assert things work.

Missing Reset of Counter in *while* Loops

It is also a classic mistake in nested *while* loops to forget to reset the counter variable of the inner loop when the outer loop is iterated:

```
int iGridSize = 10;
int iPosHor = 0;
int iPosVert = 0;
```

```
while (iPosVert < height)
{
  while (iPosHor < width)
  {
    rect(iPosHor, iPosVert, iGridSize - 2, iGridSize - 2);
    iPosHor += iGridSize;
  }
  iPosVert += iGridSize;
}
```

The loops in the code seem to be alright, but when the inner loop is done with drawing the line of squares, and the code moves to the next line to be drawn (iPosVert += iGridSize;), iPosHor should be (re-) set to 0 (i.e. iPosHor = 0;). Otherwise, we only see the very first line of squares instead of the full grid.

Omitting Braces ({ }) Around Structures

In *C*-based languages, indention is only a visual feature for the human reader, that does not mean anything for the compiler.

```
int a = 0;
if (a > 0)
    println("a is greater 0");
    println("And not equal to or less than 0");
```

   Output

```
And not equal to or less than 0
```

If the braces ({ }) are omitted, *only the first statement* after an *if* condition is recognised as being connected to the conditional check. The same issue can arise with a *for* loop. Always use braces, even for conditional checks and loops that only contain one command, then the programmer as well as the program knows what is connected to them and what is not.

Wrong Arguments in a Function or Method Call

When calling functions or methods, one needs to exactly match the number, type and order of arguments; for instance, for the text() function:

```
int posX = 20;
int posY = 40;
float valueToOutput = 210;
text(posX, posY, valueToOutput);
```

The code compiles, but does not show anything on screen, because the order of parameters is incorrect (assuming posX and posY are supposed to be screen coordinates, and valueToOutput the value the program should display on screen). The correct order of the arguments is: text(valueToOutput, posX, posY).

Uninitialised Variables

Using variables that have not yet been assigned a value should be avoided. Usually, *Processing* is nice and puts some default values into variables:

```
int n;
void setup()
{
  println(n);
}
```

Output

```
0
```

To have a (known) default value put automatically into a variable might be better than having unknown initial values in variables (as can happen in *C*, for instance). But the programmer should really be the one who puts values into variables, and he or she should not trust that the compiler is nice (or capable of making appropriate decisions). For instance, new `Strings` contain initially nothing, i.e. they contain (the literal `String`) `null`:

```
String s;
void setup()
{
  println(s);
  s += "123";   //adding "123" to presumably empty String
  println(s);
  char c = s.charAt(1);
  println("I expect the second character in the String to be '2', but it is
  '" + c + "'");
}
```

Output

```
null
null123
I expect the second character in the String to be '2', but it is 'u'
```

Missing Images

A program might fail to load files from external sources such as the hard drive (`PImage` is then `null`). A common case is attempting to load an image which is not there.[16] A popular reason is capitalised folder (`Data`) or filenames, either in the code or in the file system. This problem is specifically tricky to track because it might not occur on one system (*Windows, Mac* or *Linux*) or *Processing* version but on another.[17] A foolproof way is to only use non-capitalised letters in folders and filenames.[18]

Division by 0

Few people would write literal code that divides a number by zero. But division by 0 can happen, for instance, when one uses a random number and is not careful:

```
for (int i = 0; i < 100; i++)
{
  int rand = int(random(10));
  println(100 / rand);
}
```

There is a 10% chance that `rand` is 0 and the program crashes.

Liberal Use of the Statement Terminator

(Too) liberal use of the statement terminator (`;`) can sabotage a *for* loop:

```
for (int i=0; i<10; i++);
{
  println("Print this ten times?");
}
```

Output

```
Print this ten times?
```

The code compiles and runs fine, but the contents between the braces are executed only once (and not multiple times, as intended). The semicolon at the end of the line ends the *for* loop, and pairs of braces ({ }) can be freely used in programs without any ill effects (as long as they do not upset any structures). The same problem can happen with *while* and *if*.

Missing Return Statements in Function Bodies

Missing a `return` statement in a function body of a function that is supposed to have a return value causes a compiler error ('This method must return a result of type float'; it is a *function*, of course, not a *method*):

```
void setup()
{
  println(calcAverage(3.6, 7));
}
float calcAverage(float f1, float f2)
{
  float result = (f1 + f2) * 0.5;
}
```

In this case, `return result;` is missing from the function body.

Mixing up Local and Global Variables

Having global and local variables of the same name (with different or no content) can be confusing. In this example, the global variables (posX and posY) never receive the (random) coordinate location data:

```
int posX = 0;
int posY = 0;
void setup()
{
  size(320, 240);
  noStroke();
  int posX = int(random(width));
  int posY = int(random(height));
  println("Random position is " + posX + "/" + posY);
}
void draw()
{
  background(0);
  fill(180 + random(75), 180 + random(75), 180 + random(75));
  ellipse(posX, posY, 20, 20);
}
```

In setup(), a different set of (local) variables of the same names as the global variables are declared and assigned the values.

One can differentiate between local and global variables of the same names, though:

```
String s = "Global";
void setup()
{
  println(s);
  String s = "Local";
  println(s);
  println(this.s);
}
```

Output

```
Global
Local
Global
```

The prefix this can be used to refer to variables one level above the current structure. The example illustrates how it is used in a function to reference a global variable instead of a local variable. The prefix can also be used to reference class variables when it is used in methods, to differentiate them from local variables of the same name.

Under- and Overshooting Arrays

Under- and overshooting arrays is another classic programming error. When using arrays, one should make sure the array is what one thinks it is (specifically, that it is not empty) and that the indices one uses to access it are what one thinks they are (i.e. they are not lower than 0 (e.g. -1) or exceed array length - 1). For instance, using the length of an array to access the last element of it causes an 'ArrayIndexOutOfBoundsException: Index 5 out of bounds for length 5':

```
int[] numbers = new int[5];
for (int i = 0; i < numbers.length; i++)
{
  numbers[i] = i;
}
println(numbers[numbers.length]);
```

The length of an array read from the array.length field is correct, but the array elements are numbered 0 to length - 1 (i.e. 0, 1, 2, 3, 4 in the example); that means, the last element of an array is indexed as length -1. Note that if an array is empty, and thus has length 0, its last element cannot be accessed in this way (because the length of an empty array is 0, and 0 - 1 is -1, which is again causing an 'ArrayIndexOutOfBoundsException: Index 0 out of bounds for length 0' when used to access an array element). When an array is empty, trying to access its (non-existing) first element (i.e. array[0]) has the same result.

Generally, when a (*for*) loop goes through an array from front to back, little can go wrong. But things are more dangerous when individual items of an array are to be picked by e.g. a random number, loading values from an external data source (e.g. from disk, and values might be corrupted or somebody might have tampered with them), or by a calculation that assumes the input (and output) values to lie in a certain range. In case one cannot be 100% certain that array items exist and the values used to access them are valid, one should assert that they are by checking.

Notes

1. Compilers attempt to show errors in human-readable form, and *Processing*'s IDE has much improved in this endeavour over the years. If an error message is still unclear, one can usually find info online on what the compiler wants to say with it. Many people have probably received the same message already and wondered what it meant.

2. Locating an error is not always trivial, and *Processing*'s IDE is sometimes not very successful in locating errors, specifically when delimiters (such as braces { }) are involved.

3. A lot of these features can be helpful, and many people like and embrace them but some do not. Real-time syntax checking might immediately point out issues but can also look a bit irritating or feel intrusive; similarly, syntax highlighting – generally improves the readability of the code and helps users to quickly grasp the structure of it, but some people simply prefer a less exciting display (e.g. black-on-white for maximum contrast) (these features can be toggled in `File/Preferences` ...; Figure 23.2). Readers should try out what works best for them!

4. Sometimes people put more than one class into a tab, for instance, when inheritance is used, so that the base class and the classes which inherit from it, are located in the same tab. This works fine as long as not too many classes exist and there is not too much inheritance going on (e.g. if there is a class `GameObject`, virtually all other classes such as `Player`, `Enemy`, `BonusItem`, etc., might inherit from it; all these classes should not be put in a single tab).

5. In the *Processing* IDE, autocompletion is switched off by default. Autocompletion can be activated in `File/Preferences...`; the tickbox is titled 'Code completion with Ctrl-space' (Figure 23.2 (right)). Note that in the *Processing* IDE, for an unknown reason, autocompletion needs to be manually triggered with `Ctrl-Space` (or `Apple-Space`), which may reduce the usefulness of the feature. For class fields (methods and variables, such as `String.chatAt()` and `array.length`) suggestions are offered without a trigger, though, after typing the dot operator.

6. The development of the *Atom* editor stopped in 2022; it will continue to be available, but it is yet unclear if any future development will happen.

7. All code snippets and demo programs for this book have been created in *Processing*'s default IDE.

8. *Processing*'s documentation is fairly non-technical and very readable, to the point of making it hard to find the info one is looking in a hurry... It would be nice, for example, if the documentation for `map()` would give as the first info: `float map(float value, float start1, float stop1, float start2, float stop2)`. This is in many cases all one needs to know (or to be reminded of).

9. Such a popular mistake is to compare strings using `==` instead of `String.equals()`.

10. In an ideal scenario, the user is never be confronted with an exception (but it is still preferable that programs end with (unhandled) exceptions than just crash).

11. This list is based on personal observation and experience, and it is obviously not a comprehensive collection of programming errors (or of compiler messages).

12. Check out the buggy code available online that complements this section, for hands-on real-world examples of programs that don't work.

13. All of these bugs may look pretty obvious here, but when one is occupied with writing a program, things might not appear as clear.

14. A previous *Processing* version had 'Unterminated string constant' as an error message in this case, which is pretty spot-on.

15. One should use a *for* loop, then, anyway.

16. See the section 'Crashes at Run Time' in this chapter on catching errors such as missing files.

17. For example, loading an image from the folder `Data` in the program folder works fine on *Windows* with *Processing* 1.5.1, *Mac* with *Processing* 4.0b1 and *Linux* with *Processing* 4.2. If the folder is named data but the code specifies the folder name as `Data`, that also works. But loading an image named `Screenshot.png` with code that specifies the filename as `screenshot.png` does not work on the same *PC* and *Mac* systems ('This file is named Screenshot.png not screenshot.png. Rename the file or change your code'.), but it does work on the *Linux* system. The same situation occurs if the image is named `screenshot.png` and the code specifies `Screenshot.png`.

18. Generally speaking, folder and filenames should only use basic Latin characters, i.e. not any umlauts (ö, ø), funky symbols (/, ?, *, ", ∞) or blank spaces, in case a file system cannot handle these. Safe characters to use across most systems are: - ('minus', ASCII code 45), 0–9 (48–57), A–Z (65–90, if one wants to use capitalised letters), _ ('underscore', 95), and a–z (97–122).

24

Programming Rules of Thumb

Here we discuss principles and
conventions for writing proper code

Programs are complex artefacts, developed by one person or by a team of multiple people, over (often) long stretches of time. Programs can be written in many ways to do roughly the same thing. Even in programming languages which attempt to facilitate clear structures, programs can be written on an almost arbitrarily high level of obfuscation. In many real-life applications, there is no single, right or best way to write a (non-trivial) program.

People learn programming in many different ways and environments, and there are substantial differences with regard to, for instance, people's skill levels and programs' levels of technical sophistication. However, there is a general understanding among academics and practitioners based on shared experience to do things in certain ways. Although the detailed implementations of the conventions differ, the general agreement is largely consistent across programming languages and application domains.

It appears impractical and arguably also undesirable to educate everybody who wants to program to a level where they make such experiences themselves and can arrive at roughly similar insights about programming. Instead, it is popular to create and circulate various sets of conventions or rules for programming.[1] While they roughly pertain to identical issues and aspects, they usually differ in scope and level of abstraction (from 'write beautiful code' to 'do not use Magic Numbers'). They are informed by and reflect the insights experts have into programming, and typically aim to immediately improve the quality (such as the readability, maintainability and extendability) of the code, both for the person who writes it, and for others, who might revise it (in professional life, relatively little code is written new; the vast majority of programming work is maintaining, adapting and extending existing code). Of course, following any set of programming rules does not automatically guarantee high-quality code; but knowing some rules and considering them when coding can certainly help.

One set of conventions, based on the author's own, practical experiences, is formulated here. The five categories overlap and interact with each other; for instance, picking and using appropriate programs and data structures benefits the clarity of a program, its adaptability as well as its performance.

Coding is an art, not a science. There
are reasons to do something this way or
that way: Speed, convenience, clarity,
modularity, portability, etc. – often with

DOI: 10.1201/9781003345916-24

conflicting results. But there are some
hard-and-fast rules how to do basic things

Integrity

Programs should:

- Have headers with, for instance, (brief) info on the program, the programmer's handle or name and the date
- Cite sources, name references

Clarity

Program code should:

- Be elegant and short[2]
- Balance content and structure (e.g. when one file such as the main program approaches or exceeds 1k lines of code, introduce more structure, e.g. a manager, controller or handler object; if virtually all functionality of a program is concentrated in one function or method, introduce more program structure)
- Pick from and competently use an appropriate range of program structures and data structures for a task (functions, classes, arrays, for, while, if, else if, if &&/||, etc.)
- Use only a minimal number of variables; specifically, only a minimal number of global variables, because in non-trivial programs the presence of many global variables obfuscate things, and makes it also hard for the programmer to track which parts of the program access them
- Use multiple files to structure the code (e.g. one class per file when using classes; in *Processing* this means, to put each class in its own tab)
- Be consistent in all matters (variable and function naming, order of parameters, location of functions and methods in the program and in classes, etc.)
- Be formatted properly (e.g. indentions, placement of brackets, spaces, blank lines)
- Avoid lines longer than 80 characters. For three reasons: (1) Long lines of text (i.e. code or comments) are hard to read. (2) Most programming code happens in the first 20 characters of a line, so usually windows with code are in portrait rather than in landscape format, and nobody wants to have to use the horizontal scrollbar to be able to read code or comments. (3) It is not impossible that a compiler has a character limit per line.[3] In practice, many people prefer much shorter lines (this applies to both code and comments).

Adaptability

Programs should:

- Not depend on the computer speed (frameRate()) but use the elapsed (real) time; this applies to all programs that use movement, animation or timed events
- Be careful with boundaries (arrays, screens, etc.)
- Never repeat any code
- Access class variables from outside the object through the class interface (not directly)
- Use variables instead of Magic Numbers, for instance, for the number of bricks, aliens and bullets

- Name variables, functions and methods to indicate their use (`iLevelCurrent`, `bGetState()`)
- Declare variables at the top of structures, such as in functions, methods and loops, so they are easy to spot (not in the middle of the code)
- Have non-trivial comments that describe the big picture and the key aspects of what is going on (e.g. comment algorithms and structures such as functions, *for*-loops or *if*-statements)

Performance

Programs should:

- Get the job done (write bad code first, if there is no other way, but then revise and improve)
- Be fast (and never do any slow stuff inside of loops, e.g. loading images or fonts from disk in `draw()`)
- Also be stable, safe and all kinds of things; but all things being roughly equal, fast is important

The parts of the program where the most time is spent or where delays are most problematic, should be optimised (first). Basic optimisations for execution speed include[4]:

- Avoid doing the same thing multiple times (such as a calculation, loading images from disk)
- Addition is faster than multiplication
- Multiplication (`value * 0.5`) is faster than division (`value/2`)[5]
- Avoid doing expensive/slow calculations that are not essential (e.g. extracting square roots)
- Estimate if expensive/slow calculations are necessary before doing them (e.g. only do a pixel-perfect collision check after a collision has been detected by a bounding box collision check)
- Functions provided by the language (or by libraries) are usually faster than functions (or code) written by the programmer (for instance, `radians(degrees)` might be faster than `degrees *= (PI/180.0)`)
- Avoid declaring unneeded variables
- Functions should only require parameters which are needed
- Functions should only have a return value when it is being used; if there are two otherwise identical versions of language-supplied functions, the one without a return value is faster
- In *if-else-if* statements, test for the most likely condition first (then the other condition(s) do(es) not need to be evaluated)
- In *if* statements with multiple conditions (concatenated with `&&`), test for the most unlikely condition first (if the first condition fails, the other(s) do(es) not need to be evaluated)
- Drawing complicated shapes takes more time than drawing simple shapes (e.g. ellipses take more time than rectangles, transparent fills more than solid colours; rendering text is quite slow)
- Avoid using large images (e.g. for level backgrounds) and audio files (e.g. title music)
- Do not use console output, of course

Relevance

Programs should:

- Be expressive
- Interpret and question tasks in novel or original ways
- Make use of the unprecedented possibilities of the digital medium; for instance, one should introduce interaction (only) if there is something meaningful for the user to do

Coding Rules in Professional Life

In many companies, more or less strict internal guidelines for writing code are employed. A probably typical ruleset from a small software studio that offers web services stipulates:

- Code is to be structured visually; 20 lines of code without blank lines are hard to read
- Long lines are manually split into several lines; maximum of 100 characters per line
- Indention size: 2 spaces
- Methods/functions have a maximum of 20 lines (soft limit) or 40 lines (hard limit)
- Classes have a maximum of 150 lines (soft limit) or 200 lines (hard limit)
- Expressive names are used for all elements; the language is English
- lowerCamelCase is used for the naming of variables
- UpperCamelCase is used for the naming of classes, services and interfaces
- No specific convention for the naming of class variables is used
- Names of methods (e.g. get/set) need to be unambiguous and to describe actions
- Avoid deep class hierarchies (i.e. multiple levels of class inheritance);
- Code that is used by many classes or functions should be put into its own class or function and invoked from there;
- Only use relative file paths (e.g`../folder/file`);
- Unneeded and unused code should be removed. If the code is to be used in the future it must be clearly marked (e.g. 'TODO'); TODOs are to be realised very soon; and
- No console output in regular operation!!!

These recommendations are supplemented by numerous more specific rules for comments, documentation, interface language, services (including not to have public variables, and to only use.

Notes

1. For instance, Tim Peters, one of the contributors to *Python*, formulates 19 coding principles that can be output through a command in the language.
2. 'The key to performance is elegance, not battalions of special cases' (Jon Bentley&Doug McIlroy qtd. in Bezroukov 2014).
3. 256 characters was a limit in HTML, the author believes, at one point, although that is hardly a programming language.
4. Some of the measures are effective because of how things work technically (multiplication being faster than division), some because of simple logic (in an && concatenated *if* statement, test the most unlikely event first). It is likely that in different languages or even language implementations, the same operations or calculations take different amounts of time.
5. For instance, for *x86* CPUs, by a factor roughly between 5 and 10 (Granlund 2019); but be aware that both operations are very fast in absolute duration, and that many other factors influence performance and thus may eclipse the differences.

25

Classes and Objects

We create and use classes and objects, and immediately use them to improve the collision detection examples we have been doing already

Classes and Objects

Classes and objects are a way to organise a program (as are functions). The code uses the same parts and content as before, but the code structure now corresponds to the application structure, i.e. application objects (such as space ships or buttons) become code objects.[1]

The use of classes can result in an intuitive code structure. Intuitive in the sense that the objects in the program do not need to be handled top-down by one long program, but that each object *handles itself*! This can be achieved by using a class and creating many (more or less) self-sufficient objects from it. Revising an existing program and introducing classes to it thus usually means that functionality is transferred from the main program (the draw() function) to one class or to several classes.

Objects created from a class are called *instances* of that class. Every object holds its own data *and* the functions it uses; without classes, object data and functions are distributed in the whole program. A class structure is modular (classes can easily be copied to and used in a new project) and easy to read and modify (it is clear where one should look to find something).[2]

Example Applications of Classes

One way to understand how classes and instances work is to think in terms of baking: The class is the recipe and the instances are the breadrolls one bakes using that recipe. They all have the same ingredients (variables, functions), but they're all separate objects (with different values such as positions, sizes and colours).

We have already seen several opportunities where it would have been an advantage to have an effective way to handle many almost identical game objects: Trains moving horizontally across the screen (and this will be the first example), alien spaceships coming into the screen from the right in waves, and snowflakes falling down.[3]

DOI: 10.1201/9781003345916-25

FIGURE 25.1 Typical (and recommended) use of tabs in the *Processing* IDE: One tab for the main program (left) and another for the Train class (right)

Class Syntax

A class definition looks like this[4]:

class ClassName
{
    //variables

    //methods (functions are called *methods* in a class)
}

The use of a class definition (assuming a class `Alien` exists), i.e. the instantiation of an object a and its use, looks like this:

```
Alien a;  //object declaration
a = new Alien();  //construction
a.display();  //calling a method within object
```

First Class Example: A Train

As a first example, here is the train example again (see Code 1ff. in Chapter 15), this time using a class (Code 1, Figure 25.1). We start out with one train only.

Code 1

```
//the main program, which uses the class below (that is, it creates5 and uses
an object of the class):
//global declaration(s)
Train t;  //t is the single train object

//global functions
void setup()
{
  size(600, 100);
  t = new Train(10, 45, 2);  //the constructor is called with arguments
}
```

```
void draw()
{
  background(255, 235, 0);  //erases the background every round

  t.update();  //ask the object to move itself
  t.display();  //ask the object to display itself
}

//the class definition (usually put in its own tab):

class Train
{
  //class variables (or fields)

  int xPos = 0;
  int yPos = 0;
  int velocity = 0;

  //class methods

  Train(int x, int y, int v)  //constructor
  {
    xPos = x;  //the given values are put into class variables
    yPos = y;
    velocity = v;
  }

  void display()  //object shows itself at its position
  {
    fill(222, 22, 0);
    rect(xPos, yPos, 20, 10);

      fill(0);
      ellipse(xPos + 2, yPos + 12, 4, 4);
      ellipse(xPos + 7, yPos + 12, 4, 4);
      ellipse(xPos + 13, yPos + 12, 4, 4);
      ellipse(xPos + 18, yPos + 12, 4, 4);
  }

  void update()  //object moves itself to the right
  {
    xPos += velocity;
  }
}
```

Note that virtually no new code was written; the existing code (e.g. for displaying the train, and for moving it across the screen) has merely been transferred from the main program to the class.

One beautiful aspect of objects is, that they usually can take care of themselves. For instance, in Code 1, the train draws itself simply at the position where it currently is (in the display() method, using the class variables (or fields) xPos and yPos.

Example: Space Aliens

Here is the space alien example again (see Code 11ff. in Chapter 15, with simplified movement in a straight line), this time using a class (Code 2). To make things more clear, only one alien is present.

Code 2

```
Alien a;
void setup()
{
  size(300, 200);
  a = new Alien();
}
void draw()
{
  background(0);
  a.move();
  a.display();
}

class Alien
{
  float velocityX = -2;
  float posX = (width + 10);
  float posY = (height * 0.5);

  Alien()  //constructor⁶
  { }
  void display()
  {
    ellipse(posX, posY, 20, 20);
  }
  void move()
  {
    posX = posX + velocityX;
    if (posX < -10) { posX = (width + 10); }
  }
}
```

Now, of course, one wants to have more than one alien on the screen. One could use several named variables to handle several objects, but a more efficient approach is to use an array for the class objects. Often, one wants to access each of the objects, for instance, to move them or to check collision; if one uses an array this can quite easily be done through a (*for*) loop.

Recall: Arrays

An array is a collection of objects of a single data type. The twist is, that the individual objects are not named but numbered (i.e. indexed). Often it is much more convenient to access (many) numbered items than named ones.[7]

An array definition consists of a type specifier (e.g. int), an identifier (e.g. `favoriteNumbers`), and a dimension (e.g. 5):

```
int[] favoriteNumbers = new int[5];
```

Arrays can use the standard data types, e.g. int and float; but also custom-made data types, for instance, our Alien class.[8] We can thus make an array that efficiently stores the class objects:

```
Alien[] aliens = new Alien[5];
```

Multiple Objects from a Class with an Array

The next examples demonstrate how to put objects into an array. Starting with the above codes, we only need to modify the main programs: The single objects t (in the train example) and a (in the alien example) are replaced with arrays that hold multiple objects. The particle example is new and uses an array from the start to store particles.

In Code 3, the single alien object a is removed and an array of aliens is added. In technical terms: The main program now declares a (global) array instead of a variable; the objects in the array are constructed (in setup()) and accessed (in draw()) in *for* loops.

In principle, the above Alien class can be re-used as it is. Classes do not care how many objects are created from them (just as baking recipes do not care how many breadrolls are baked from them). Here, however, the class is slightly modified to prevent all aliens from stacking up in the same spot. To facilitate this, the constructor is extended to accept a parameter so every object can be given a different horizontal starting position.

Code 3

```
//global declaration(s)
Alien[] aliens = new Alien[5];

//global functions
void setup()
{
  size(300, 200);
  for (int i = 0; i < aliens.length; i++)
  {
    aliens[i] = new Alien(i * 45);  //parameter is used to offset the aliens
    from each other
  }
}
void draw()
{
  background(0);
  //all objects display and update themselves:
  for (int i = 0; i < aliens.length; i++)
  {
    aliens[i].move();
    aliens[i].display();
  }
}
```

```
class Alien
{
  //class variables
  float velocityX = -2;
  float posX = width + 10;
  float posY = height * 0.5;

  //class methods
  Alien(float offsetX)  //constructor; the given parameter is here used to
  set the initial x position of the alien
  {
    posX += offsetX;
  }

  void display()
  {
    ellipse(posX, posY, 20, 20);
  }

  void move()
  {
    posX = posX + velocityX;

    if (posX < -10) { posX = (width + 10); }
  }
}
```

Particle Systems

A popular application of object-based programming is Particle systems. Roughly speaking, particle systems are sets of many small things that do some simple stuff and look intriguing because they are so many. Particle systems can be used, for instance, to visually simulate explosions, smoke, bubbles, rain, snowflakes and rocket boosts.

The next example (Code 4) shows a particle system. It uses an array with 100 particles. The constructor takes four parameters (the screen position of the particle and its velocity in x and y directions). All particles start in the middle of the screen, and they are only different from each other in the velocity with which they move (and their random colours).

Code 4

```
Spark[] sparks = new Spark[100];

void setup()
{
  size(200, 200);
  strokeWeight(2);

  for (int i = 0; i < sparks.length; i++)
  {
    sparks[i] = new Spark((width * 0.5), (height * 0.5), random(-3, 3),
    random(-6, 0));
  }
}
```

```
void draw()
{
  background(0);
  for (int i = 0; i < sparks.length; i++)
  {
    sparks[i].move();
    sparks[i].display();
  }
}

class Spark
{
  float posX = 0;
  float posY = 0;

  float velocityX = 0;
  float velocityY = 0;

  color c = color(int(random(128, 256)), int(random(128, 256)),
  int(random(128, 256)));

  float gravity = 0.3;

  //constructor gets position in pixels and x and y velocities, and sets the
  class variables accordingly
  Spark(float x, float y, float vX, float vY)
  {
    posX = x;
    posY = y;

    velocityX = vX;
    velocityY = vY;
  }
  void display()
  {
    stroke(c);
    point(posX, posY);
  }
  void move()
  {
    posX += velocityX;
    posY += velocityY;

    velocityY += gravity;
  }
}
```

Code 5 shows another application of a particle system: Bubbles. The code has the same structure, with a slightly different setup (i.e. constructor parameters), and different visuals than Code 4.

Code 5

```
Bubble[] bubbles = new Bubble[100];

void setup()
{
  size(320, 240);
  stroke(220);
  fill(255, 128);

  for (int i = 0; i < bubbles.length; i++)
  {
    bubbles[i] = new Bubble(random(width), height + random(120), random(-1, 1));
  }
}

void draw()
{
  background(0);
  for (int i = 0; i < bubbles.length; i++)
  {
    bubbles[i].move();
    bubbles[i].display();
  }
}

class Bubble
{
  float posX = 0;
  float posY = 0;
  float velocityX = 0;
  int size = int(random(16, 32));

  Bubble(float x, float y, float vX)
  {
    posX = x;
    posY = y;
    velocityX = vX;
  }

  void display()
  {
    ellipse(posX, posY, size, size);
  }

  void move()
  {
    posX += velocityX;
    posY -= (size * 0.05);
  }
}
```

Here is the train example with an array of five trains instead of a single train object (Code 6). Only the main program has been modified, the `Train` class is unchanged from Code 1.

Code 6

```
Train[] trains = new Train[5];

void setup()
{
  size(600, 100);
  for (int i = 0; i < 5; i++)
  {
    trains[i] = new Train(10, 5 + (i * 20), i + 1);
  }
}

void draw()
{
  background(255, 235, 0);  //erases the background every round
  for (int i = 0; i < 5; i++)
  {
    trains[i].update();
    trains[i].display();
  }
}
```

Now let's add collision detection to the train example. The trains should move in opposite directions when they hit the window edge (Code 7). The main program from Code 6 remains the same (it does nothing else than to tell the trains to move). But this time, we extend[9] the `Train` class from Code 1 to include a check if the train exceeds the window dimension on either side; if this happens, the velocity (i.e. the movement over time in x direction) of the train is inverted.

Code 7

```
//the class definition (usually put in its own tab):

class Train
{
  //class variables
  int xPos = 0;
  int yPos = 0;
  int velocity = 0;

  //class methods
  Train(int x, int y, int v)  //constructor
  {
    xPos = x;  //the given values are put into class variables
    yPos = y;
    velocity = v;
  }
```

```
  void display()   //show the object at its position
  {
    fill(222, 22, 0);
    rect(xPos, yPos, 20, 10);

    fill(0);
    ellipse(xPos + 2, yPos + 12, 4, 4);
    ellipse(xPos + 7, yPos + 12, 4, 4);
    ellipse(xPos + 13, yPos + 12, 4, 4);
    ellipse(xPos + 18, yPos + 12, 4, 4);
  }
  void update()   //move the object to the right
  {
    xPos += velocity;

    if ((xPos < 0) || (xPos >= width))   //invert speed of train when it
    reaches either window edge
    { velocity = -velocity; }

  }
}
```

Note that each object moves, is tested, collides, etc. on its own, and is independent of the other objects of the class.

A potential issue with this sketchy implementation is that the collision with the right edge of the window does not take into account the length of the wagon. This can be fixed, though (because we know how long it is, or rather, the train object knows how long it is).

The *this* Prefix

When one looks at code, one sometimes sees variables prefixed with this, for instance, this.posX. Usually, this is used to differentiate and avoid naming ambiguities between several variables of the same name. Often, the situation arises in class constructors. Class constructors regularly receive parameter values that are to be transferred into class variables, such as on-screen positions and colours.

Let's assume we have an example in which a constructor is given the initial position of a player's spaceship. If one uses a fully consistent naming convention, the parameter could be called posX, the same name as the class variable, which could also be called posX. When prefixed with this, e.g. within the constructor, the variable signified is the *class variable* (in contrast to a *local variable* of the same name, such as a parameter; Code 8).

Code 8

```
//main program
Spaceship ship = null;
void setup()
{
  noStroke();
  ship = new Spaceship(40, 60);
}
```

```
void draw()
{
  background(20, 80, 0);
  ship.display();
}

//class definition
class Spaceship
{
  int posX = 0;
  int posY = 0;

  Spaceship(int posX, int posY)
  {
    this.posX = posX;   //the class variable is assigned the value from the
    parameter
    this.posY = posY;
  }
  void display()
  {
    fill(40, 180, 0);
    rect(posX, posY, 24, 24);
  }
}
```

Note that one can immediately confirm if the above description is correct, and this.posX indeed refers to the class variable, and posX without a prefix refers to the local variable (the parameter given to the constructor): Is the spaceship at the intended position of (40, 60) or at the unintended position of (0, 0)?

In this book, the examples usually avoid using this and instead use (slightly) different names for parameters and class variables (such as x for the parameter in a class constructor, and posX for the corresponding class variable; see e.g. Code 4 for an example).

Game Example: *Dangerous Ducks*

Now we take a look at some stuff we can do with objects – (part of) an implementation of an action game with ducks, and a *BreakOut*–style game.

Let's program a game in which the player shoots dangerous ducks which are coming towards him/ her! First thing, is, of course, a (dangerous) Duck class; then we need a main program to use it (Code 9).

Code 9

```
Duck[] ducks = new Duck[6];

void setup()
{
```

```
    size(640, 480);
    for (int i = 0; i < ducks.length; i++) {
      ducks[i] = new Duck((i * 100), 100, 1);
    }
}

void draw()
{
  background(255, 255, 200);

  for (int i = 0; i < ducks.length; i++)
  {
    ducks[i].update();
    ducks[i].display();
  }
}

class Duck
{
  float posX = 0;
  float posY = 0;
  float velocityY = 0;

  Duck(float x, float y, float vy)
    {
      posX = x;
      posY = y;
      velocityY = vy;
  }

  void display()
  {
      fill(255, 255, 120);
      rect(posX, posY, 40, 40);
  }

  void update()
  {
      posY += velocityY;
  }
}
```

This is already very scary, but it would be nice if the ducks looked more like ducks and grew bigger as they approached the player.

Modify Code 9 so the player can shoot 'em! The mousePressed() function is automatically called when a mouse button is pressed; then pass the pointer coordinates mouseX and mouseY to each duck which then can find out if it was hit!

With classes, the question arises, wherein a program data and logic should be located, in the main program or in a class. Generally, put functionality directly related to objects into the class (e.g. movement, display, collision detection); and put other, general or unrelated functionality (e.g. mouse interface, starting or winning the game) into the main program. This makes the class modular and reusable in other projects because it contains all (and only) essential code.

Now we do (part of) another iconic game
with classes, and see how they can share
variables and functionality with each other

Game Example: *BreakOut*-Style Game

In a *BreakOut*-style game, usually there is a paddle, a ball and many bricks. All of these should be implemented as objects.

The first code snippet (Code 10) implements several bricks as objects.

Code 10

```
//main program

Brick[] bricks = new Brick[8];

void setup()
{
  size(320, 240);
  noFill();
  stroke(0, 220, 0);

  for (int i = 0; i < bricks.length; i++) {
    bricks[i] = new Brick(48 + (i * 28), 50);
  }
}

void draw()
{
  background(0);

  for (int i = 0; i < bricks.length; i++) {
    bricks[i].display();
  }
}


//class definition

class Brick
{
  int posX = 0;
  int posY = 0;
  int sizeX = 28;
  int sizeY = 8;

  Brick(int x, int y)
  {
    posX = x;
    posY = y;
  }

  void display()
  {
    rect(posX, posY, sizeX, sizeY);
  }
}
```

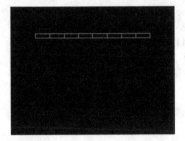

Nothing happens when the program is run except that eight bricks are displayed on the screen.

To keep the code short, a new, separate program is made to create a ball that bounces off the window edges (Code 11).

Code 11

```
//main program
Ball b;
void setup()
{
  size(320, 240);
  fill(0, 220, 0);
  b = new Ball(10, 20, 1, 2);
}
void draw()
{
  background(0);
  b.update();
  b.display();
}

//class definition
class Ball
{
  //class variables
  int xPos = 0;
  int yPos = 0;
  int velocityX = 0;
  int velocityY = 0;
  int size = 10;

  //class methods
  Ball(int x, int y, int vX, int vY)  //constructor
  {
    xPos = x;   //the given values are put into class variables
    yPos = y;
    velocityX = vX;
    velocityY = vY;
  }

  void display()  //show the object at its position
  {
    rect(xPos, yPos, size, size);
  }
```

```
  void update()   //move the object to the right
  {
    xPos += velocityX;
    yPos += velocityY;

    if ((xPos < 0) || (xPos + size >= width))   //invert x speed of ball when
    it reaches either left or right window edge
    { velocityX = -velocityX; }

    if ((yPos < 0) || (yPos + size >= height))  //invert y speed of ball when
    it reaches either top or bottom window edge[10]
    { velocityY = -velocityY; }
  }
}
```

If one wanted to combine Code 10 and Code 11, and add collision detection between the ball and the bricks, one can add code similar to the one shown in Code 12 to the update() method of the Ball class:

Code 12

```
//add to update() method in Ball class

for (int i = 0; i < bricks.length; i++)
{
  if ((xPos >= bricks[i].getX()) &&
      (xPos < bricks[i].getX() + bricks[i].getWidth()) &&
      (yPos >= bricks[i].getY()) &&
      (yPos < bricks[i].getY() + bricks[i].getHeight()))
  {
      velocityY = -velocityY;
  }
}
```

Note that this collision check requires several methods in the Brick class to return values. There are also some compromises in function; for instance, the code assumes the ball is a square, and it only bounces the ball off in y-direction on collision. But the collision between two rectangular objects is successfully (if roughly) implemented.

Class Inheritance[11]

Classes already cleared up the program structure a lot. But still, there are many redundancies (i.e. duplicated code). For instance, in a *BreakOut*-style game, the bricks, the ball and the paddle all use more or less the same kind of data, such as a position on screen, size and colour (Code 13).

Code 13 shows the rudimentary code structure of a *BreakOut*-style game with classes (not yet using class inheritance). Note how much of the code is identical in the Ball, Brick and Paddle classes!

Code 13

```
//main program

Ball myBall = null;
Brick[] myBricks = null;
Paddle myPaddle = null;

void setup()
{
  size(320, 240);
  strokeWeight(2);
  stroke(0);
  fill(220, 240, 0);
  myBall = new Ball();
  myBricks = new Brick[6];
  for (int i = 0; i < myBricks.length; i++)
  {
    myBricks[i] = new Brick(40 + (i * 40), 40);
  }
  myPaddle = new Paddle();
}

void draw()
{
  background(0);
  myBall.vDisplay();
  for (int i = 0; i < myBricks.length; i++)
  {
    myBricks[i].vDisplay();
  }
  myPaddle.vDisplay();
}

//class definitions

class Ball
{
  int iPosX = 0;
  int iPosY = 0;
  int iWidth = 10;
  int iHeight = 10;

  Ball()
  {
    iPosX = int((width * 0.5) - (iWidth * 0.5));
    iPosY = int((height * 0.5) - (iHeight * 0.5));
  }

  int iGetPosX()
  {
    return iPosX;
  }

  int iGetPosY()
  {
    return iPosY;
  }

  void vDisplay()
  {
    rect(iPosX, iPosY, iWidth, iHeight);
  }
}
```

```
class Brick
{
  int iPosX = 0;
  int iPosY = 0;
  int iWidth = 40;
  int iHeight = 20;

  Brick(int iX, int iY)   //gets x and y coordinates, so every bricks knows
  where it sits
  {
    iPosX = iX;
    iPosY = iY;
  }

  int iGetPosX()
  {
    return iPosX;
  }

  int iGetPosY()
  {
    return iPosY;
  }

  void vDisplay()
  {
    rect(iPosX, iPosY, iWidth, iHeight);
  }
}
class Paddle
{
  int iPosX = 0;
  int iPosY = 0;
  int iWidth = 50;
  int iHeight = 12;

  Paddle()
  {
    iPosX = int((width * 0.5) - (iWidth * 0.5));
    iPosY = height - 25;
  }

  int iGetPosX()
  {
    return iPosX;
  }

  int iGetPosY()
  {
    return iPosY;
  }

  void vDisplay()
  {
    rect(mouseX - (iWidth * 0.5), iPosY, iWidth, iHeight);
  }
}
```

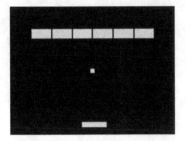

While the `Ball`, `Brick` and `Paddle` classes are different, they all have very similar and even fully redundant parts. For instance, in a *BreakOut*-style game, all graphical game entities may have position, size and colour variables, as well as display and getter methods. These parts can well be written once, in a general class, that can serve as a base class for other classes in the game that share such parts. This is called *class inheritance*.

Class inheritance allows a class to 'inherit' (or simply to use) variables and methods from another (base or parent or super) class (e.g. the position variables in Code 14). In the *BreakOut*-style game, one can create a base class (for instance, for all such graphical game entities) and then other classes can extend it (i.e. they inherit its class variables (also called fields) and methods from it). In Code 14, a `GameObject` class implements the most basic aspects, and the classes `Brick`, `Ball` and `Paddle` inherit them.

Child classes (or subclasses) can overwrite variables and methods that they inherit from their parent class.[12] In Code 14, the `Paddle` class has a different display method than the `GameObject` class.

Code 14

```
//main program same as above in Code 13[13] (except for the fill colour)
//class definitions
class GameObject
{
  int iPosX = 0;
  int iPosY = 0;
  int iWidth = 0;
  int iHeight = 0;

  int iGetPosX()
  {
    return iPosX;
  }

  int iGetPosY()
  {
    return iPosY;
  }

  void vDisplay()  //methods of the base class can be overwritten by child
  classes
  {
    rect(iPosX, iPosY, iWidth, iHeight);
  }
}
```

```
class Ball extends GameObject
{
  Ball()
  {
    iPosX = int((width * 0.5) - (iWidth * 0.5));
    iPosY = int((height * 0.5) - (iHeight * 0.5));
    iWidth = 10;
    iHeight = 10;
  }
}
class Brick extends GameObject
{
  Brick(int iX, int iY)  //gets x and y coordinates, so every bricks knows
  where it sits
  {
    iPosX = iX;
    iPosY = iY;
    iWidth = 40;
    iHeight = 20;
  }
}
class Paddle extends GameObject
{
  Paddle()
  {
    iPosX = int((width * 0.5) - (iWidth * 0.5));
    iPosY = height - 25;
    iWidth = 50;
    iHeight = 12;
  }

  void vDisplay()  //this method overwrites the vDisplay() method that is
  present in the parent class
  {
    rect(mouseX - (iWidth * 0.5), iPosY, iWidth, iHeight);
  }
}
```

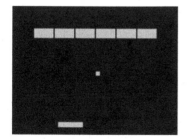

Note how substantially shorter the code now ist, because the redundant code from example Code 13 is almost completely gone.

Of course, each class can also have its special, additional, diverse abilities; for instance, the Ball class may have collision detection, and the Brick class is a boolean variable that reflects if a brick is still on or has been destroyed by the ball already.

It is possible for classes to inherit from each other over several generations. For instance, a GameObject class can be extended by a Button class, which can be extended by a ToolButton class. However, at some point, things are no longer very obvious, and too much structure might also get in the way of programming.[14]

Solution

Modify Code 9 so the player can shoot 'em! The mousePressed() function is automatically called when a mouse button is pressed; then pass the pointer coordinates mouseX and mouseY to each duck which then can find out if it was hit!

We are going to use the mouse pointer position, the state of the mouse buttons and the mouse pointer icon to convey the impression to the player that he/she can shoot down attacking ducks.

When the game starts, we change the mouse pointer from the system default arrow to a custom crosshair. During game play, the plan is, as soon as a mouse button is pressed, to find out the current pointer coordinates, pass these on the all ducks on screen, then every duck can check if it was clicked (or hit by the shot).

Switching off the display of the default mouse pointer can be done in setup() with noCursor(). Now we do not see anymore where the mouse is. To draw a crosshair at the pointer position we can add the following code towards the end of the draw function:

```
noFill();
ellipse(mouseX, mouseY, 20, 20);
line(mouseX, mouseY - 12, mouseX, mouseY + 12);
line((mouseX - 12), mouseY, (mouseX + 12), mouseY);
```

Processing automatically runs a function when a mouse button is pressed; this function is called mousePressed(). We can add the following function definition to the main program which sends the current mouse pointer position to all ducks:

```
void mousePressed()
{
  //inform all ducks of the shot:
  for (int i = 0; i < ducks.length; i++)
  {
    ducks[i].shot(mouseX, mouseY);
  }
}
```

Correspondingly, we now need to extend the Duck class to feature a method called shot() which takes two arguments[15] (the mouse pointer position) and checks if the duck was hit:

```
void shot(int shotX, int shotY)
{
  if ((clickX >= posX) && (clickX < posX + 40) &&
      (clickY >= posY) && (clickY < posY + 40))   //we are hit
  {
      alive = false;   //[16]
      score++;
  }
}
```

Done this way, the main program handles the player interaction, and the Duck class handles collision detection – a clear division. The duck does not even need to know it is reacting to mouse input, it simply checks collision when given a screen location.

It is also conceivable that each duck reacts to mouse events, or reads the mouse coordinates when triggered by a call from the main program, but I feel that the roles of the main program and the class then become less clear, and the class less modular.

Chapter End Exercises

0. The Flower Stand

   Make a class `FlowerStand` that models a flower stand. The stand sells one (unspecified) type of flower, receives flower deliveries (to re-stock supplies), and stands at a specific location in town. The class has three variables (i.e. two ints and one string), and all of them have initial default values; for example, the stand can start with 50 flowers, 20 money and be located 'next to the history museum'. The class has an output method that prints all available info about the stand (money, flower count, location) to the console. The class has also a sell method (one flower is sold for 7 money), a method to receive a flower delivery (one flower is bought for 4 money), and a method to change location; each of these methods takes arguments as needed (e.g. the number of flowers to be sold), and adjusts the class variables to accurately reflect the current state of the stand. It is not necessary to verify sensible use of the class (for instance, that the stand's number of flowers or money is always positive). Instantiate one object from the class, and call the methods to demonstrate that the stand can sell flowers, receive flower deliveries and change location.

1. Three Dices

   Make a class for a dice game with three six-sided (D6) dice. Implement a class method to roll a dice and return the result, and a function that rolls three dice and displays the result on the screen.

Notes

1. The class structure in programming can thus be seen as a retake of Walter Gropius' maxim that an artefact's appearance and technical logic should be aligned harmoniously.
2. There have been attempts to align the structure of the code with the structure of the application before (e.g. the struct structure in *C* holds only data but no functions), but classes are the most accepted and widely used technique so far.
3. In a *Pong* implementation, one would use classes/objects for the two paddles and also for the ball, even if there is only a single ball.
4. Note that, by convention, class names are capitalised.
5. The geeky term is to *instantiate* a class object; because the object is an instance of the class.
6. Nothing to do in the constructor; it will be used in the next example, Code 3. Constructors have no return type.
7. See Chapter 13 for more info on arrays.
8. We have already seen that it is possible to make an array that holds a `String`, which is actually not a data type but a class provided by *Processing*.
9. 'Extent' the class in the ordinary sense of adding to it; extent is also a specific operation in class inheritance (see the section 'Class Inheritance' in this chapter).
10. Actually, in *BreakOut*-style games, there usually is no collision with the bottom border of the screen.
11. If readers have just now started to learn about classes, they may want to skip this section and come back to it later, after they used classes for a while, and can see and appreciate the benefits of inheritance.
12. An interface (class) can specify variables and/or methods that child classes *need* to implement – this is omitted here.
13. Code 14 only shows the (revised) class definitions, not the main program. The main program is identical, whether or not class inheritance is employed.
14. *Processing* (and *Java*) only support single inheritance, i.e. a class can only inherit from one other class (in my view, this is not a major limitation). Other languages may also support multiple inheritance.
15. An (actual) argument is said to be put into a (formal) parameter.
16. The `alive` and `score` class variables are added also; one to mark ducks as dead (e.g. draw them in green instead of yellow), the other to hold the number of hits the player scored.

26

Event-Driven Programming and Game Controls

Outline

- Event-Driven Programming
- Game Controls
- Game Examples
- Mouse Events in *Processing*
- Keyboard Events in *Processing*

Here we see how player actions can be used
to control the flow of a program, and look
into typical real-time game control schemes,
and how they can be implemented in code

Event-Driven Programming

The idea of event-driven programming is that the flow of a program mirrors the flow of the interaction between a user and the system.

Events are notifications within a program. Events correspond to something that lies without the program's direct control. One part of the program creates (or *raises*) an event, another part of the program attends to (or *handles*) it. The part that raises an event is the *publisher*, the part that handles it is the *subscriber* (e.g. in *C#*) or *event listener* (in *Java*). Both communicate only through the event; the publisher's job is to raise it or not, the subscriber's job is to handle it if it occurs. There can be more than one subscriber for an event; and one subscriber can register for multiple events. There can be several event queues in a program. In an application, events are queued in an event queue as they happen, and taken off it when they are attended to.

The difference of events to routine function calls is that:

- Events are only raised when actually something happens (not when nothing happens);
- Events are relatively infrequent compared to regular e.g. screen updates; and
- Events are a special type of communication within the program (e.g. using the `eventObject` class in *Java* or the `EventArgs` class in the *.NET* framework).

What Are Events' Properties?

Events can be user-initiated or system-initiated. Events triggered by user action include key presses, mouse movement and mouse button presses, joystick and joypad directional input and button presses, screen/window resizes and GUI interaction (button clicks, menu selections). Events triggered by the system include the elapsing of real time and errors such as running out of memory or hard disk space. Some events are raised automatically by a language (e.g. key presses), and other, custom events can be added (e.g. network status).

DOI: 10.1201/9781003345916-26

Much of programming today is to some extent event-driven. The basic premise is that the flow of the program is directed by user action.[1] The program is notified if something relevant happens and can then react to the event. The advantage is that the program only does something when necessary, and only precisely what is necessary (e.g. redraw the screen only after there was a change to display).

Alternatives to Events

The more traditional way is that a program routinely and actively checks if a condition has yet changed. This is called *polling*. Naturally, that means that, depending on the frequency of an event, the program might often work for nothing and thus waste resources.

For interaction, the author would generally advise to use events as an elegant (in terms of organisation of the code) and efficient (speed) alternative to polling. A typical desktop application easily waits more than 95% of the time for user input, and even in a fast-paced action game, the author cannot quite see why the program should keep checking conditions constantly if changes are relatively infrequent (such as user input). The author can imagine only a few other types of events, that change very often (e.g. reading from the serial port), for which things would be different.

Specifically for games, a second reason is that with polling (e.g. in the game loop), the speed of player-controlled game objects depends on the speed of the computer. Players who own faster computers thus have more agile in-game avatars; this is undesirable.[2]

Processing's Support for Event-Driven Programming

Processing offers some basic event functionality such as mouse, keyboard, serial port, network and video and movie events that implement the concept with very little overhead.[3] Other languages offer similar functionality, sometimes through libraries (for instance, *Python*[4]).

Game Controls

One application of the event-driven programming paradigm is, of course, game controls.

In digital games, many different controllers are utilised. In arcade games, controllers are often custom-made for a specific game. Arcade controllers include light guns, trackballs, multiple joysticks, multiple buttons, step-on buttons, steering wheels, pedals and gear shifters and full-size controllers modelled after, e.g. skies, planes and motorbikes. For computers and consoles, controllers are usually more general and shared between multiple games. There still exist a large number of different controllers, including various models of joysticks and joypads, mice with extra buttons, flight sticks, steering wheels, and fitness controllers.

Popular Control Schemes in Games

Many control schemes exist that translate players' controller manipulations into actions in games. In 2D action games, for example, four control schemes appear to be popular (here discussed with keyboard or joystick controls):

- Immediate action; on key press execute or initialise an action at once and only once (a shot in *Space Invaders*, a jump in *Super Mario Bros.*, moving the bird up a specific pixel distance in *Flappy Bird*, moving a token in a board game);
- Continuous movement; while a key is pressed keep moving a figure on screen (e.g. the space ship in *Space Invaders*, paddles in *Pong*);
- Autofire; while a key is pressed, intermittently trigger an action, e.g. fire bullets (in many classic shoot 'em up games); and
- Charge and trigger; while a key is pressed, e.g. charge a weapon and trigger it on key release (such as the wave cannon in *R-Type* (Irem, 1987)).

Control schemes are often mixed; for instance, in 2D jump n' run games, there is usually a continuous movement for horizontal movement, but immediate action for jumps; in *Space Invaders*, there is continuous horizontal movement, combined with immediate shots.

Other control schemes and combinations of schemes exist and can be created. One advantage of coding games from (more or less) scratch and not using high-level frameworks or tools, is the freedom designers have, for instance, to make up custom control schemes for particular games.

Immediate Action

Immediate action is probably the most straightforward control scheme. The player presses a key, and at once, and only once, a change in the game is triggered. It would be unintuitive, if, for instance, the bird in *Flappy Bird* would continue to move upwards while a key is kept pressed; Flappy should only flap and move upwards a few pixels *once per keypress*.

Continuous Movement

The first approach to continuous movement in games might be to duplicate the immediate action scheme; for instance, initiate an action such as a movement by a certain pixel distance, as soon as a key pressed event is detected. In this way, in a *Space Invaders*-style game, the player's ship would be moved a certain distance every time a key is pressed. If the player wanted to move the ship across the screen, he/she would need to press and release the key repeatedly. It is also possible, that the computer's operating system automatically creates a key repeat event every few milliseconds if a key is kept pressed (likely after an initial delay). The settings related to keyboard input are usually adjusted in the operating system's Control Panel or Settings app (Windows), System Preferences (Mac) or similar.

Because the settings lie outside of the control of the program, it might happen that on some systems game objects move faster than on others.[5] Also, things get more complex when several keys are pressed at the same time, and the program might exhibit unexpected or (on different systems) varying behaviour. All of this should obviously be avoided.

I advocate, as good practice, to employ mediated control. With this, the movement of player-controlled game objects can be seen as an extension of the movement of computer-controlled game objects, such as we have seen already (trains, boxes, aliens, ducks in Chapters 15 and 25). Instead of automatic movement that is always on, the movement is switched on and off by player input. In *Space Invaders*, the ship moves after a key pressed event has been registered and as long as no key release event is registered.

Autofire, and Charge and Trigger

The autofire, and the charge and trigger schemes are variations of the continuous movement scheme. A timer is used to trigger an action every x milliseconds in the autofire scheme.

A timer is also used in the charge and trigger scheme to progressively modify a game condition (such as charging a cannon for a specially powerful shot) and to trigger an (immediate) event (such as shooting the cannon) on key release.

Real-time Input with and without Classes

Real-time input can be (and has been) realised with and without using classes, of course. The examples given here without classes are really for reference only. The author would argue that pretty much all of the objects in games that are moved about by players should also be implemented as class objects (see, for instance, Code 3 and Code 5 and the demo programs *TiledPlatformer* and *No Man's Lane* (online, book web site)).

Using classes, real-time control schemes can be implemented in at least two different ways: One, in which the main program checks which keys are pressed and released, and informs the player objects the keys refer to (the players-keys combinations are usually hard-coded in the main program in this case; if e.g. more players are added, new code needs to be written).

Another, more modular, possibility is to forward all key actions to all player objects, and the player objects figure out if the keys are relevant for them (the keys player objects listen to are usually provided to the class constructor, and the object takes over from there). This method makes it easy to add more players and controls, and no new code needs to be written.

Game Examples

First an example for immediate action, then one for continuous movement. Both are iteratively improved (as would happen in a development process).

Immediate Action

Code 1 draws a chess board and a static token, without classes.

Code 1

```
int posX = 50;
int posY = 90;
int size = 20;

void setup()
{
  size(160, 160);
  noStroke();
}

void draw()
{
  background(10, 120, 10);  //draw chess board
  fill(255, 200, 20);
  for (int i = 0; i < 64; i += 2)
  {
    int rectX = ((((i / 8) % 2) * size) + ((i % 8) * size));
    int rectY = ((i / 8) * size);
    rect(rectX, rectY, size, size);
  }
  fill(220, 60, 10);  //draw token
  ellipse((posX + size), (posY + size), (size * 0.5), (size * 0.5));
}
```

Code 2 implements a chess board and a movable token, with the immediate action scheme, and without classes. On my *Windows* PC, the system's key repeat function kicks in and keeps moving the token if the key is kept pressed.

Code 2

```
int posX = 50;
int posY = 90;
int size = 20;

void setup()
{
  size(160, 160);
  noStroke();
}

void keyPressed()
{
  if (keyCode == LEFT) { posX -= size; }
  else if (keyCode == RIGHT) { posX += size; }
  else if (keyCode == UP) { posY -= size;  }
  else if (keyCode == DOWN) { posY += size; }
}

void draw()
{
  background(10, 120, 10);  //draw chess board, short version
  fill(255, 200, 20);
  for (int i = 0; i < 64; i += 2)
  { rect((((i/8)%2)*size)+(i%8)*size, (int(i/8)*size), size, size); }

  fill(220, 60, 10);  //draw token
  ellipse((posX + size), (posY + size), (size * 0.5), (size * 0.5));
}
```

How can one defeat the automatic and unwanted repetition of key presses by the operating system (in Code 1), for instance, in a game such as *Flappy Bird*?

Code 3 implements a chess board and a moveable token, with the immediate action scheme, and with a class. Again, on my *Windows PC*, the system's key repeat function kicks in and keeps moving the token if the key is kept pressed. This program is an improvement over Code 2 because it appropriately uses a class, but it is still not ideal; if more players were involved, new (repetitive) code would need to be added (and the keys hardcoded).

Code 3

```
//main program

int size = 20;
Token t;

void setup()
{
  size(160, 160);
  noStroke();
  t = new Token(50, 90);
}

void keyPressed()
{
  if (keyCode == LEFT) { t.moveLeft(); }
  else if (keyCode == RIGHT) { t.moveRight(); }
  else if (keyCode == UP) { t.moveUp(); }
  else if (keyCode == DOWN) { t.moveDown(); }
}
```

```
void draw()
{
  background(10, 120, 10);  //draw chess board, short version
  fill(255, 200, 20);
  for (int i = 0; i < 64; i += 2)
  { rect((((i/8)%2)*size)+(i%8)*size, (int(i/8)*size), size, size); }
  t.display();  //draw token
}

//class definition
class Token
{
  int posX = 0;
  int posY = 0;

  Token(int x, int y)
  {
    posX = x;
    posY = y;
  }
  void display()
  {
    fill(220, 60, 10);  //draw token
    ellipse(posX + size, posY + size, size * 0.5, size * 0.5);
  }
  void moveLeft()
  { posX -= size; }
  void moveRight()
  { posX += size; }
  void moveUp()
  { posY -= size; }
  void moveDown()
  { posY += size; }
}
```

Continuous Movement

Code 4 shows a *Space Invaders*-style example for continuous movement, with a ship controlled by the player, without classes. Two boolean variables are used to keep track of the keys currently pressed and to move the ship. Note how the code differs from the examples above (Code 2, Code 3) which demonstrate immediate action.

Code 4

```
boolean keyLeft = false;
boolean keyRight = false;

float shipX = 0;
float shipY = 0;
float speed = 2;

void setup()
{
  size(320, 240);
  shipY = (height - 10);  //height only now available
  fill(0, 180, 0);
}
```

```
void keyPressed()
{
  if (keyCode == LEFT) { keyLeft = true; }
  else if (keyCode == RIGHT) { keyRight = true; }
}

void keyReleased()
{
  if (keyCode == LEFT) { keyLeft = false; }
  else if (keyCode == RIGHT) { keyRight = false; }
}

void draw()
{
  background(0, 40, 0);
  text("Aliens go here", 10, 20);

  if (keyLeft) { shipX -= speed; }
  if (keyRight) { shipX += speed; }

  triangle(shipX, (shipY - 10), (shipX - 7), shipY, (shipX + 7), shipY);
}
```

Code 5 is slightly a long code snippet, and demonstrates a class-based, modular solution for continuous movement, that is easily extendable to include more players (see the comments in the code) because it implements the keys used to control the ships as variables (or arguments). This technique could also be used to improve Code 3.

It is straightforward to add shot functionality to this code, that immediately fires a bullet on fire button press (then a class for bullets and an array that holds all bullet objects should be added, too).

Code 5

```
//main program
Ship[] ships = new Ship[2];   //or 3, for another player

void setup()
{
  size(320, 240);
  fill(0, 180, 0);

  //init objects by hand because keys need to be given (which can't easily be
  done in a loop)
  ships[0] = new Ship(0, (height - 10) - (20 * 0), 'a', 'd');
  ships[1] = new Ship(0, (height - 10) - (20 * 1), 'j', 'l');
  //ships[2] = new Ship(0, (height - 10) - (20 * 2), 'f', 'h');
}

void keyPressed()
{
  for (int i = 0; i < ships.length; i++)
  { ships[i].pressedKey(key); }
}
```

```
void keyReleased()
{
  for (int i = 0; i < ships.length; i++)
  { ships[i].releasedKey(key); }
}

void draw()
{
  background(0, 40, 0);
  text("Aliens go here", 10, 20);

  for (int i = 0; i < ships.length; i++)
  {
    ships[i].display();
    ships[i].update();
  }
}

//class definition
class Ship
{
  int posX = 0;
  int posY = 0;
  int speed = 2;

  char left=' ';
  char right=' ';

  boolean keyLeft=false;
  boolean keyRight=false;

  Ship(int x, int y, char l, char r)
  {
    posX = x;
    posY = y;
    left = l;
    right = r;
  }

  void display()
  { triangle(posX, (posY - 10), (posX - 7), posY, (posX + 7), posY); }

  void pressedKey(char c)
  {
    if (c==left) { keyLeft = true; }
    else if (c==right) { keyRight = true; }
  }

  void releasedKey(char c)
  {
    if (c==left) { keyLeft = false; }
    else if (c==right) { keyRight = false; }
  }

  void update()
  {
    if (keyLeft) { posX -= speed; }
    if (keyRight) { posX += speed; }
  }
}
```

All examples given above are programmed within an event-based paradigm and use *Processing*'s functions keyPressed(), mousePressed(), etc. There are no examples that use *Processing*'s variables keyPressed, mousePressed, etc., because, as argued above, an event-based paradigm has several advantages, certainly in games.

Events are a powerful way of handling interaction in
a program, interrupting the program flow to trigger
reactions. Practically, in many cases I prefer to only
set an (e.g. boolean) variable in the event handler,
and react to it when it makes sense

Mouse Events in *Processing*

In both mouse and keyboard access, the author would like to only use minimal and basic functionality provided by *Processing*. *Processing* might offer more elaborate access with language-specific convenience functions, but other languages or libraries might not. Also, the more control over the interaction lies within our own program and not within language-specific functions whose implementation and behaviour might change with the next version or release, the better.

Processing appears not to offer a function or variable that says if a specific keyboard key is currently pressed or not.[6] Therefore, using the keyPressed() and keyReleased() functions in combination with a set of boolean variables to keep track of the state of keys, appears to be the most accurate way to handle keyboard input. This is also the standard way to do so.[7]

Here, we are going to focus on the functions mousePressed(), mouseReleased() and mouse-Wheel(), and the variables mouseX, mouseY and mouseButton for mouse interaction; and on the functions keyPressed() and keyReleased(), and the variables key and keyCode for keyboard interaction.[8]

Mouse Pointer Position

In *Processing*, the mouse is easy to access, both the pointer position on the screen (i.e. relative to the top-left corner of the *Processing* window) and the state of the (three) buttons. We have already seen mouse input used occasionally (interactive Bézier curve, the *Breakout* paddle, possibly the *Duck Attack* game).

The pointer position is the location on the screen in pixels where the tip of the mouse pointer currently is. It can easily be read by programs because *Processing* provides it in the variables mouseX and mouseY. Code 6 demonstrates their use.

Code 6

```
void setup()
{ }

void draw()
{
  background(0);

  fill(255);
  ellipse((width * 0.5), (height * 0.5), (width - 10), (height - 10));

  fill(0);
  ellipse(mouseX, mouseY, 50, 50);
}
```

Note that the mouse pointer is omitted from the screenshots.
The mouse pointer coordinates can also be printed to the screen (Code 7), or to the console.

Code 7

```
void setup()
{
  size(200, 100);
  fill(255);
}

void draw()
{
  background(0);

  text("Mouse pos x is " + mouseX + ", y is " + mouseY, 10, 50);
}
```

Recall that the values go from (0, 0) to (199, 99) in a window that is sized 200x100 pixels.

Applications

In games (and other applications), the mouse pointer position is often used to do collision detection with in-game objects such as ducks, aliens, balls or with interface elements such as buttons. In some games, the mouse position is directly translated into a (e.g. screen) position or orientation within the game. In first-person shooters, for instance, usually the WASD keys move the player character in the game world, and the mouse position rotates him/her horizontally and vertically and allows aiming with a weapon.

Of course, the mouse position can be used in other, more experimental ways, e.g. for scaling, colours, transparency or movement speed. Code 8 shows some of these possibilities.[9] Note that not all applications of the pointer coordinates are equally intuitive.

Code 8

```
int ballWidth = 0;
int ballHeight = 0;

float ballX = 0;
float ballY = 0;

float speedX = 1.2;
float speedY = -10;

float gravity = 0.3;

void setup()
{
  strokeWeight(3);
  ballY = height;  //height is only now available
}

void draw()
{
  background(0, 12, 240);

  ballWidth=(10 + int(mouseX * 0.5));
  ballHeight=(10 + int(mouseY * 0.5));
  stroke((50 + mouseX), 128, 128);
  fill(128, (255 - mouseY), 128);
  ellipse(ballX, ballY, ballWidth, ballHeight);

  ballX += speedX;
  ballY += speedY;
  speedY += gravity;

  if ((ballX - (ballWidth * 0.5)) < 0) { speedX = -speedX; ballX = (ballWidth *
  0.5); }  //collides with left border
  else if ((ballX + (ballWidth * 0.5)) >= width) { speedX = -speedX; ballX =
  (width - (ballWidth * 0.5)); }  //collides with right border

  if ((ballY - (ballHeight * 0.5)) < 0) { speedY = -speedY; ballY =
  (ballHeight * 0.5); }  //collides with top border
  else if ((ballY + (ballHeight * 0.5)) >= height) { speedY = -speedY; ballY =
  (height - (ballHeight * 0.5)); }  //collides with bottom border
}
```

Code 9 demonstrates clicking on a button which then changes colour using *Processing*'s mousePressed() function which is automatically called when a mouse button is pressed.

Code 9

```
int buttonLeftX = 10;
int buttonTopY = 20;

int buttonWidth = 80;
int buttonHeight = 60;

color buttonColor = color(200, 128, 255);

void setup()
{ }
void mousePressed()
{
  if ((mouseX >= buttonLeftX) &&
      (mouseX < (buttonLeftX + buttonWidth)) &&
      (mouseY >= buttonTopY) &&
      (mouseY < (buttonTopY + buttonHeight)))
  {
      buttonColor = color(random(255), random(255), random(255));
  }
}
void draw()
{
  background(120, 70, 20);

  fill(buttonColor);
  rect(buttonLeftX, buttonTopY, buttonWidth, buttonHeight);
}
```

Code 9 uses some event-driven parts, that is, when the `mousePressed()` function is triggered when a mouse button is pressed and the program acts on this; but the rectangle is drawn and redrawn in `draw()` all the time, regardless if there was, indeed, a colour change or not.

Button State

Processing can access the state of three mouse buttons. Code 10 keeps track of which button is pressed and which is not (Figure 26.1), by using three boolean variables. The variables are set in the two functions `mousePressed()` and `mouseReleased()` which are automatically called when the state of one of the mouse buttons changes. Many languages provide such functions.

Code 10

```
boolean pressedLeft=false;
boolean pressedMiddle=false;
boolean pressedRight=false;
```

```
void setup()
{
  size(300, 100);
}

void mousePressed()
{
  if (mouseButton==LEFT) { pressedLeft=true; }
  else if (mouseButton==CENTER) { pressedMiddle=true; }
  else if (mouseButton==RIGHT) { pressedRight=true; }
}

void mouseReleased()
{
  if (mouseButton==LEFT) { pressedLeft=false; }
  else if (mouseButton==CENTER) { pressedMiddle=false; }
  else if (mouseButton==RIGHT) { pressedRight=false; }
}

void draw()
{
  background(20, 40, 170);

  if ((pressedLeft) || (pressedMiddle) || (pressedRight)) {
      text("One or several mouse buttons are pressed", 10, 20); }
  else {
      text("No mouse buttons are pressed", 10, 20); }

  if (pressedLeft) { text("The left button is pressed", 10, 40); }
  if (pressedMiddle) { text("The middle button is pressed", 10, 60); }
  if (pressedRight) { text("The right button is pressed", 10, 80); }
}
```

One or several mouse buttons are pressed
The left button is pressed

The right button is pressed

Processing also provides variables (instead of functions) to check the state of mouse buttons pressed (Code 11 demonstrates this). It shortens the example code considerably – but the feature is a *Processing* special[10] and it does not work well (it misses simultaneously pressed buttons because mouseButton can (like all variables) only hold one value, i.e. the most recently pressed button). Many games have higher requirements than office software when it comes to interaction; it is usually essential for the program to have complete, accurate and fast access to player input.

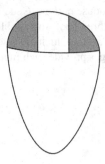

FIGURE 26.1   Left and right mouse buttons are pressed

Code 11

```
void setup()
{
  size(300, 100);
}
void draw()
{
  background(20, 40, 170);
  if (mousePressed) {
      text("One or several mouse buttons are pressed", 10, 20); }
  else {
      text("No mouse buttons are pressed", 10, 20); }
  if ((mousePressed) && (mouseButton==LEFT)) { text("The left button is
  pressed", 10, 40); }
  if ((mousePressed) && (mouseButton==CENTER)) { text("The middle button is
  pressed", 10, 60); }
  if ((mousePressed) && (mouseButton==RIGHT)) { text("The right button is
  pressed", 10, 80); }
}
```

Mouse Wheel

Code 12 shows how a mouse wheel can be read with the mouseWheel() function.

Code 12

```
float e = 10;
void setup()
{
  size(100, 200);
  noStroke();
}
void mouseWheel(MouseEvent event)
{
  e += (3 * event.getCount());
}
void draw()
{
  background(255);
  fill(255, 230, 0);
  rect(0, 0, width, 40);
  fill(0);
  rect(0, 135, width, 65);
  fill(255);
  rect(25, 135, 50, 65);
```

```
  fill(40, 70, 220);
  ellipse(30, 60, 20, 20);
  ellipse(70, 60, 20, 20);

  fill(255, 0, 0);
  ellipse((width * 0.5), 82, 20, 20);

  fill(155, 0, 40);
  ellipse((width * 0.5), 110, 70, 25);

  if (e > 0)
  {
    fill(255, 0, 0);
    rect(40, 110, 20, e);
    triangle(40, (110 + e), (width * 0.5), (110 + e + 10), 60, (110 + e));
  }
  else { e = 0; }
}
```

Pointer Icon

In many applications, the standard, operating system-supplied pointer (an arrow, presumably) does not fit. In a program, one can turn off the display of the pointer, and replace it with something else.[11]

Code 13 shows how to have either no pointer or a pointer constructed from primitive graphical shapes.

Code 13

```
void setup()
{
  noCursor();

  noFill();
}
void draw()
{
  background(10, 190, 70);

  if (mouseX > (width * 0.6)) { line(mouseX, (mouseY - 10), mouseX, (mouseY + 10)); line((mouseX - 10), mouseY, (mouseX + 10), mouseY); }

  else if (mouseX > (width * 0.3)) { ellipse(mouseX, mouseY, 20, 20);
  ellipse(mouseX, mouseY, 4, 4); }

}
```

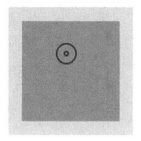

Above, we have already seen how an image file can be loaded (from the project's data folder) and used as a pointer graphics (Code 3 in Chapter 22).

Code 14 shows off the six mouse pointers that *Processing* provides.

Code 14

```
void setup()
{ }
void draw()
{
  background(10, 190, 70);

  if (mouseX >= (width * 0.83)) { cursor(WAIT); }
  else if (mouseX >= (width * 0.67)) { cursor(TEXT); }
  else if (mouseX >= (width * 0.5)) { cursor(MOVE); }
  else if (mouseX >= (width * 0.33)) { cursor(HAND); }
  else if (mouseX >= (width * 0.17)) { cursor(CROSS); }
  else { cursor(ARROW); }
}
```

Keyboard Events in *Processing*

Keys on the keyboard can be read much in the same way as mouse buttons. *Processing* offers two functions (keyPressed() and keyReleased()) and several variables (keyPressed, key, keyCode) to access it.

Coded Keys

The cursor keys and other specialty keys use the keyCode variable to check if they are pressed. Letters and digits etc. would use the key variable. Both are demonstrated in Code 15.

Code 15

```
boolean keyArmLeft=false;
boolean keyArmRight=false;
boolean keyLegLeft=false;
boolean keyLegRight=false;

void setup()
{
  size(160, 220);
}

void keyPressed()
{
  if (key == CODED)
  {
    if (keyCode == LEFT) { keyLegLeft = true; }
    else if (keyCode == RIGHT) { keyLegRight = true; }
  }
  else
  {
    if ((key == RETURN) || (key == ENTER)) { keyArmLeft = keyArmRight =
    keyLegLeft = keyLegRight = true; }
    else if (key == '1') { keyArmLeft = true; }
    else if ((key == 'a') || (key == 'A')) { keyArmRight = true; }
  }
}

void keyReleased()
{
  if (key == CODED)
  {
    if (keyCode == LEFT) { keyLegLeft = false; }
    else if (keyCode == RIGHT) { keyLegRight = false; }
  }
  else
  {
    if ((key == RETURN) || (key == ENTER)) { keyArmLeft = keyArmRight =
    keyLegLeft = keyLegRight = false; }
    else if (key == '1') { keyArmLeft = false; }
    else if ((key == 'a') || (key == 'A')) { keyArmRight = false; }
  }
}

void draw()
{
  background(255);

  //arms:

  fill(255);
  if (keyArmLeft) { rect(63, 60, -50, 10); }
  else { rect(53, 60, 10, 50); }

  if (keyArmRight) { rect(97, 60, 50, 10); }
  else { rect(97, 60, 10, 50); }

  //legs:

  fill(0, 160, 0);
  if (keyLegLeft) { rect(87, 120, -80, 15); }
  else { rect(58, 120, 15, 80); }

  if (keyLegRight) { rect(71, 120, 80, 15); }
  else { rect(86, 120, 15, 80); }
```

```
//body:

fill(255, 250, 0);
quad(63, 60, 97, 60, 105, 135, 55, 135);

fill(255, 220, 220);
ellipse((width*0.5), 44, 36, 36);

fill(200, 20, 20);
quad(75, 10, 85, 10, 98, 40, 62, 40);
rect(54, 38, 52, 4);
}
```

Note that non-capitalised and capitalised letters are not the same and need each to be checked; also be aware that *Macs* and *PCs* differ in their naming of the RETURN and ENTER keys (check for both to make programs run on both systems).

ASCII Code

Instead of comparing a pressed or released key with characters, one can also use ASCII values.

Letters and digits and symbols are represented internally by the computer as numbers. But it is not obvious, which characters to use, and how they should be numbered. The capital letter A, for instance, can be encoded in all kinds of ways. When computers were still few in number and used as stand-alone machines, it did not matter much, which of the many different (and incompatible) encodings was used. But in the 1950s and 1960s, when computers became integrated into networks and began to communicate with each other, the problem became evident.

The most widely used character-encoding system is ASCII (American Standard Code for Information Interchange). The first ASCII code version was created between 1960 and 1963 by a committee of the American Standards Association (ASA[12]) based on earlier codes used for teleprinters. Usually, these codes could describe 26 letters (the ones used in English) in lower and upper case, ten digits, about 20 symbols such as colons and quotation marks, and some control characters such as end of transmission and line feed.

The fewer bits are needed to encode one character, the less memory and network bandwidth texts take up. To describe up to 128 different characters, 7 bits are needed (6 bits or 64 characters are too few if every character is to be encoded independently[13]). The distribution of the characters within the 128 spaces (Table 26.1) was determined by existing standards and by technical considerations (e.g. to maximise the Hamming distance between control characters, to arrange the digits 0–9 so their location in the code would correspond to their binary values when prefixed with 011, and to have upper and lower letters to differ from each other in only a single bit) (ASCII History 2017).

But ASCII catered only to English. Various attempts have been made to accommodate other (e.g. non-Latin) languages, such as localised versions of ASCII. In the 1970s, 8 bits instead of 7 began to be used by the increasingly popular microcomputers. The extra bit that was available was never standardised, and the codes between 128 and 255 contained in, for instance, IBM's 8-bit ASCII, describe letters and

TABLE 26.1

7-bit ASCII Table

0: null	32: [space]	64: @	96: `
1: SOH (start of header)	33: !	65: A	97: a
2: STX (start of text)	34: "	66: B	98: b
3: ETX (end of text)	35: #	67: C	99: c
4: EOT (end of transmission)	36: $	68: D	100: d
5: ENQ (enquiry)	37: %	69: E	101: e
6: ACK (acknowledge)	38: &	70: F	102: f
7: BEL (bell)	39: '	71: G	103: g
8: BS (backspace)	40: (	72: H	104: h
9: TAB (horizontal tab)	41:)	73: I	105: i
10: LF (line feed)	42: *	74: J	106: j
11: VT (vertical tab)	43: +	75: K	107: k
12: FF (form feed)	44:,	76: L	108: l
13: CR (carriage return)	45: -	77: M	109: m
[...]	46:.	78: N	110: n
	47: /	79: O	111: o
	48: 0	80: P	112: p
	49: 1	81: Q	113: q
	50: 2	82: R	114: r
	51: 3	83: S	115: s
	52: 4	84: T	116: t
	53: 5	85: U	117: u
	54: 6	86: V	118: v
	55: 7	87: W	119: w
	56: 8	88: X	120: x
	57: 9	89: Y	121: y
	58: :	90: Z	122: z
	59: ;	91: [	123: {
	60: <	92: \	124:	
	61: =	93:]	125: }
	62: >	94: ^	126: ~
	63:?	95: _	127: DEL

accents for the most popular (Western) languages, some mathematical symbols and some graphical symbols (such as borders) (Tero 2012). Since this time, ASCII could be read using different *character sets*, and they are still with us today.[14,15]

From the 1980s on, Unicode, a new encoding standard that provides each language with all its letters was conceived. As a compromise between international standardisation bodies and (mostly US) industry, a variable-length (1 to 4 byte, 8-bit code units) version (UTF-8) is now the accepted standard on modern computers. The 1-byte version corresponds to the ASCII standard. *Processing* (since release 0134) writes (and reads) all files in UTF-8 encoding.

Using ASCII values, Code 15 would work when the else clause in keyPressed() is changed to

```
if (key == 10) { keyArmLeft = keyArmRight = keyLegLeft = keyLegRight = true; }
else if (key == 49) { keyArmLeft = true; }
else if ((key == 97) || (key == 65)) { keyArmRight = true; }
```

and when the else clause in keyReleased() is changed to

```
if (key == 10) { keyArmLeft = keyArmRight = keyLegLeft = keyLegRight = false; }
else if (key == 49) { keyArmLeft = false; }
else if ((key == 97) || (key == 65)) { keyArmRight = false; }
```

Coded keys are keys that have no ASCII equivalent (the left and right cursor keys in this case).

Solution

How can one defeat the automatic and unwanted repetition of key presses (in Code 2), for instance, in a game such as *Flappy Bird*?

After a bit of investigative work (e.g. printing when key press and key release events are registered), it becomes clear that the system only simulates key *presses* that are factually not happening, but not key *releases*.

The revised code (below) uses a boolean variable that tracks key releases, to make sure key presses are only recognised after a key was released (changes are highlighted). The code could be improved to accommodate several keys pressed at the same time (by adding one boolean variable per key that is relevant).

```
int posX = 50;
int posY = 90;
int size = 20;
boolean anyKeyDown = false;

void setup()
{
  size(160, 160);
  noStroke();
}

void keyPressed()
{
  if (anyKeyDown) { return; }
  anyKeyDown = true;

  if (keyCode == LEFT) { posX -= size; }
  else if (keyCode == RIGHT) { posX += size; }
  else if (keyCode == UP) {  posY -= size; }
  else if (keyCode == DOWN) { posY += size; }
}

void keyReleased()
{
  anyKeyDown = false;
}

void draw()
{
  background(10, 120, 10); //draw chess board, short version
  fill(255, 200, 20);
  for (int i = 0; i < 64; i += 2)
  { rect((((i/8)%2)*size)+(i%8)*size, (int(i/8)*size), size, size); }
  fill(220, 60, 10); //draw token
  ellipse((posX + size), (posY + size), (size * 0.5), (size * 0.5));
}
```

Chapter End Exercises

0. The Secret Self

   Draw a little figure on the screen that, when clicked with the mouse for at least 2.27 seconds, reveals its secret self. Extend the code to also recognise pressing the space bar. Implement this in two different ways: Once with polling (using *Processing*'s special variables such as mousePressed) and once within an event-driven paradigm (using functions such as mousePressed()). For which applications is each technique typically used? Which technique is appropriate for this exercise, and why?

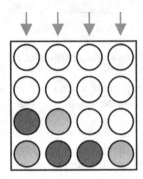

FIGURE 26.2   *Connect 3* game sketch

1. The Dame Simulator

   Implement a 2-player Dame game simulator: Players click on pieces to pick them up, and click on fields (or beside the board) to set them down. There is no AI. Use classes for the 64 fields and the pieces. The program turns a piece (permanently) into a queen on reaching the final row.

   The Dame simulator is really only a simulator of the gaming equipment; there are no game mechanics such as a jump; just players picking up a piece (hopefully one of their own pieces) and putting it down somewhere (there is only one mechanic: If a piece reaches the opposite final row it is turned (graphically) into a queen; everything else is managed by the players).

   Potential extra features: The program keeps track of who's turn it is, elapsed time, number of pieces statistics, winning condition, and checks for or indication of valid moves.

2. *Connect 3* (2 player)

   Create a simplified version of *Connect 4* (Figure 26.2) that can be played with another person using hotseat multiplayer (both players taking turns on the same screen, swapping the mouse between them). The game is played on a 4x4 grid of circles. During their turn, a player selects one of the four columns to place their coloured token in. The token appears in the lowest possible row in that column, stacking on top of any other tokens previously placed. If a column is full then it is not a valid choice. The aim of the game is for a player to align three of their tokens in a row either vertically, horizontally, or diagonally. The game ends when one player has lined up three of their tokens or if the grid is full. The game displays which player won (or *draw* in the case of a draw), and can then be restarted with a click.

3. The 2D Pixel Art Drawing Program

   Implement a pixel-based 2D image editor (Figure 26.3). Desirable features include 16 (or more) different colours (including black, white and greys) and different drawing tools (one of them is a simple draw tool, i.e. dragging the mouse pointer draws pixels in the selected colour; other tools could be, e.g. a pipette, straight line, rectangle, spray paint or ellipse tool). One tool or colour can be assigned to each of the (left and right) mouse buttons; the default behaviour is to draw a pixel with the current foreground colour on the left mouse button click and with the current background colour on the right click. A tool or colour is assigned to the left or right mouse button by clicking on it. Load (you may want to re-use your code from exercise 1 in Chapter 22) and save the image in PNG format. The image file (filename `image.png`) is loaded automatically on program start, and saved on program exit, and on clicking a save button. The image has a fixed size of 32 by 32 pixels. There are two views of the image: An editable view which is enlarged to fit the (fixed) window size (scale the image with the `image()` function when displaying it on screen); and a preview which is in actual (i.e. not enlarged) size. All program functions can be triggered by mouse: It is used to manipulate the image, and to click on GUI buttons to select tools and colours and to invoke functions such as saving the image. Do not use any libraries (e.g. for the graphical interface).

   Potential extra features: Different pointer symbols for different tools, undo, transparent colour and keyboard shortcuts.

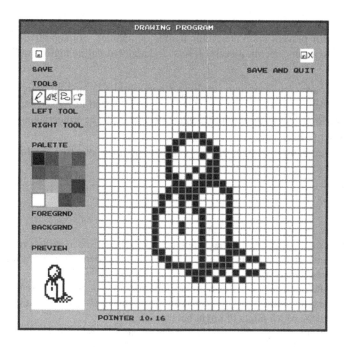

FIGURE 26.3 Pixel art program screen layout sketch

4. The Animation Editor

Make an animation editor with eight frames (Figure 26.4). Each frame has a fixed size of 24x24 pixels (internally, all eight frames are located in one `PImage spriteSheet` of size 192x24 pixels). The animation is continuously looped; each frame is shown for 100 milliseconds in a preview display. The editable view is enlarged to fit the (fixed) window size (scale the image with the `image()` function when displaying it on one screen); the preview is in real size. There is only one drawing tool that sets a pixel, black with the left mouse button, white with the right. All functions can be triggered by the mouse.

Potential extra features: Start/stop preview, load and save sprite sheet file(s), colour palette (picking buttons) with 16 colours and transparency, more drawing tools (e.g. lines, rectangles and ellipses), different pointer symbols for different tools, undo function, keyboard shortcuts, and changing the animation speed.

5. Flappy Flies Again

Make a game similar to the infamous *Flappy Bird* (dotGears 2013, iOS); that is, an endless, one-button, single-player, 3rd person-view, side-scrolling, fast action game.[16] The player's avatar is displayed in two different states: Wings down as long as the button is pressed, wings up otherwise. Flappy dies on collision with an obstacle (I recommend to create a little explosion with a particle system for the visual effect). Flappy has no jetpack.[17] The difficulty increases noticeably over time. The game can be restarted with, for instance, a key press.

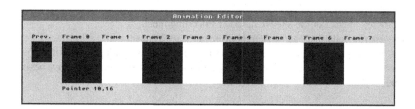

FIGURE 26.4 Animation editor screen layout sketch

Potential extra features: A highscore list with ten items which is sorted by score, and into which successful players can enter their names or handles, collaborative multiplay, sound, bonus extras, weapons, enemies, secret levels, and a global online highscore list.

6. Mario Forever

Make a single-player, endless, auto scrolling,[18] horizontal, 2D, side-view and tiled jump n' run game. The game is essentially fast and fluid. The scroll speed increases noticeably over time. The game world is on-the-fly randomly generated. The player collects items such as stars to increase his/her score.

Potential extra features: Collaborative multiplay, enemies, shooting and hidden gems.

Notes

1. Imagine a *Processing* program with an empty `draw()` function.
2. Modern computers are pretty fast, so the differences in absolute time as well as in practical, observable or measurable effects are minor; but, apart from efficiency considerations, events are more elegant than polling, for interactive applications such as games.
3. If desired, one could implement one's own event framework in *Processing*, or use the *Java* class.
4. The *pygame* library provides access to screen and (e.g. keyboard) input, and even some convenience classes such as bullets, which might or might not be useful.
5. Even if the language or library offers control over key repeats (as does *SDL*, for instance), it appears more elegant to read a pressed key by individual key pressed and key released events, than by way of simulated key presses that do not actually happen.
6. The key variable contains the last key that was either pressed or released; it says nothing about the state of other keys.
7. For instance, when using *C++* with the *Simple Directmedia Layer* (*SDL*, libsdl.org) library.
8. Omitted from the text are language-specific convenience functions such as `mouseMoved()`, `mouseDragged()`, `mouseclicked()` and `keyTyped()`, and variables such as `pmouseX` and `pmouseY` that might nevertheless be useful in some programs.
9. Note that the speed of the ball steadily increases because gravity is constantly added, and the speed never reset (e.g. on collision with the bottom border).
10. That is, it is *Processing*-specific. One should rather use the above method, using one's own variables to keep track of things, and not rely on language-specific features that might not be present in other languages.
11. *Processing* versions before 3 could compile into *Javascript*, and *Processing* sketches would thus run inside web browsers. But in these cases, the mouse pointer could not be reliably hidden or changed (processing.org/reference/cursor_.html, processing.org/reference/noCursor_.html (Feb 28, 2015)). Compiling into *Javascript* is no longer supported by *Processing*. According to the *Processing* documentation, in *Processing 3*, 'setting or hiding' the pointer 'does not generally work with "Present" mode', that is, when 'running full-screen' (processing.org/reference/cursor_.html, processing.org/reference/noCursor_.html (Feb 28, 2017)). I cannot confirm this; in presentation mode, cursor commands appear to work fine in *Processing* 3.2.3 and 4.2 (both on *Linux*).
12. Later the *American National Standards Institute* (*ANSI*).
13. A Baudot-like shift function that would have allowed to use 6 bits was considered not reliable enough (ASCII History. www.liquisearch.com/ascii/history (Mar 3, 2017)).
14. As anybody can witness when receiving emails with (non-English) letters and accents that turned into weird symbols.
15. In a web browser, check out the View/Character Encoding menu.
16. Do not (re-) use the code that can be found online but start from scratch.
17. This means, pressing and holding the button does not keep increasing Flappy's vertical position on screen.
18. The screen moves automatically with a certain speed; the player's avatar cannot move beyond the left edge of the screen.

27

Hardware Speed Independence for Movement

Outline

- Elapsed Time
- Movement Speed in Games

Elapsed Time

`millis()` returns the number of milliseconds that have elapsed since the program (or *sketch*, in *Processing* lingo) began running. That might not sound very exciting or useful, but it is!

The basic assumption here is that `millis()` (and time) run at the same speed on all computers. That means that values returned by `millis()` can be used e.g. in graphics, and things will look the same on different machines, slow and fast (see the sections 'Frame-Based Animation' and 'Timed Events' in Chapter 28). For instance, the values can be used to cycle through the colours of the rainbow (Code 1).

Code 1

```
void setup()
{
  frameRate(999999999);  //to defeat the speed limit Processing imposes by
  default

  noStroke();
  colorMode(HSB);
  background(0);
}
void draw()
{
  int hue = int((millis() % 10000) / 39.215686275);  //scale the hue value to
  lie between 0 and 255 (39.216 is 10000 / 255)
  fill(hue, 255, 255);
  ellipse(50, 50, 25, 25);
}
```

The values from `millis()` can also be used for movement; the circle in moves in exactly the same way regardless of hardware speed, because it uses the values from `millis()` for its (vertical) location (moderated by the `sin()` function, see the discussion of sine and cosine in Chapter 15).

Code 2

```
void setup()
{
  frameRate(999999999);   //to defeat the speed limit Processing imposes by
  default
}

void draw()
{
  background(0);

  int y = (50 + int(sin(millis() * 0.001) * 50));
  ellipse(50, y, 25, 25);
}
```

The number of elapsed milliseconds can also be used to test how long things take (such as graphical output), for moving and animating objects, and for timed events (see Chapters 15 and 28).

Code 3 shows how many milliseconds the program is running.

Code 3

```
void setup()
{
  size(210, 90);

  frameRate(999999999);   //to defeat the speed limit Processing imposes by
  default

  textSize(72);
  strokeWeight(5);
  strokeCap(SQUARE);
  stroke(255);
}

void draw()
{
  background(0);

  text(millis(), 10, (height - 20));

  line(((millis() * 0.1) % width), (height - 10), ((millis() * 0.1) % width) +
  40, (height - 10));
}
```

5672

Now let's use the `millis()` function to measure something. How long does it take to draw 100000 ellipses (Code 4)?

Code 4

```
int startTicks = millis();
for (int i = 0; i < 100000; i++) { ellipse(50, 50, 10, 10); }
println(millis() - startTicks);
```

Output (on my machine):

```
2953
```

Drawing 100000 ellipses of diameter 10 take just under 3 s. Larger ellipses (of diameter 50) take a lot more time, just over 13 s on my computer. Even ellipses with a diameter of 0 take time (about 1.1 s), as does drawing outside of the visible area (regardless of diameter, about 1 s).

What about the claim that on computers multiplication is faster than division (Code 5)?

Code 5

```
int startTicks = millis();
float a = 0;
for (int i = 0; i < 1000000000; i++) { a = (i * 0.1); }
println(millis() - startTicks);
```

Output (on my machine):

```
453
```

For division (a = (i/10)), I have a dramatically different result (4344 ms, on the same machine[1]). The claim thus appears to be confirmed by this experiment.[2]

In Chapter 20 on Text and Fonts, two ways of outputting text to the screen were described: One method using `createFont()` and another method using `loadFont()`. The first renders fonts at run-time from a (ttf) font file, the other uses pre-rendered graphics files. Using one or the other is not only a question of preference or convenience, but also of speed.

Rendering fonts at run-time might (and can be expected to) be slower than using prepared bitmapped graphics. On my friend Max' computer, and with a random RGB, non-transparent fill, the bitmapped font is faster than the rendered font by about 30% (0.21 vs. 0.32 ms). On my computer, using bitmapped fonts is, however, not faster than rendering them at run-time: When transparency is involved, rendering is a bit faster (on my computer 0.13 vs. 0.18 ms per output line); with a random colour fill, rendering is much faster (0.07 vs. 0.24 ms); with a plain fill still quite a bit (0.07 vs. 0.18 ms).[3]

Modify Code 3 and Code 5 from Chapter 20 (the author recommends to integrate them into one program for a proper comparison) and speed test the machine!

Movement Speed in Games (The Time Fix for Movement)

*Here we see how to make programs
run the same speed on slow machines
and on fast ones*

   Computers have different speeds. Even the same computer might run faster or slower, depending on how many processes are on-going at a certain moment in time. This is problematic for games, because game speed plays a major role, for instance, for how the interaction with a game feels, and for game difficulty.

   The time fix discussed here addresses the problem that programs run with different speeds on different computers. The time fix is relevant for any program that includes movement or animation (such as games, of course). There are two similar but different time fixes: One is used for movement (below), and one for animation and timed events (see the sections 'Frame-Based Animation' and 'Timed Events' in Chapter 28).

   Processing already offers a function that is supposed to work as a time fix, called frameRate(). The problem with frameRate() is, that it does not work well. It cannot speed up a slow machine, so, on a slow computer, a program will just run slow. What frameRate() can do, is, make a fast machine run slower. And that is something we probably don't want. We want all the computing power we can get to make a game as fast, responsive and smooth as possible. There is not anything else important going on, on that computer anyway, that the game cares about. By default, and hidden from view, *Processing* limits the speed of programs to 60 executions of the draw() function per second (confirm this with frameratetest.pde program available online). That means, if one wants to harness all the available computing power and to go full send, one should always set frameRate() to some extraordinarily high number in setup(). Then use the movement timefix to achieve maximum movement smoothness.

   So far, moving things was done rather crudely, by trial-and-error, adjusting how fast something moves by tinkering with Magic Numbers (see the section 'Magic Numbers' in Chapter 4; e.g. in setting the speed), and nobody knew how fast, in fact, things move on players' computers. This applies to both, objects controlled by the player (e.g. the spaceship in *Space Invaders*) and to objects controlled by the computer (e.g. space aliens).[4]

   In Code 6 a butterfly moves back and forth, in a straight line, between the left and right screen (or window) boundaries, with speed 1, whatever that is. We have already seen such examples (e.g. Code 2 in Chapter 15).

Code 6

```
float posX = 0;
float speedX = 1;

void setup()
{ }

void draw()
{
  background(254, 148, 96);
  fill((posX * 1.7), (posX * 2.5), (posX * 2.1));
  rect(posX, 40, 20, (sin(posX) * 10));

  posX += speedX;

  //collision with left and right wall:
  if ((posX < 0) || ((posX+20) >= width)) { speedX = -speedX; }
}
```

A problem with Code 6 is, the butterfly moves with different speeds, depending on how fast the computer hardware is. Code 7 avoids this, by using the time fix. We have used real time before. Here, it is used to scale movement by elapsed milliseconds; that is, a turtle is moved depending on how much time elapsed since the last update.

Whatever one's hardware, the turtle reaches the right border of the screen in 50 seconds (500 pixels distance, with a speed of 10 pixels per second). The only difference between different computers is, how many updates are made, and how far the turtle moves in each update.

Code 7

```
float turtleX = 0;
float turtleSpeed = 10;  //speed in pixels per second
int ticksLastUpdate = millis();

void setup()
{
  size(500, 40);
  frameRate(999999999);  //to defeat the speed limit Processing imposes by
  default
}

void draw()
{
  background(190, 225, 45);
  arc(turtleX, 25, 20, 16, PI, (2 * PI), CHORD);
  ellipse((turtleX + 12), 20, 6, 6);

  turtleX += turtleSpeed * (millis() - ticksLastUpdate) * 0.001;
  ticksLastUpdate = millis();
}
```

An identical speed for the turtle on slow and fast machines is achieved by the object's position being updated less often on slow computers but the object moving farther each time; on fast computers, the object's position is updated very often but the object only moving a tiny bit each time (Figure 27.1). To be able to move an object the correct amount of pixels, one needs to calculate the elapsed time from update to update. When one knows the time difference and when the speed is given (e.g. as pixels per second), is it possible to calculate how far (e.g. how many pixels) the object should be moved?

Now there can be a race between the reader's and my computer hardware (Code 8)! On my computer, both texts reach the right window border at approximately the same time. But only the movement of the upper text is time fixed. The lower text moves as fast as the hardware allows. That means, the reader's computer is faster than mine, if the lower text moves faster than the upper. Try it out!

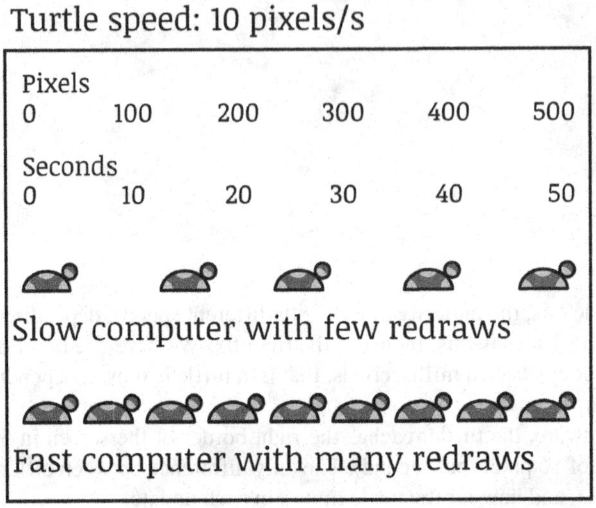

Turtle speed: 10 pixels/s

Pixels					
0	100	200	300	400	500

Seconds					
0	10	20	30	40	50

Slow computer with few redraws

Fast computer with many redraws

FIGURE 27.1   Slow and fast computers displaying a turtle which is moving with the same speed of 10 pixels per second

Code 8

```
float myCompX = 0;
float myCompSpeed = 10;
int ticksLastUpdate = millis();

float yourCompX = 0;
float yourCompSpeed = 0.0038;   //Magic Number to model my computer's speed

void setup()
{
  size(500, 50);
  frameRate(999999999);   //to defeat the speed limit Processing imposes by
  default
}

void draw()
{
  background(190, 225, 45);

  text("My computer", myCompX, 20);
  myCompX+= myCompSpeed * (millis() - ticksLastUpdate) * 0.001;
  ticksLastUpdate = millis();

  text("Your computer", yourCompX, 40);
  yourCompX += yourCompSpeed;   //not time fixed
}
```

My computer

Your computer

Code 9 shows how little code is needed to implement the time fix in a class. We know that a bear should move, say, 10 pixels per second. If since the last update only 0.5 seconds elapsed, we only move it 5 pixels (i.e. 10 * 0.5).[5]

Code 9

```
class Bear
{
  float fX = 0;   //moving in x direction only
  float fPixelsPerSec = 10;
  int iTicksLastUpdate = 0;
  //other class variables not relevant for the time fix...

  void vUpdate()
  {
    int iDelta = (millis() - iTicksLastUpdate);
    fX += fPixelsPerSec * iDelta * 0.001;
    //iTicksLastUpdate = millis();
    iTicksLastUpdate += iDelta;   //slight optimisation
  }

  //other methods not relevant for the time fix...
}
```

When using classes, the time fix goes into the class. Each object keeps track of its own time. There is only one variable (int iTicksLastUpdate) required; it stores when the last update happened. Using this variable, one can calculate the time difference between the last update and this update happening now (millis() - iTicksLastUpdate), stored in a local (int iDelta) variable. The difference in milliseconds (iDelta) is then multiplied with the speed (float fPixelsPerSec). The speed is given in pixels per second, so when multiplying, this needs to be taken into account (i.e. * 0.001). After the change in position is done, the current time is stored (iTicksLastUpdate = millis(), or slightly optimised, iTicksLastUpdate += iDelta) to be used in the next update.[6]

The 'optimisation' to add iDelta to iTickLastUpdate (and not to assign millis()), is done to avoid adding up a (small) inaccuracy (i.e. each update losing a tiny amount of milliseconds when newly assigning millis() to iTickLastUpdate); also, it saves one function call (to millis()).

Note that this style of time fix works exactly the same for objects controlled by the computer (such as bears, Code 9), and for objects controlled by the player (such as space ships). Only a space ship is only moved for as long as a key is pressed (i.e. a boolean variable is true), but the rest of the code is virtually identical.

Solution

Modify Code 3 and Code 5 from Chapter 20 (the author recommends to integrate them into one program for a proper comparison) and speed test the machine!

```
void setup()
{
  size(600, 400);
  frameRate(999999999);   //to defeat the speed limit Processing imposes by
  default⁷
  int iMillisStart = 0;
  int iMillisEnd = 0;
  int iDiff = 0;
  int iRepeat = 10000;
  //fill(255, 10);

  //rendered font
  PFont fontRender = createFont("Times-Roman", 48);
  textFont(fontRender);
  background(0);
```

```
iMillisStart = millis();
println("Rendered font: Start at " + iMillisStart);
for (int i = 0; i < iRepeat; i++)
{
  fill(random(0, 255), random(0, 255), random(0, 255));
  //fill(i % 255);
  text("abcdefghijklmnopqrstuvwxyz0123456789", 10, random(10, (height-20)));
}
iMillisEnd = millis();
iDiff = (iMillisEnd - iMillisStart);
println("End at " + iMillisEnd + ", " + iRepeat + " repeats took " +
iDiff + " milliseconds, i.e. one text output took " + (float(iDiff) /
float(iRepeat)) + " ms");

//bitmapped font
PFont fontBitmapped = loadFont("Times-Roman-48.vlw");
textFont(fontBitmapped);
background(0);
iMillisStart = millis();
println("Bitmapped font: Start at "+iMillisStart);
for (int i = 0; i < iRepeat; i++)
{
  fill(random(0, 255), random(0, 255), random(0, 255));
  //fill(i%255);
  text("abcdefghijklmnopqrstuvwxyz0123456789", 10, random(10, (height - 20)));
}
iMillisEnd = millis();
iDiff = (iMillisEnd - iMillisStart);
println("End at " + iMillisEnd + ", " + iRepeat + " repeats took " + iDiff +
" milliseconds, i.e. one text output took " + (float(iDiff) /
float(iRepeat))+" ms");
}
void draw()
{ }
```

Chapter End Exercises

0. Algorithmic Art

   Create an algorithmic, graphical artwork. Identify some of the particular characteristics of
   an early computer artist's style and make an interactive or animated homage.[8] Play with the
   parts, colours or patterns of the artwork and use *Processing*'s (or your own) drawing functions
   (e.g. 2D shapes and curves). For instance, if one took image 5 from *144 Trapèzes* (1974) by
   Vera Molnár as a starting point, one could make the quad-looking shapes move sideways, with
   varying sizes and speeds. Do not load and display an image of the artwork and e.g. filter it.
   The program should neither be trivial nor fully predictable (nor both; for instance, a program
   that displays part of an artwork, and the rest of it on mouse click); but involve some degree of
   surprise, exploration or discovery. Pick an artwork that does not require to spend 90% of the
   time on recreating it, but pick one that allows you to focus on the interaction or animation. Use
   the time fix and classes and objects.

1. Get Moving

   Make a figure such as a droid bee, droid bear or droid pig appear next to one screen edge.
   Move the figure across the screen with a speed of exactly 100 pixels per second (use the
   'multiplication-style' movement time fix). Test that the figure traverses 600 pixels in 6 seconds.
   Implement the figure as a class object. Use an image off a sprite sheet to display the figure[9].

2. Walking the Droid

   Modify the code of exercise 1. Fit the figure with an (e.g. walking) animation with 8 or more frames; each frame is shown for 100 milliseconds (use the 'if style' animation time fix). Use a sprite sheet.

Notes

1. With *Processing* 1.5.1 on a PC (other versions might be optimised).
2. Note that outputting the results of the calculations to the console with `println()` (or to the screen) is omitted, because this takes a long time and might interfere with the measuring of the actual operation.
3. There is a lot of optimisation going on behind the scenes, specifically with graphics, so speed comparisons are not always straightforward.
4. For example, in *Pong*, the ball would have a time fix, as it is moved by the computer. The paddles would have a time fix if they are controlled through relative positioning devices, e.g. key or button presses or digital joysticks – they would of course not need a time fix if they are controlled through absolute positioning devices such as potentiometers ('turning knobs') or mice.
5. Because the calculation is done not with elapsed seconds but with milliseconds, it actually is `10 * 500 * 0.001`, with the same result.
6. There is the possibility of using an *if* statement instead, i.e. if time difference > 1000 milliseconds, change position i.e. `xPos += 10`. There are two problems with this solution. The first is that the speed (e.g. displacement in pixels) is fixed; it does not utilise fast hardware for a smooth display. The other problem is, that it adds up an error. The time difference is probably 1015 or 1040 instead of exactly 1000. Because this check is performed very often, the error adds up, and the object is actually moving slower than anticipated. This can be fixed (see Code 6 in Chapter 28) – but the other method appears to be more elegant and scales the displacement with the available hardware performance, so I recommend using that for movement. For animation and timed events, the *if* method works fine (see the sections 'Frame-Based Animation' and 'Timed Events' in Chapter 28).
7. This is has little effect in this program, because `draw()` does not run (and it appears only the `draw()` function is effected by the `frameRate()` setting (but not the `setup()` function)).
8. Focus on algorithmic art, do not pick any random artwork such as the Mona Lisa...
9. Free game assets such as sprite sheets and tile sheets can pretty easily be found online.

28

Sprites, Frame-Based Animation and Timed Events

Outline

- Sprites
- Frame-Based Animation
- Timed Events

A lot of 2D games use pixel-based graphics.[1] Roughly, there are two types of in-game objects that have graphical representations in such games, i.e. things that move, and things that do not move. Things that move are often shown using *sprites*, i.e. little pieces of (often animated) graphics, such as a space ship in a shooter, or a little figure running and jumping in a platformer. Things that do not move are usually shown using *tiles*, which are also little pieces of (often not animated) graphics, such as platforms, walls, trees and diamonds.

Technically, sprites and tiles are similar, and both are regularly used together in games. For instance, in a platform-style game, the player's figure and enemies are sprites, the level platforms and in-game items are tiles. There is an overlap between sprites and tiles: A fire-throwing plant, for instance, should be part of a level layout but also be animated. A med pack could be stationary in a level (in a top-down *Gauntlet*-style game (Atari, 1985)), or it can move across the screen (in a space shooter).

Sprites are discussed in the next section, animation in the following section 'Frame-Based Animation', and tiling in Chapter 29.

Sprites

So far we have been using rather simple graphics to represent entities in our programs, such as rectangles. And for some games, it is perfectly fine to draw entities with graphical primitives (e.g. a triangular space ship in *Space Invaders*). This typically results in rather simple graphics (Code 1).

Code 1

```
int playerPosX = 32;
int playerPosY = 92;
int size = 10;

void setup()
{
  size(320, 240);
}

void draw()
{
  background(0);
  noStroke();
  fill(20, 160, 0);
  triangle(playerPosX - size, playerPosY - size, playerPosX + size, playerPosY,
  playerPosX - size, playerPosY + size);
}
```

DOI: 10.1201/9781003345916-28

But 2D games usually use sprites to represent moving entities, for instance, the player, enemies, bullets and bonus items such as med packs. Sprites are typically preferred over geometrical shapes in games, because they are more detailed, and rather straightforward to create (e.g. with popular graphics programs) as opposed to graphics created from geometrical shapes (which need to be programmed).[2]

Code 2 shows the player's space ship on screen using a sprite from a sprite sheet.

Code 2

```
PImage spriteSheet = null;
int playerPosX = 32;
int playerPosY = 92;

void setup()
{
  size(320, 240);
  spriteSheet = loadImage("data/spritesheet.png");
}

void draw()
{
  background(0);
  image(spriteSheet.get(0, 0, 24, 24), playerPosX, playerPosY);
}
```

The sprite sheet ('spritesheet.png'; Figure 28.1) is located in the data folder which is in the program folder. The get() function grabs a rectangular (or square, in this case) piece of the sprite sheet. This piece (the sprite) is then shown on screen (at the player's position).

Sprite sheets contain a (sometimes large) number of 2D graphics.[3] A game only needs to load a single file for all the sprite graphics. Access to the individual sprites in the sprite sheet is usually trivial, because in many games, most (or even all) entities have the same size (often square[4]), and the graphics are arranged in a regular grid in the sprite sheet (Figure 28.1).

How to Store Sprites on Disk and in Memory

When a game uses sprites, there is often a considerable number of them. There are several possibilities to store these images on disk and in memory.

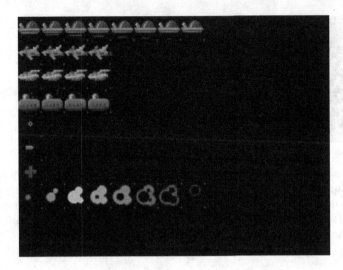

FIGURE 28.1   A basic sprite sheet, containing sprites for the player's space ship and three for enemy space ships, two kinds of bullets, a med pack and an explosion on a black background[5]; the player's space ship and the explosion have eight animation frames, the enemy space ships have four, the bullets and the med pack have only one.[6]

As files **on disk**, sprites can be saved in separate files (such as `spaceship.png`) or in sprite sheets. Separate image files are typically only used in rare, special cases, not for fully-fledged games. Separate image files are often only used for:

- Games which only need a minimal number of sprites (such as board games);
- Initial game sketches and games in development; and
- Games for play tests in which graphics should not distract from other aspects of the game such as the controls or the level design.

In probably most 2D games, sprite sheets are used. A sprite sheet typically contains all sprites a game uses; in cases in which there are so many or so large sprites that a single sprite sheet cannot practically hold them (e.g. the size of the sprite sheet would be several thousand pixels, with a very large file size), several sprite sheets can be employed (e.g. one for each type of entity in the game).

In memory, programs can store sprites in a variety of ways. Structures include separate, named variables that contain single images, arrays and sprite sheets.

Separate image variables (e.g. `PImage spaceship`) should only be used in the most simple cases, where only a handful of images are shown in the game. For instance, in a chess game, each piece can be an object, and each object can have one named variable that contains its sprite (such as a pawn or queen; the image can be loaded in the constructor and used every time when the object displays itself).

One-dimensional or two-dimensional **arrays** (e.g. `PImage[][] sprites`) can hold multiple sprites, similar to sprite sheets. Arrays are an improvement over separate, named variables, but are somewhat tedious to set up (i.e. to load the images and assign them to array indices), and involve an abstraction from graphical coordinates to indices.[7]

Sprite sheets (e.g. `PImage spriteSheet`) are a possibility to store a large number of images in memory in an organised, accessible and efficient manner. They offer several practical advantages over the use of separate variables and arrays. The use of a sprite sheet may:

- Shorten the game's code. Games often use a stunning number of images, and to handle (e.g. load) a large number of separate graphics files in the program can be tedious;
- Make creating and editing the sprites (in a graphics program) more efficient than having to load and save a large number of files;

- Be intuitive; one can think of sprites in a context (e.g. of a character or scene), instead of the individual images; one can also visually inspect the sprite sheet to locate where a sprite (or animation frame) is located;

- Be faster than, for instance, images in arrays, because the handling in memory (and in graphics memory) is more efficient[8,9]; and

- Speed up the loading time of the game; loading a few large graphics files is certainly faster than loading very many small ones.

Sprite Examples

Code 3 uses a sprite sheet (Figure 28.1) and displays five different sprites (i.e. the player's space ship, three enemy space ships and a bullet; no animation is used).

Code 3

```
PImage spriteSheet = null;

int playerPosX = 32;
int playerPosY = 92;
int enemy1PosX = 220;
int enemy1PosY = 128;
int enemy2PosX = 186;
int enemy2PosY = 44;
int enemy3PosX = 149;
int enemy3PosY = 181;
int bulletPosX = 66;
int bulletPosY = 92;

void setup()
{
  size(320, 240);
  spriteSheet = loadImage("data/spritesheet.png");
}

void draw()
{
  background(0);
  image(spriteSheet.get(0,  0, 24, 24), playerPosX, playerPosY);
  image(spriteSheet.get(0, 24, 24, 24), enemy1PosX, enemy1PosY);
  image(spriteSheet.get(0, 48, 24, 24), enemy2PosX, enemy2PosY);
  image(spriteSheet.get(0, 72, 24, 24), enemy3PosX, enemy3PosY);
  image(spriteSheet.get(0, 96, 24, 24), bulletPosX, bulletPosY);
}
```

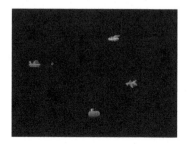

Note that Code 3 only produces static screen output; it is not a framework for a space shooter game. A game should employ a class structure (with classes for the player, enemies, bullets and med packs) and use arrays to store class objects such as multiple enemies, among other things. Code 4 sketches how to start with a Player class and object.

Code 4

```
//main program
PImage spriteSheet = null;  //sprite sheet is globally available so all
classes can access it
int size = 24;  //everything has size of 24 by 24 pixels
Player player = null;
void setup()
{
  size(320, 240);
  spriteSheet = loadImage("data/spritesheet.png");
  player = new Player(32, 92, 0, 0);  //position of player and position of
  sprite on sprite sheet
}
void draw()
{
  background(0);
  player.display();
}

//class definition
class Player
{
  int posX = 0;
  int posY = 0;
  int spriteSheetPosX = 0;
  int spriteSheetPosY = 0;

  Player(int x, int y, int sheetX, int sheetY)
  {
    posX = x;
    posY = y;
    spriteSheetPosX = sheetX;
    spriteSheetPosY = sheetY;
  }

  void display()
  {
    image(spriteSheet.get(spriteSheetPosX, spriteSheetPosY, size, size), posX,
    posY);
  }
}
```

Transparency for Sprite Sheets

Often, sprites have transparent backgrounds; this is useful, for instance, when they overlap each other, or when a background is drawn behind them. *Processing* reads png format graphics files, and the png format affords transparency (see the section on graphics formats in Chapter 22).[10]

Occasionally, graphics formats without transparency are used, or (rarely) a programming language or library cannot read transparency.[11] In that case, the background colour of a sprite sheet should use a colour that is not employed in the sprites (such as bright pink, rgb code (255, 0, 255)), so a program can decide which pixels belong to sprites and should be shown, and which pixels belong to the background and should not.

Code 5 loads a sprite sheet with a non-transparent background and then creates a copy of that sprite sheet which contains only the pixels that should be transparent (highlighted). The colour that is to be transparent is not hard-coded (e.g. as pink), but the program takes the colour of the pixel at screen coordinates (0, 0) and assumes that this is the background colour intended to be transparent.

Code 5

```
void setup()
{
  size(330, 580);
  noStroke();

  PImage graphicsNonTrans = loadImage("spritesheet_pinkbg.png");  //this is
  only loaded, and not modified, and shown for comparison
  PImage graphicsTrans = createImage(graphicsNonTrans.width,
  graphicsNonTrans.height, ARGB);  //empty bitmap with alpha channel, same
  size as original sprite sheet

  //go through sprite sheet and copy all non-background pixels to the PImage
  that should have a transparent background:
  color transColour = graphicsNonTrans.get(0, 0);  //assuming that pixel 0, 0
  is the background colour we don't want to see
  for (int j = 0; j < graphicsTrans.height; j++)
  {
    for (int i = 0; i < graphicsTrans.width; i++)
    {
      if (graphicsNonTrans.get(i, j) != transColour)  //if pixel is not
      background colour…
      {
        graphicsTrans.set(i, j, graphicsNonTrans.get(i, j));  //...copy it
        to new bitmap
      }
    }
  }

  background(20, 50, 0);
  for (int i = 0; i < 100; i++) { int starSize = int(1 + random(3));
  ellipse(random(width), random(height), starSize, starSize); }  //draw star
  background
  text("Original image as loaded from disk with non-\ntransparent
  background", 10, 20);
  image(graphicsNonTrans, 10, 50);
  text("Image created with only the pixels that are not in\nbackground colour "
  + int(red(transColour)) + ", " + int(green(transColour)) + ", " +
  int(blue(transColour)) + ", " + int(alpha(transColour)) + " (RGBA)", 10, 20 +
  250 + 40);
  image(graphicsTrans, 10, 260 + 40 + 40);
}
```

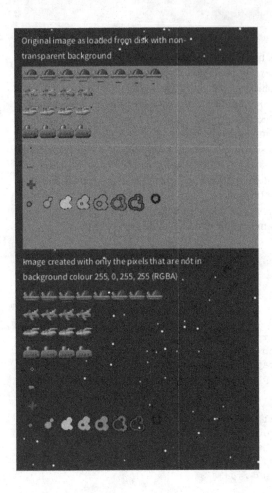

Pixel-level operations are relatively slow. Thus, the pixel-exchange should of course only be done once, i.e. when the image is loaded (once). Also, note that get() and set() are (according to *Processing*'s documentation) slower than using the pixels[] array, so this code is clearly not optimised for speed.

Frame-Based Animation

We do frame-based animation
and time-fix it

In very simple games, game demos and certain game genres (such as board games) sprites are sometimes not animated (see, e.g. Code 2), but in many games and game genres (such as platform-ers) they are. This is usually done by frame-based animation.[12] Frame-based animation is realised by showing several images (i.e. frames) right after each other in the same (or a similar) position on screen, so that the impression (or illusion) of, for instance, a smooth movement is achieved (such as walking).

Animations need to be time fixed, because each animation frame is to be shown for an exact amount of time, for instance, 1/10th of a second. Code 6 demonstrates a time fixed explosion animation that uses eight animation frames (each sized 24x24 pixels, Figure 28.2) from the sprite sheet (Figure 28.1) from the previous code snippets (Code 2–Code 4).

FIGURE 28.2   The eight explosion animation frames are part of the sprite sheet (Figure 28.1) used in Code 6

Code 6

```
int durationOneFrame = 100;  //in milliseconds
int frame = 0;
int frameMax = 8;
int size = 24;  //size of sprite in pixels
int ticksLast = millis();
PImage spriteSheet = null;

void setup()
{
  size(320, 240);
  frameRate(999999999);  //to defeat the speed limit Processing imposes by
  default
  spriteSheet = loadImage("data/spritesheet.png");
}

void draw()
{
  background(0);

  //display explosion frame from sprite sheet; frame 0 starts at (0, 168),
  frame 1 at (24, 168), etc.):
  PImage sprite = spriteSheet.get((frame * size), 168, size, size);
  image(sprite, 20, 60);

  int delta = millis() - ticksLast;

  if (delta >= durationOneFrame)
  {
     frame++;
     if (frame >= frameMax) { frame = 0; }
     //ticksLast = millis();  //adds up time overshooting error
     ticksLast += delta;  //avoids adding up error[13]
  }
}
```

The animation time fix is different from the one used for movements (Chapter 27). In movements, the elapsed time can be multiplied with the speed of an object for smooth movement; but animations have discrete frames. Therefore, an *if* structure is used to check if one should advance to the next frame; then the timer is reset.

Timed Events

Timed events are actions that happen after a specific amount of time, for instance, regularly.

Times events also need to be time fixed. For example, if there is a 10% chance every minute, that an alien appears on the screen, the calculation should rely on real time.

The time fix for timed events is virtually identical to the one for animation. Code 7 demonstrates a timed event: A circle is drawn every 5 seconds.

Code 7

```
int frequency = 5000;  //in milliseconds
int ticksLast = millis();

void setup()
{
  frameRate(999999999);  //to defeat the speed limit Processing imposes by
  default
}

void draw()
{
  int delta = millis() - ticksLast;

  if (delta >= frequency)
  {
    ellipse(random(width), random(height), 10, 10);

    ticksLast += delta;  //avoids adding up error (thus preferred over
    ticksLast = millis())
  }
}
```

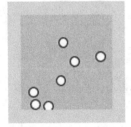

Chapter End Exercise

0. Random Appearances

Implement a timed event: Make a figure such as a droid bee, droid bear or droid pig appear every 3 seconds at a random location on screen (use the 'if style' time fix). The figure is a class object. Use an image of a sprite sheet to display the figure.[14] There are at most 10 figures on screen. Potential extra feature: Take each figure of the screen after 5 seconds.

Notes

1. Examples of games that do not use pixel-based graphics are text-based games and games that draw all graphics from geometrical shapes.
2. An advantage of geometrical shapes over sprites is that they easily can be rotated and scaled (see footnote 12).

3. Always use a loss-less graphics format for sprite sheets (such as png); compression artefacts (e.g. of the jpeg format) ruin the graphics on repeated loads and saves during creation, and make animations look terrible.

4. In classic games with a low resolution of 320 by 240 pixels, a popular size for sprites is 24 by 24 pixels.

5. Note the pink dots that form a grid on the sprite sheet; the grid helps to position sprites (e.g. when drawing them) but should eventually be removed, of course.

6. The player's ship has eight animation frames, while the enemy space ships only have four animation frames. This is not unusual. The player's sprite is the most important item on screen, so a bit more effort can be expended on it than on other items. Of course, everything should still look coherent together, so avoid too stark differences in level of detail, for instance.

7. A case where arrays might be efficiently used, is for storing a relatively low number of large images, for instance, background images for various game screens (such as main menu, game over and highscore screens). Of course, background images are not sprites.

8. One could write a short program to compare if displaying (in nerd speak, *blitting*) graphics from a sprite sheet is faster than from an array.

9. If sprite sheets (or arrays) are very large (several megabytes), the program might have difficulty to manage (position, access) such large chunks of data efficiently and quickly in memory, and it might sense to split them up into several sprite sheets.

10. The example sprite sheet used here (Figure 28.1) does not feature transparency, but a black (rgb (0, 0, 0)) background. The sprite sheet in Figure 30.2 in Chapter 30 uses transparency.

11. If the programming language does not know transparency at all, the last resort is to go through all pixels of a sprite when it is to be displayed and only show the ones that are not of the background colour. This is possible but slow.

12. An alternative to frame-based animation is geometrical animation, for instance, by drawing avatars such as cars or planes from primitive shapes. Frame-based animation is usually more detailed, but is tied to a specific pixel resolution and size (such as 24 by 24 pixels) and orientation (i.e. it does not rotate). Geometrical animation can easily be scaled and also rotated but is often rather bland or clunky looking (see footnote 2).

13. Overshooting the threshold on each frame change minimally by a few milliseconds results in a (probably insignificant) delay over time; bit this can be avoided.

14. Free game assets such as sprite sheets and tile sheets can pretty easily be found online.

29

Tiling

Outline

- Tiling with Text Files and Image Files
- Game Example
- Tiling and Optimisation

*Here we organise 2D game
graphics effectively with a
technique called tiling*

Tiling is a technique to efficiently store and access data about the locations of 2D graphical elements in games. Tiling can handle level layouts (such as walls, pits, level start, and level end), locations of items (such as stars), as well as positions of entities (such as enemies). Functionality is not limited to static graphical display but can include animation and collision detection (e.g. when the player's figure collides with walls or uses portals/teleporters).[1,2]

A major advantage of tiling is that when each tile is created as an object (see Chapter 25), it can take care of itself, e.g. display an animation, move, and do collision detection. Another advantage of tiling is, that it allows quick iteration and freedom for designers to implement levels without relying on programmer assistance.

Two limitations of tiling are that it puts everything on a grid, and everything has (or at least many things have) the same size. For many games this appears to be acceptable, and tiling is the standard way of building levels in almost all 2D genres such as jump n' run (*Mario*), shoot 'em ups (*R-Type*, Irem, 1987), and top-down action (*Gauntlet*, Atari, 1985). Tiling is also a widely-used solution for building 3D game levels, and a designer can use an editor to puzzle together premade 3D pieces into a larger level.

With tiling, the layout of the game (such as levels and race tracks) is determined by data files (not hardcoded into the program; see the next section), and the visuals are supplied by a graphics file called a *tile sheet* (Figure 29.1).

Tiling with Text Files and Image Files

When using tiling, the layout of game levels, stages or tracks can be stored in text files or image files. As a developer, one can define a sort of key or code that the program uses to understand either text documents or images that one gives it, then the program will be able to interpret the info to construct a level. There is a base amount of setup that must be done for each object one would like to be a tile in a game but it will make level design easier down the line. Hard-coding level info in a program is possible, but is less convenient than level data in separate and easily editable files.

DOI: 10.1201/9781003345916-29

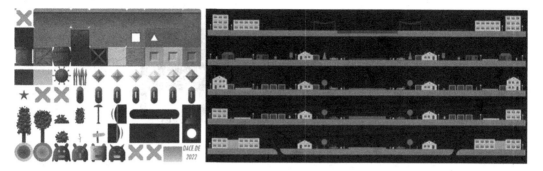

FIGURE 29.1 Example tile sheets; one with level elements for a platformer (left), the other with elements for a space shooter (right)[3]

Code 1 loads text, and then prints it to the screen, one char at a time. With some trial and error, the author found out that each character in the used font was approximately 7 to 9 pixels wide and 14 pixels high.

Code 1

```
void setup()
{
  size(70, 70);
  background(0);
  fill(0, 255, 0);
  textAlign(LEFT, TOP);

  // loadStrings() returns an array of strings where each item is a line from
  the text file⁴
  String[] lines = loadStrings("level.txt");

  // printing text to the screen by reading each individual character and
  writing it to the screen
  for (int j = 0; j < lines.length; j++)  //goes through lines
  {
    for (int i = 0; i < lines[j].length(); i++)  //goes through rows
    {
      text(lines[j].charAt(i), i * 7, j * 14);
    }
  }
}
```

The next step is to interpret the chars and use them for something else, for instance, to display a filled rect for each '1', and an empty rect for each '0'; or select and display graphics from a tile sheet.

FIGURE 29.2 Image with coded level data used by Code 2 and Code 5

Code 2 also reads a file and displays its contents on screen; but it is an image and not a text file as in Code 1. The program loads an image from disk, goes through it pixel by pixel, and for each pixel in the image draws a rect based on the pixel colour unto the screen. The image is 10 by 4 pixels large (Figure 29.2).

Code 2

```
void setup()
{
  noStroke();
  PImage levelImage = loadImage("level.png");

  for(int x = 0; x < levelImage.width; x++)
  {
    for (int y = 0; y < levelImage.height; y++)
    {
      fill(levelImage.get(x,y));
      rect(x * 10, y * 10, 10, 10);
    }
  }
}
```

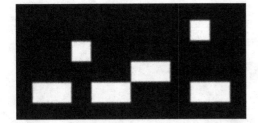

The above examples read files, and display their contents on screen. But only little structure is introduced (a `String` array in Code 1, and a `PImage` in Code 2). But levels should be class objects, and the parts the levels are made up of (such as bricks) should also be class objects.

Code 3 shows how such a structure could look like, with a `Level` class and a `Brick` class.[5] The (single) Level object holds a number of `Brick` objects (in an array).

Code 3

```
//main program

Level = null;
String[] levelInfo = new String[] {
  "0010000100",
  "0000100100",
  "0011110000",
  "0010010000" };
```

```
void setup() {
  size(400, 200);
  level = new Level(levelInfo);
}
void draw() {
  background(0);
  level.display();
}

class Level {
  int id = -1;
  Brick[] bricks = new Brick[100];

  Level(String[] levelString) {
    for (int i=0; i<bricks.length; i++) { bricks[i] = new Brick(); }

    println("there are " + levelString.length + " levelStrings");

    for (int i = 0 ; i < levelString.length; i++) { println(levelString[i]); }

    int currentBrick=0;
    for (int j = 0; j < levelString.length; j++) {  //goes through
    levelString array

      for (int i = 0; i < levelString[j].length(); i++) {  //goes through
      each String letter by letter
        if (levelString[j].charAt(i) == '1') {
            bricks[currentBrick].switchOn(i*40, j*20);
            currentBrick++;
        }
      }
    }
  }

  void display() {
    for (int i = 0; i < bricks.length; i++) { bricks[i].display(); }
  }
}

class Brick {
  int x = 0;
  int y = 0;
  int w = 40;
  int h = 20;
  boolean isOn = false;

  Brick() { }

  void display() {
    if (isOn) { rect(x, y, w, h); }
  }
  void switchOn(int posX, int posY) {
    x = posX;
    y = posY;
    isOn = true;
  }
  void switchOff() {
    isOn = false;
  }
}
```

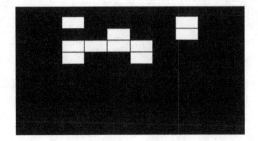

TABLE 29.1

Text File That Is Loaded for Level 0 (`level0.txt`)

```
0000000000
0111111110
0111111010
0000001010
0111101110
```

Code 4 combines Code 1 and Code 3 and showcases loading a text file (Table 29.1) as an array of strings and then converting that data into brick objects that are used as a *BreakOut* level. Right now the level only knows if there is a brick or if there is not a brick but the code could be expanded to have the text file tell the program how many hits a brick takes to disappear or what colour a brick should be, or both.

It has 5 lines of 10 characters each; any 1s will show up as bricks and any 0s will be gaps in the level. Note that for Code 4 to run, the files `level1.txt` and `level2.txt` are needed as well, with similar contents.

Code 4

```
//main program
Level[] levels = new Level[3];
int weAreInLevel = 0;

void setup() {
  size(400, 200);

  for (int i = 0; i < levels.length; i++) { levels[i] = new Level(i); }
}
void keyPressed() {
  if (keyCode == UP) {
    weAreInLevel++;
    if (weAreInLevel >= levels.length) { weAreInLevel = 0; }
  }
}
void draw() {
  background(0);
  levels[weAreInLevel].display();
}

class Level {
  int id = -1;
  Brick[] bricks = new Brick[100];

  Level(int l) {
    id = l;
```

```
    //load level id:
    String[] lines = loadStrings("level" + id + ".txt");
    println("there are " + lines.length + " lines");

    for (int i = 0; i < lines.length; i++) { println(lines[i]); }

    for (int i = 0; i < bricks.length; i++) { bricks[i] = new Brick(); }

    int currentBrick = 0;
    for (int i = 0; i < lines.length; i++) {  // goes through lines
      for (int j = 0; j < lines[i].length(); j++) {  // goes through rows
        if (lines[i].charAt(j) == '1') {
          bricks[currentBrick].switchOn(j * 40, i * 20);
          currentBrick++;
        }
      }
    }
  }

  void display() {
    for (int i=0; i<bricks.length; i++) { bricks[i].display(); }
  }
}

class Brick {
  int x = 0;
  int y = 0;
  int w = 40;
  int h = 20;
  boolean isOn = false;

  Brick() { }

  void display() {
    if (isOn) { rect(x, y, w, h); }
  }

  void switchOn(int posX, int posY) {
    x = posX;
    y = posY;
    isOn = true;
  }

  void switchOff() {
    isOn = false;
  }
}
```

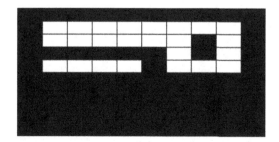

Code 5 does the same as Code 4 but the information is loaded into the program as a png image with the different pixel colours storing different data (black is no brick, white is a brick; Figure 29.2). In a similar fashion as Code 4, this could be expanded to have different colours mean (more) different things (such as brick health, colour or both).

Code 5 shows only the constructor for the Level class because everything else is the same as in Code 4 (i.e. the main program, the Brick class and the rest of the Level class).

Code 5

```
class Level
{
  //...

  Level(int l) {
    id = l;
    for (int i = 0; i < bricks.length; i++) {
      bricks[i] = new Brick();
    }

    PImage levelImage = loadImage("level" + id + ".png");
    int currentBrick = 0;
    color pxCol = color(0,0,0);
    int avgCol = 0;

    for (int x = 0; x < levelImage.width; x++) {
      for (int y = 0; y < levelImage.height; y++) {
        pxCol = levelImage.get(x,y);     // loop through all the pixels in the
        image with nested for loops
        avgCol = (int)(red(pxCol) + green(pxCol) + blue(pxCol)) / 3; // get the
        average colour value⁶

        if (avgCol >= 200) {  // check if the average colour value is greater
        than a threshold
            bricks[currentBrick].switchOn(x * 40, y * 20);
            currentBrick++;
        }
      }
    }
  }
  //...
}
```

TABLE 29.2

Data File That Holds the Info for Level 0 (level0.txt)

```
1111111111111111111111111111111111
1   1         1                    1
1 P 1         1          1         1
1             1 11111111     111    1
1     1 111              1          1
1     1   1              1          1
1     1   1                         1
1     1                  1          1
1     11111              111111 1111
1                                   1
1                                   1
1                        1111       1
1                        1  111 1111
1111   111   111111     1           1
1          1 1          1           1
1          1 1          1           1
1111   111              1           1
1.        1   1  111111              1
1             1                     1
1111111111111111111111111111111111111
```

Game Example

Code 6 is a quick maze game example with simple logic. The levels are written out as text files by the designer with '1' as walls, 'P' as player start and everything else as an empty space (Table 29.2).

The Level class transforms this text information into a 2D array of booleans as a way to know where the walls and the player are.

Code 6

```
// main program
int levelToLoad = 0;
Level loadedLevel = null;
int playerPosX = -1;
int playerPosY = -1;

void setup() {
  size(640, 400);
  loadedLevel = new Level(levelToLoad);
}

void keyPressed() {
  if ((keyCode == LEFT) && (!loadedLevel.IsThereAWallAt(playerPosX - 1,
  playerPosY))) { playerPosX--; }
  else if ((keyCode == RIGHT) && (!loadedLevel.IsThereAWallAt(playerPosX +
  1,playerPosY))) { playerPosX++; }
  else if ((keyCode == UP) && (!loadedLevel.IsThereAWallAt(playerPosX,
  playerPosY - 1))) { playerPosY--; }
  else if ((keyCode == DOWN) && (!loadedLevel.IsThereAWallAt(playerPosX,
  playerPosY + 1))) { playerPosY++; }
}

void draw() {
  background(0);
  loadedLevel.display();
  ellipse((playerPosX * 20) + 10, (playerPosY * 20) + 10, 17, 17);
}

class Level {
  int playerStartPosX = -1;
  int playerStartPosY = -1;
  boolean[][] walls = null;

  Level(int levelID) {
    String[] lines = loadStrings("level" + levelID + ".txt");
    walls = new boolean[lines[0].length()][lines.length];

    for (int x = 0; x < walls.length; x++) {
      for (int y = 0; y < walls[x].length; y++) {
        walls[x][y] = (lines[y].charAt(x) == '1');

        if ((lines[y].charAt(x) == 'P')) {
          playerPosX = x;
          playerPosY = y;
        }
      }
    }
  }
}
```

```
void display()
{
  for (int x = 0; x < walls.length; x++) {
    for (int y = 0; y < walls[x].length; y++) {
      if (walls[x][y]) {
        rect(x * 20, y * 20, 20, 20);
      }
    }
  }
}
boolean IsThereAWallAt(int x, int y) {
  return walls[x][y];
}
}
```

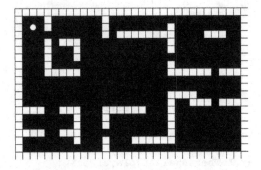

The player (dot) can move around with the cursor keys, except when moving into a spot where a wall is.[7]

Tiling and Optimisation

Tiling is not only an effective way of storing and accessing game data (such as level layouts), but it also offers potentials for optimisation. For instance, let's assume a 2D jump n' run platform game. The levels consist of 80 x 8 (square) tiles (of size 32 pixels, in this example; Figure 29.3); the tiles are numbered 0 to 639 starting at the top left (Figure 29.4). The player's figure is a square sprite (of the same size; Figure 29.5). The task is to do the collision detection of the player's figure with the (non-moving) objects in the level, such as the platforms.

Since the level is tiled, there is extra information available that might be helpful when designing the collision detection: (1) We know that the level tiles do not overlap. That means that finding one collision for a given point is enough, after that, we can stop checking. (2) A second piece of information is that the tiles do not move (at least in this example), that they are ordered, and that they are all the same size, and also the same size as the player's sprite. That means that the sprite can only collide (i.e. overlap) with (at most) four tiles (Figure 29.6). When checking for collision with the tiles of the level, there is thus no need to go through all 640 tiles. Checking four tiles is enough, a massive saving in terms of computational load.

In a given game, we would need to identify which tile contains the top-left corner of the sprite. Let us assume this is tile number 245 (given that the level is 80 tiles wide and 8 tile high, this tile is located

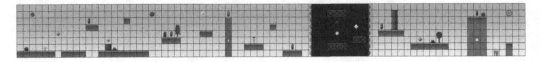

FIGURE 29.3   Complete view of a tiled level with 80 x 8 tiles

0	1	3	.	.	.	.	.	.	77	78	79
80	.	.	.	.	.	.	.	.	.	.	159
160	.	.	.	.	.	.	.	.	.	.	239
240	.	.	.	.	.	.	.	.	.	.	319
320	.	.	.	.	.	.	.	.	.	.	399
400	.	.	.	.	.	.	.	.	.	.	479
480	.	.	.	.	.	.	.	.	.	.	559
560	561	562	.	.	.	.	.	.	637	638	639

FIGURE 29.4　Tiles numbered from 0 to 639

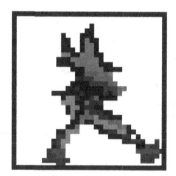

FIGURE 29.5　Square sprite

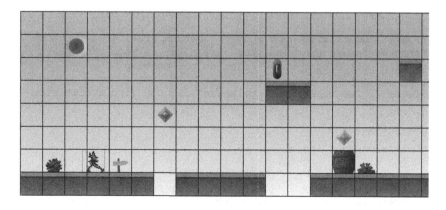

FIGURE 29.6　Collision of the player's sprite with (at most four) tiles

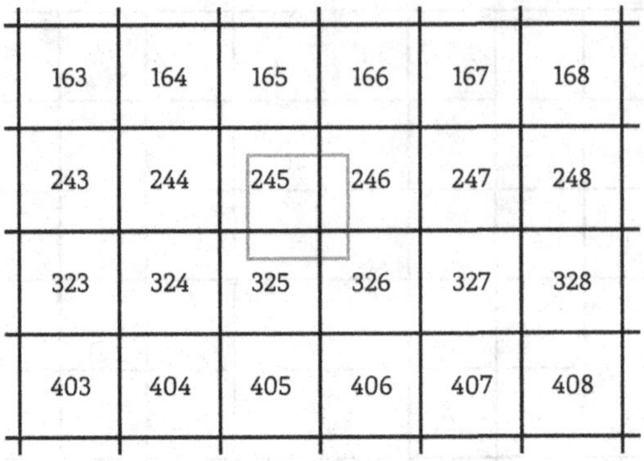

163	164	165	166	167	168
243	244	245	246	247	248
323	324	325	326	327	328
403	404	405	406	407	408

FIGURE 29.7   Checking possible collisions of the sprite with four tiles

somewhere left on the level). Tile 245 is then the first of the four tiles we need to check for collision (it might be a platform, so there is a collision, or it might be a background tile, and there is none). The other three tiles are then also easily identified: The one to the right is number 246, the one below is 325 (i.e. 245 + 80) and the one to the right of that is 326 (Figure 29.7).

There are special cases if the tile which contains the top-left corner of the sprite is located at the border of the level, i.e. in the last column on the right edge of the level (tiles numbered 79, 159, 239, etc.) or in the last row of the level (tiles numbered 560, 561, 562, etc.), or in both (i.e. tile 639 at the very right bottom corner of the level; Figure 29.4).

But it even gets better; usually, one is not asking for a collision of a whole sprite with the tiles of a level. Usually, one only wants to check collision for a single point; for instance, the bottom center point when the figure is falling down, to check if it lands on a tile.

If we check collision for a point, we only need to check *a single tile* for collision. To find that tile, we do not need to go through all tiles and compare pixel coordinates, but we can *calculate* the number of that tile. Code 7 demos an approach that does not take into account (most of) the extra information we have available, and Code 8 demos a more optimised approach that makes use of it.

Assume point (x, y) is the point we want to check for collision with the tiles of a level. We call a method in the Level class because the Level class owns the Tile class. Code 7 works, but is unnecessarily inefficient, because it goes through all tiles, and then compares coordinates for each tile.

Code 7

```
//in the level class:
boolean bCollisionCheck(int x, int y)
{
  for (int i = 0; i < tiles.length; i++)   //go through all tiles
  {
    if (tiles[i].bCollisionCheck(x, y)) { return true; }   //if there is a
    collision we return true and stop searching; we know that there can only
    be one tile colliding because tiles do not overlap
  }
  return false;   //we checked all tiles and did not find a collision
}

//in the tile class:
boolean bCollisionCheck(int x, int y)
{
  if ((bCollidable) &&
      (x >= iTilePosX) && (x < (iTilePosX + iTileSize)) &&
      (y >= iTilePosY) && (y < (iTilePosY + iTileSize))) { return true; }
  return false;
}
```

Code 8 gets the same data, but it is much more efficient because it only checks the collision with a single tile, and only checks if this tile is on, i.e. if it is something the player figure can collide with. We know already that the point lies within the tile.

Code 8

```
//in the Level class:

boolean bCollisionCheck(int x, int y)
{
  int iTileX = (x / iTileSize);  //calculate the tile coordinates for the
  given point
  int iTileY = (y / iTileSize);
  int iTileToCheck = iTileX + (iTileY * iHorizontalTilesInLevel);  //convert
  the coordinates into a tile number
  return tiles[iTileToCheck].bCollisionCheck(x, y);
}

//in the Tile class:

boolean bCollisionCheck()
{
  if (bCollidable) { return true; }
  return false;
}
```

The examples assume that the tiles as well as the sprite are 100% filled with their objects (i.e. platforms, player's figure), which is not unusual in classic games. If, for instance, the player's figure is not fully square, but more rectangular, the collision detection should take that into account (e.g. by allowing a few pixels of horizontal overlap of the sprite with a platform tile on both sides without triggering a collision); similarly, a more accurate collision detection might be needed to pick up items that are smaller than a full tile. This functionality can be added to the method, of course.

Chapter End Exercise

0. The Level Editor

   Make a basic tiled level editor (Figure 29.8).[8] The editor shows the level (in the example in the top part of the screen, with a light blue background) and the tile sheet (bottom, with a pink background); and a status bar (in dark blue, with a SAVE button). Users pick a tile type in the tile sheet by left-clicking on it; they can then place this type of tile in the level by left-clicking (multiple copies of the selected type can be placed in the level ('painted') by moving the pointer while the mouse button is pressed across the level).

   The level is shown in part, and can be scrolled left/right with the mouse wheel. The editor features mouse-only controls. The editor loads a level file automatically from the disk on program start and saves this file on on-screen button press. Loading and saving use the same file.[9] The editor uses a text file (Table 29.3) for the level data; it uses a tile sheet for the graphics (Figure 29.1). Use classes for the level tiles and for the button.

   The dimensions can be freely chosen; the tile editor shown in Figure 29.8 uses 32 by 32 pixel tiles, and a level size of 80 by 8 tiles. The tile sheet holds 10 x 8 tiles. The coding of the tile types in the level text file uses ASCII codes starting with . (char(46)) for a blank/empty tile.

FIGURE 29.8 A tiled level editor: The level is shown in the top (horizontally scrollable) part of the window, the available tiles in the bottom part

TABLE 29.3

Level Text File (`level.txt`)

```
..............m.....S...........m.............................................cUU..........
.......P..../50....S....c[..../0.........................TT......./560.....u..
.......Pb.........1..../0...........................]....2563..^..............
......./50.........................................c....:>9:.m............_....
..........................................Q..26666663..9:995653.............b
..a..................a...Q..26663..\.......b::999999..:9::9:::........25553
..k.n.........c....n..bk.266669:9:9.......2555::999999...999:999..255553.99999
2655655665655653MM2666666:9:9999:9:55553..::::::999999..9:9::9::..9:99:9.99999
```

Notes

1. For a brief discussion of tiling as a popular technique in digital games, and of the problems to realise it on the Atari *VCS/2600* console, see Montfort/Bogost 2009:68.
2. Technically, in today's game developers' lingo, the notions of tile and sprite overlap or are even equivalent. Both refer to (a part of) a 2D bitmap; tiles are used for levels, sprites for moving entities (see Montfort/Bogost 2009:70). Multiple tiles for a game are usually combined in a tile sheet or several tile sheets (e.g. for different levels); the same applies to sprites.
3. Always use a loss-less graphics format for tile sheets (such as png); compression artefacts (e.g. of the jpeg format) ruin the graphics on repeated loads and saves, and make tiled levels look terrible.

4. To save a text file, use, for instance, `saveStrings()` which also works on `String` arrays. However, while `loadStrings()` looks for the file to load, by default, in the program's data folder (e.g. `String[]` `lines = loadStrings("level.txt")`), `saveStrings()` needs the addition of `data` in the file path to save the file in the `data` folder (e.g. `saveStrings('data/level.txt', lines)`). The `data` folder is located within the program's folder (see the section 'Loading and Saving Data' in Chapter 20).

5. To demo the functionality a global string array is used, in which the level data (the location of the tiles) is hard-coded (in the program code), which should usually be avoided.

6. Or use the `colour.brightness()` method, as discussed in the section 'Colour Components' in Chapter 19.

7. For info on real-time game controls, see Chapter 26.

8. For inspiration, read the *Gamasutra* interview with John Romero about his tile editor *TEd* (www. gamasutra.com/blogs/DavidLightbown/20170223/289955/Classic_Tools_Retrospective_John_Romero_ talks_about_creating_TEd_the_tile_editor_that_shipped_over_30_games.php).

9. On startup, the editor automatically loads the level file it also can save. When the SAVE button is clicked, the editor saves the current level layout to the file it will automatically load on the next startup (not to a separate, different file).

30

Scrolling and Split-Screen Displays

Scrolling

Scrolling (of graphics) is a technique for 2D games to show worlds bigger than one screen to players. Scrolling means that a game world such as a level is moved smoothly across the screen, either automatically or dependent on avatar movement; there are no hard cuts. Scrolling is almost always limited to orthogonal movement (horizontal, vertical or both) without rotation (which is done, if it is possible at all, by the avatar (as in *Super Cars 2*, Gremlin 1991)).

Scrolling is done in horizontal and vertical directions and used for side-view as well as for top-view games. Scrolling is usually used in (but not limited to) games with a third-person perspective.[1] Popular game genres using scrolling are jump n' run games such as *Super Mario Bros.* (side-view, horizontal scrolling; Nintendo 1985) and *Turrican II* (side-view, multi-directional scrolling; Rainbow Arts 1991), and shooters such as *R-Type* (side-view, horizontal scrolling; Irem 1987), *Silkworm* (ditto; Tecmo 1988) and *Uridium* (ditto; Graftgold 1986) and *Xenon 2* (top-view, vertical scrolling; Image Works 1989).

An alternative to scrolling is switching screens when the player's avatar reaches screen borders (as in *Adventure* (Atari 1980), *Stairway to Hell* (Software Invasion 1986), *Bad Cat* (Rainbow Arts 1987), and *Rick Dangerous* (Firebird 1989)). Many early games used screen switching; screen switching is technically easier and requires fewer graphical resources.

There are several popular specific combinations of (avatar) movement and (world) scrolling:

- The avatar can move in all directions, and the world is moved with a constant speed across the screen. This is a common modality in space shooters, which employ either side-view horizontal scrolling (*Katakis*, Rainbow Arts 1987) or top-view vertical scrolling (*Xenon 2*).
- The avatar is fixed in the screen centre, and the world is effectively the only thing that moves, in any direction, controlled by the avatar.
- The avatar has an area around the screen centre in which it can move around freely, and scrolling happens only when the avatar approaches one of the screen borders (as in *Ghosts 'n Goblins* (*Amstrad* version – the arcade, Commodore *64* and *NES* versions scroll immediately; Capcom 1985) and *Turrican II*). Often, the movement of the screen is limited to the level; that means, the scrolling stops when the border or end of the level is reached (e.g. *Gauntlet* (Atari 1985), and *Leonardo* (Starbyte 1989)).
- The avatar is horizontally fixed in the screen centre but can move vertically independent of the scrolling (as in *Uridium*); horizontal movement is conveyed by horizontal scrolling of the world. Or the avatar is vertically fixed, and can move horizontally, while the world scrolls vertically, as in *Jumping Jack'son* (Infogrames 1990).

DOI: 10.1201/9781003345916-30

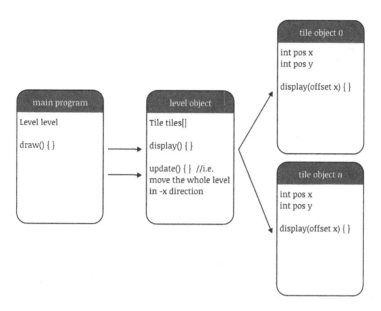

FIGURE 30.1 The main program, the level object and the tile objects and their interactions with regard to displaying and scrolling

FIGURE 30.2 The (rather minimal) tile sheet[2] used in Code 1

- In 2D, side-scrolling games, the avatar is horizontally fixed in the screen centre when moving forward (right, usually); but the screen does not scroll backwards (left). When the avatar moves backwards, the scrolling stops (*Super Mario Bros.*). That means that the avatar can only go back within the boundaries of the screen.

If a game has a tiled level (see Chapter 29), implementing scrolling is quite straightforward: All visible tiles should not only display themselves but also move (Figure 30.1). Technically, this movement is very similar to how avatars, items and enemies move.

Code 1 demonstrates horizontal scrolling with a constant speed. It uses a tiled level similar to the one developed for *BreakOut* (Code 4 in Chapter 29). Each tile object holds its own position relative to the level origin; the level object holds the global offset, i.e. the movement in -x direction. The tile graphics are loaded from a tile sheet (Figure 30.2).

Code 1

```
// main program
float fSpeed = -50;   //scrolling speed in pixels/second
int tileSize = 32;
Level level = null;

void setup()
{
  size(320, 240);
  frameRate(999999999);  //to defeat the speed limit Processing imposes by
  default
  level = new Level(width);
}
```

```
void draw()
{
  background(180, 210, 255);
  level.display();
  level.update();
}

class Level
{
  Tile tiles[] = new Tile[1024];
  float fOffsetX = 0;
  int iTicksLast = 0;

  Level(float offsetX)
  {
    for (int i=0; i<tiles.length; i++) { tiles[i] = new Tile(); }  //init all
    tiles

    int tileNumber = 0;
    String[] lines = loadStrings("level.txt");  //loadStrings() returns an
    array of strings where each item is a line from the text file
    for (int j = 0; j < lines.length; j++)  //goes through lines
    {
      for (int i = 0; i < lines[j].length(); i++)  //goes through rows
      {
        tiles[tileNumber].init(tileNumber, i * tileSize, j * tileSize,
        int(lines[j].charAt(i)));
        tileNumber++;
      }
    }
    fOffsetX = offsetX;
    iTicksLast = millis();
  }
  void display()
  {
    for (int i = 0; i < tiles.length; i++) { tiles[i].display(fOffsetX); }
  }
  void update()
  {
    int delta = millis() - iTicksLast;
    fOffsetX += fSpeed * delta * 0.001;
    iTicksLast += delta;
  }
}

class Tile
{
  int iId = -1;
  boolean bOn = false;
  float fPosX = 0;
  float fPosY = 0;
  int iType = 0;
  PImage pPic;

  Tile()
  { }
```

```
void init(int id, int x, int y, int type)
{
  iId = id;
  fPosX = x;
  fPosY = y;
  iType = type - 48;  //to convert ASCII to int
  PImage tileSheet = loadImage("tilesheet.png");
  pPic = tileSheet.get((iType * tileSize), 0, tileSize, tileSize);
  bOn = true;
}

void display(float offsetX)
{
  if ((bOn) && (iType != 0)) { image(pPic, round(fPosX + offsetX),
  round(fPosY)); }
}
}
```

Note that only a single level object (instead of an array of levels) is present and that all (used) tiles are drawn every time, whether they are actually (at least partially) visible on screen or not. Much housekeeping functionality such as resetting the level position is omitted, of course. Collision detection and animation could be added to each tile. The text file that specifies the level layout is shown in Table 30.1.

Split-Screen Displays

Split-screen displays are usually used in multi-player games to give each player an appropriate (albeit somewhat small) view of the game (Figure 30.3). Split-screen displays usually scroll; there are but a few split-screen games that have a single screen for a game world (e.g. *Tennis Cup* (Loriciel 1989) and *Lotus Turbo Challenge* (Gremlin 1990), which are both pseudo-3D). Popular applications of split-screen multi-player modes are 2D and 3D racing games and 3D action games.

An alternative is a single-screen view with multiple players such as in *Gauntlet* and *Double Dragon* (Taito 1987). Both variants can be attractive depending on the game; the chosen display technique also

TABLE 30.1

Level text file (`level.txt`)

```
00000000000000700000077005600007770000000000077700000560000000000000007000000900
05600000056000700000000000000002130000000000213000000000000000560070700000800
000000770000021300000230000000000000000023000000002130021300000070407000213 0
0000000000000000000000000000000000000777000000000000007770000000000040404 0000000
000002113000000000000700700002130000000000000002130000077700000021300404040 000000
000000000000000000007400470000000000211130070000000000044000000070004040400 00000
000000000000000000074400447000000000000000000000000000000440000000000004040400 00000
21111111111111111111130021111111111113000002111111113000230002113021130402111 1113
```

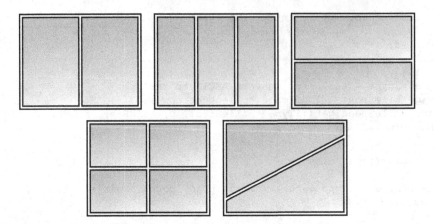

FIGURE 30.3 Popular arrangements of split-screen displays are side-by-side (as in *Super Cars 2*), three wide (*Nitro*, Psygnosis 1990, split-screen only in the car selection screen), horizontal (*Alcatraz*, Infogrames 1992), four-way (*Borderlands*, 2K, 2009), and dynamic (*Lego Jurassic World*, Warner 2015)[3]

influences gameplay. For instance, in *Gauntlet* and *Double Dragon*, players can only spread out as much as the display allows. In many 2D top-down racing games, the view follows and centres around the leading (human) player. In *Nitro*, for instance, players who drop out of the screen are beamed back into view, but this costs expensive fuel.

One challenge of split-screen displays compared to single-screen displays is to cut-off graphical objects at the border(s) between the multiple displays. The cut-off happens automatically when using a single screen (i.e. what is outside of the window is neither displayed nor seen), but of course, it does not happen automatically on the border between, say, a side-by-side split-screen display.

One solution is displaying only parts of the graphics such as tiles, but that requires some computation. A more convenient way might be to use a background surface of the required size, which cuts off everything not needed automatically; this is demonstrated in Code 2.

For each player a background graphical surface is created. Everything relating to a player is then first drawn onto that surface, and not directly onto the screen. After all graphical items (i.e. the tiles, in this example) have been drawn to a player's surface (and automatically cut off by *Processing*), the surface is copied to the screen; this is done for all players. The background surface is located in each view, and each view passes it on to the track object which passes it on to each tile object, and each tile object draws on it (Figure 30.4); then the view object copies the surface onto the screen.

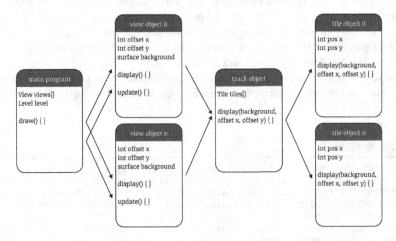

FIGURE 30.4 The main program, the view objects, the level object and the tile objects and their interactions with regard to displaying and scrolling

Code 2 shows three different views of the same 2D, top-down racing track. This is a somewhat long example, but one can clearly observe how it implements the structure sketched in Figure 30.4 in real code. The main program talks to the (three) views, but the views talk to the *same* level object, i.e. in each of the views the same level and the same tiles should be displayed: The players want to race on the same track, and see each other, etc. The views scroll in random directions; in a game, the views would be controlled by the players' cars or similar. The starting coordinates are arbitrarily chosen and hard-coded. Players' avatars (and everything else) are omitted.

Code 2

```
// main program

int tileSize = 32;
Track track = null;
View views[] = new View[3];

void setup()
{
  size(320, 240);
  frameRate(999999999);   //to defeat the speed limit Processing imposes by
  default
  track = new Track();
  for (int i = 0; i < views.length; i++) { views[i] = new View(-240, -40,
  random(-10, 10), random(-10, 10)); }
  views[0].init(0, 0, 106, 240);   //do by hand for each of the three views
  views[1].init(107, 0, 106, 240);
  views[2].init(214, 0, 106, 240);
}

void draw()
{
  for (int i=0; i<views.length; i++)
  {
    views[i].display();
    views[i].update();
  }
}

class View
{
  int iScreenTopLeftX = 0;
  int iScreenTopLeftY = 0;
  float fOffsetX = 0;
  float fOffsetY = 0;
  float fSpeedX = 0;
  float fSpeedY = 0;
  int iTicksLast = 0;
  PGraphics pBackground = null;

  View(float x, float y, float speedX, float speedY)
  {
    fOffsetX = x;
    fOffsetY = y;
    fSpeedX = speedX;
    fSpeedY = speedY;
    iTicksLast = millis();
  }
```

```
  void display()
  {
    pBackground.beginDraw();
    pBackground.background(60, 255, 20);
    pBackground.endDraw();
    track.display(pBackground, fOffsetX, fOffsetY);
    image(pBackground, iScreenTopLeftX, iScreenTopLeftY);
  }

  void init(int screenX, int screenY, int sizeX, int sizeY)
  {
    iScreenTopLeftX = screenX;
    iScreenTopLeftY = screenY;
    pBackground = createGraphics(sizeX, sizeY);
  }

  void update()
  {
    int delta = millis() - iTicksLast;
    fOffsetX += (fSpeedX * delta * 0.001);
    fOffsetY += (fSpeedY * delta * 0.001);
    iTicksLast += delta;
  }
}

class Track
{
  Tile tiles[] = new Tile[512];

  Track()
  {
    for (int i=0; i<tiles.length; i++) { tiles[i] = new Tile(); }  //init all
    tiles
    int tileNumber = 0;
    String[] lines = loadStrings("track.txt");
    for (int j = 0; j < lines.length; j++)  //goes through lines
    {
      for (int i = 0; i < lines[j].length(); i++)  //goes through rows
      {
        tiles[tileNumber].init(tileNumber, i * tileSize, j * tileSize,
        int(lines[j].charAt(i)));
        tileNumber++;
      }
    }
  }

  void display(PGraphics surface, float offsetX, float offsetY)
  {
    for (int i = 0; i < tiles.length; i++) { tiles[i].display(surface,
    offsetX, offsetY); }
  }
}

class Tile
{
  int iId = -1;
  boolean bOn = false;
  float fPosX = 0;
  float fPosY = 0;
  int iType = 0;
  PImage pPic;
```

```
Tile()
{ }
void init(int id, int x, int y, int type)
{
  iId = id;
  fPosX = x;
  fPosY = y;
  iType = type - 48;   //to convert ASCII to int
  PImage tileSheet = loadImage("tilesheet.png");
  pPic = tileSheet.get((iType * tileSize), 0, tileSize, tileSize);
  bOn = true;
}
void display(PGraphics surface, float offsetX, float offsetY)
{
  if ((bOn) && (iType != 0))
  {
    surface.beginDraw();
    surface.image(pPic, round(fPosX + offsetX), round(fPosY + offsetY));
    surface.endDraw();
  }
}
}
```

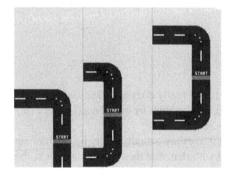

Note that all movement functionality is now located in the View class (no longer in the Level class); this might be a cleaner structure than the one in Code 1. Here, the level is solely organising the arrangement of the tiles.

Notes

1. *Operation Wolf* (Taito 1988) is an example of a game with a first-person view and scrolling.
2. A graphics file in png format is used, with transparency, which is recognised by *Processing* (see the section 'Images' in Chapter 22).
3. The variable separation even vanishes when both players are close to each other.

31

Movement in Curves

Now we move stuff along
lines and curves

Graphics by Hand

- Lines parallel to x or y axis
- Diagonal lines

To see that one does not need to rely on other people's code if one really does not want to (or cannot), let's assume, we only had a `point()` function, and needed to do all graphics by ourselves (i.e. not using any of *Processing*'s graphics primitives such as `line()` and `rect()`)!

Computers are pretty bad at drawing curves. Thinking about it, they are actually pretty bad at drawing anything that is not a horizontal or vertical line.[1] So we'll start with that, and then see that we get to the more interesting things fast! We'll later see multiple ways to generate curves ('Curves', in this chapter).

Lines Parallel to x or y Axis[2]

Let's draw a horizontal line from adjacent points; we have done this already when discussing loops (see Chapters 5 and 12). Code 1 below uses a *for* loop.

Code 1

```
void setup()
{
  strokeWeight(3);
}

void draw()
{
  for (int i = 10; i < (width - 10); i++)
  {
    point(i, (height * 0.5));
  }
}
```

DOI: 10.1201/9781003345916-31

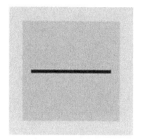

Each straight line has a slope. The slope of a line is the proportion of vertical to horizontal change. By dividing the vertical change by the horizontal change, the slope of a line can be calculated.

In the case above (Code 1), which is a horizontal line, the vertical change is always 0, and 0 divided by anything is still 0. So, unsurprisingly, horizontal lines have no (i.e. 0) slope.

A vertical line can be drawn similarly (changes are highlighted, Code 2).

Code 2

```
void setup()
{
  strokeWeight(3);
}
void draw()
{
  for (int i = 10; i < (height - 10); i++)
  {
    point(i, (width * 0.5));
  }
}
```

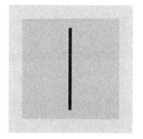

The slope of vertical lines is undefined because there is no (or 0) horizontal change. Anything divided by 0 is undefined in math.

Diagonal Lines

Now, the program would be more versatile if it could draw not only orthogonal lines but also diagonal lines with given slopes.

One way to describe a line that has a slope is the *slope-intercept form* $y = mx + b$. In this form, x is the x coordinate, m is the slope, and b is the constant vertical displacement (i.e. the point of interception with the y-axis).

The slope of a line can be calculated if the start and end points are given (Figure 31.1). The same line described using the slope-intercept form is $y = 0.7x - 2.5$.[3]

Diagonal lines are not special cases like vertical and horizontal lines, so the code must be revised. Code 3 uses a *for* loop, Code 4 uses the repetition of the draw() function to do essentially the same

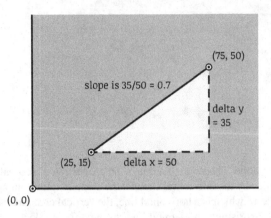

FIGURE 31.1   Calculating the slope of a line

things. In both cases, the points are calculated independent of each other; i.e. one does not need to calculate the first, say, ten points to draw the eleventh.

Code 3

```
float m = 0.5;
float b = 20;

void setup()
{
  strokeWeight(3);
}

void draw()
{
  for (int x = 10; x < (width - 10); x++)
  {
    float y = (m * x) + b;  //slope-intercept form y = mx + b
    point(x, y);
  }
}
```

Code 4

```
float x=10;
float m=0.5;
float b=20;

void setup()
{
  strokeWeight(3);
}
```

```
void draw()
{
  float y = (m * x) + b;  //slope-intercept form y = mx + b
  point(x, y);
  if (x < (width - 10)) { x++; }
}
```

An iterative way to draw a line is demonstrated in Code 5. In each step, the point position is advanced by a delta x and a delta y. To draw the next point one needs to know where the previous one was.

If delta y is 1.5 and delta x is 3, the slope is 0.5.

Code 5

```
float x = 10;
float y = 20;
float deltaX = 3;
float deltaY = 1.5;

void setup()
{
  strokeWeight(3);
}

void draw()
{
  point(x, y);

  if (x < (width - 10))
  {
    x += deltaX;
    y += deltaY;
  }
}
```

Note that the graphics look more coarse than the previous ones because fewer points are used to draw the line.

One can probably already guess how this line can be turned into a curve.

Curves

- The first (iterative) curve
- Drawing curves using trig
- Drawing curves with polynomials
- *Processing*'s curve functions

Lines cannot only be drawn as graphics but also as diagrams to represent, for instance, movement (i.e. time and distance). Constant speeds, then, are perfectly represented by straight lines (such as in Code 3ff.). But as soon as acceleration (or deceleration) happens, curved lines are needed.

Curves can be tricky to handle, and we now see three ways to draw them (using only *Processing*'s point() function).

The First (Iterative) Curve

One can draw a curve in an iterative fashion, i.e. move from one point to the next, modifying the position of the point little by little (same as in Code 5). Code 6 uses addition in the x direction, but multiplication in the y direction, to create a curved line.

Code 6

```
float x = 10;
float y = 0;
float speedX = 1;
float speedY = 0.98;

void setup()
{
  y = (height - 20);   //height is only now available
  strokeWeight(3);
}

void draw()
{
  point(x, y);
  if (x < (width - 10))
  {
      x += speedX;
      y *= speedY;
  }
}
```

Drawing Curves Using Trig

Another way to draw curves is to use trig functions such as sine and cosine, which we have used already before (e.g. Code 9–Code 13 in Chapter 15).

Code 7

```
void setup()
{
  strokeWeight(3);
}

void draw()
{
  for (int x = 10; x < (width - 10); x++)
  {
    float y = (height * 0.5) + (sin(x * 0.07) * 40);
    point(x, y);
  }
}
```

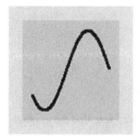

The Magic Numbers of `0.07` and `40` have arbitrarily been selected to generate a smooth curve (`0.07`) and to scale it up to somewhat to fill the window (`40`).

Drawing Curves with Polynomials

A third possibility to generate curves is using polynomials. We have already used a polynomial in Code 3 to draw a straight line.

Zero-degree polynomials draw orthogonal lines, first-degree polynomials draw straight lines, second-degree polynomials draw curved lines (or rather, parabolas), and third-degree polynomials draw parabolas with inflection points (Figure 31.2).

Code 8 shows a second-degree polynomial; note that very little has changed from Code 3, and that the y dimension is scaled.

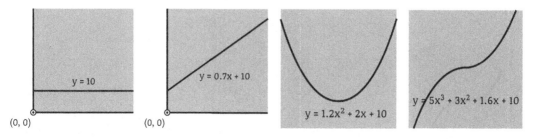

FIGURE 31.2 Zero-degree, first-degree, second-degree (moved) and third-degree (moved, scaled) polynomials

Code 8

```
float n = 1.2;
float m = 2;
float b = 10;

void setup()
{
  strokeWeight(3);
}

void draw()
{
  for (int x = 10; x < (width - 10); x++)
  {
    float y = (n * pow(x, 2)) + (m * x) + b;  //second-degree polynomial⁴
    point(x, (y * 0.01));  //scaled in y dimension
  }
}
```

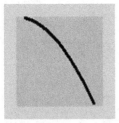

Code 9 uses a third-degree polynomial to draw a curve with an inflection point. Note that the graphics are moved and scaled to fit the window.

Code 9

```
float o = 5;
float n = 3;
float m = 1.6;
float b = 10;

void setup()
{
  strokeWeight(3);
}
void draw()
{
  for (int x = -40; x < 40; x++)
  {
    float y = (o * pow(x, 3)) + (n * pow(x, 2)) + (m * x) + b;
    point((50 + x), (50 + (y * 0.0001)));
  }
}
```

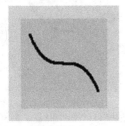

Processing's Curve Functions

Processing offers a number of functions to draw curves. Of course, these can only be used for drawing, not for moving objects. `arc()`, `curve()` and `bezier()` are 2D shape primitives; `curveVertex()` and `bezierVertex()` can be used within shape structures.

It is ok to use *Processing's* functions, but better to know how to do things on your own. The internet might break down, or you might come across a programming language which is not so convenient to use as *Processing*, or face a programming challenge where you want total control. Also, and probably most relevant, for moving things along curves you have to have access to all the points on them

Drawing curves is nice, but how can objects move, in curves, with a certain (real-time) speed?[5]

A race of a butterfly against a (flying) sausage is shown in Code 10. The butterfly moves in a sine wave (borrowed from Code 7), the sausage moves diagonally upwards (borrowed from Code 5).

Code 10

```
float butterflyX = 0;
float butterflySpeed = 50;

float sausageX = 0;
float sausageSpeed = 100;

int ticksLastUpdate = millis();

void setup()
{
  size(500, 50);
  frameRate(999999999);  //to defeat the speed limit Processing imposes by
  default
}

void draw()
{
  background(190, 225, 45);

  rect(butterflyX, 20 + (sin(butterflyX*0.1) * 4), 20, (sin(butterflyX)*10));
  butterflyX += butterflySpeed * float(millis()-ticksLastUpdate) * 0.001;

  rect(sausageX, 35 - (sausageX * 0.1), 20, 10, 10);
  sausageX += sausageSpeed * float(millis() - ticksLastUpdate) * 0.001;

  ticksLastUpdate=millis();
}
```

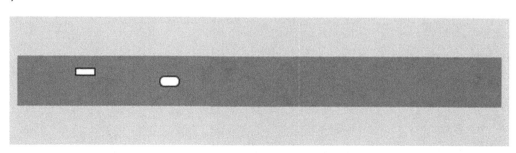

Notes

1. Since raster displays took over from vector displays in the second half of the 20th century.
2. The rocket science notion for that kind of lines is *orthogonal*.
3. Note that on screens, the coordinate system origin is usually located in the top-left corner. To arrive at the slope-intercept form y = mx + b one can insert a point on the line and the slope:

   ```
   15 = 0.7 * 25 + b
   15 = 17.5 + b
   b = -2.5
   ```

4. `pow(x, y)` is the programming way of writing x^y; square root is `sqrt()`.
5. Moving an object in a straight line along one axis with a certain speed can be done without too much trouble (see the examples above); moving it in two dimensions, in a curve, is a bit more involved, and is omitted here.

32

Pixel-Perfect Collision Detection

In many cases, a rough and fast bounding box collision check is good enough to establish collisions between 2D graphical objects such as sprites. In cases where it is not accurate enough, collision can be checked pixel-by-pixel. This is computationally expensive (Figure 32.1) and should only be used selectively, e.g. in cases where a bounding box collision check has already indicated an overlap.[1]

Even on modern machines, and with low screen resolutions, the computational load of pure pixel-perfect collision checking without optimisations (such as the use of bounding box checking to limit or completely avoid pixel-perfect checking) is substantial.[2] In Code 1, depending on the used graphics, the 32x32 pixels of the ship image are checked with 32x32 pixels in each of the ten tiles; that are up to 10.485.760 pixels to check every redraw (compared to 80 conditional checks for a much less accurate bounding box collision check); and the example is rather trivial with only one ship and ten tiles. Adding more objects such as enemy space ships or bullets would increase the computational load exponentially.

Code 1 shows a pixel-perfect collision check of a space ship with a row of houses and other objects. It is checked if any non-transparent pixel of the ship happens to be in the same spot as any non-transparent pixel of a tile. Collisions are shown by red pixels. The relevant code is in the `collisionCheck()` method in the `Ship` class (highlight).

Code 1

```
int tileSize = 32;
Tile tiles[] = new Tile[10];
Ship ship = null;

void setup()
{
  size(320, 240);
  for (int i = 0; i < tiles.length; i++) { tiles[i] = new Tile(i); }
  ship = new Ship();
  noFill();
}
```

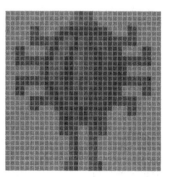

FIGURE 32.1 Checking each pixel of these two 32x32 pixels objects with each other for collision results in 1024 checks

DOI: 10.1201/9781003345916-32

```
void keyPressed()
{
  if (key == CODED)
  {
      if (keyCode == LEFT) { ship.move(-2, 0); }
      else if (keyCode == RIGHT) { ship.move(2, 0); }
      else if (keyCode == UP) { ship.move(0, -2); }
      else if (keyCode == DOWN) { ship.move(0, 2); }
  }
}

void draw()
{
  background(0);

  for (int i = 0; i < tiles.length; i++) { tiles[i].display(); }

  ship.display();
  if (ship.collisionCheck()) { text("collision", 10, 15); }
}

class Tile
{
  int iId = -1;
  int iPosX = 0;
  int iPosY = 0;
  int iType = 0;
  PImage pPic = null;

  Tile(int id)
  {
    iId = id;
    iPosX = id * tileSize;
    iPosY = height - 48;
    PImage tileSheet = loadImage("tilesheet.png");
    pPic = tileSheet.get((int(random(8)) * tileSize), 0, tileSize, tileSize);
  }

  void display()
  {
    stroke(60, 60, 0);
    rect(iPosX, iPosY, tileSize, tileSize);
    image(pPic, iPosX, iPosY);
  }

  color[] getPixelsArray()
  {
    pPic.loadPixels();
    return pPic.pixels;
  }

  int getPosX() { return iPosX; }

  int getPosY() { return iPosY; }
}

class Ship
{
  int iPosX = tileSize;
  int iPosY = tileSize;
  PImage pPicShip = null;
```

```
Ship()
{
  pPicShip = loadImage("ship.png");
}

boolean collisionCheck()
{
  boolean pixelCollision = false;
  stroke(220, 0, 0);
  int pixelNumber = tileSize * tileSize;
  pPicShip.loadPixels();

  for (int i = 0; i < tiles.length; i++)  //go through all tiles
  {
    color tilePixels[] = tiles[i].getPixelsArray();  //get tile's pixels array

    for (int p = 0; p < pixelNumber; p++)  //take a pixel from the array and...
    {
      if (alpha(tilePixels[p]) != 0)  //if pixel is not transparent...
      {
        for (int o = 0; o < pixelNumber; o++)  //...check it with each
        pixel from the ship
        {
          if (alpha(pPicShip.pixels[o]) != 0)  //is pixel not transparent?
          {
            int posInImageShipX = o % tileSize;
            int posInImageShipY = o / tileSize;
            int posInImageTileX = p % tileSize;
            int posInImageTileY = p / tileSize;

            if (((iPosX + posInImageShipX) == (tiles[i].getPosX() +
            posInImageTileX)) && ((iPosY + posInImageShipY) == (tiles[i].
            getPosY() + posInImageTileY)))  //are both pixels' positions
            identical?

            {
              //println("collision at "+(iPosX + posInImageShipX)+"/"+
              (iPosY + posInImageShipY));
              point(iPosX + posInImageShipX, iPosY + posInImageShipY);
              if (!pixelCollision) { pixelCollision = true; }  //if there
              is any pixel collision we want to return true
              break;  //if we have found the overlaping pixel we can stop
              checking any more ship pixels against this tile pixel
            }
          }
        }
      }
    }
  }
  return pixelCollision;  //return true if any pixels overlap, otherwise
  returns false
}

void display()
{
  stroke(0, 60, 60);
  rect(iPosX, iPosY, tileSize, tileSize);
  image(pPicShip, iPosX, iPosY);
}
```

```
void move(int x, int y)
{
  iPosX += x;
  iPosY += y;
}
}
```

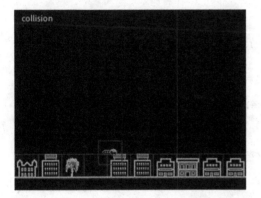

Note that the ship's controls are hard-coded[3] as are many other things; the ship's movement is also not time-fixed.[4] There is no scrolling. Although there is one `break` to avoid unnecessary checks, and the pixel array `image.pixels[]` is used instead of the (slower, according to the *Processing* documentation) `get()` method to access singular pixels, the code is not optimized for speed.

Notes

1. For basic (bounding box) collision detection, see Chapter 16.
2. Except when it can be offloaded to hardware as on the Atari *VCS/2600* (Montfort/Bogost 2009:54).
3. For a much superior way of implementation see the section 'Continous Movement' in Chapter 26.
4. See the (movement) time fix in the section 'Movement Speed in Games (The Time Fix for Movement)' in Chapter 27.

33

Vectors

A vector is a variable that can hold multiple values in multiple components at the same time (one value per component).[1] If one uses vector math in a program, vectors are an elegant alternative to using multiple named variables.[2]

In *Processing*, vectors are called PVectors. A PVector can hold either two or three values. For instance, it can contain two values that describe 2D pixel coordinates on screen (Code 1).

Code 1

```
PVector myVector = null; //creates a new PVector with no data, cannot (yet)
be used³

myVector = new PVector(20, 60); //assigns data to a PVector that has been
previously created

rect(myVector.x, myVector.y, 20, 20);
```

As with the data types described (section 'Data Types' in Chapter 4), there is a more compact form of creating a new PVector and assigning initial values (Code 2).

Code 2

```
PVector newVector = new PVector(20, 60); //creates a new PVector with values
in one line

rect(newVector.x, newVector.y, 20, 20);
```

If a PVector holds two values (in geek speak, has two *components* or *fields*), they are accessed with the suffixes x and y; if it holds three values, with the suffixes x, y and z (Code 3).

Code 3

```
PVector vector3 = new PVector(70, 60, 10);

println(vector3.x + ", " + vector3.y + ", " + vector3.z);
```

A PVector contains values of type float.[4] In that aspect the PVector is quite similar to the data types described above (in the section 'Data Types' in Chapter 4). But the PVector is actually a class, which explains the funky way of creating it (see e.g. Code 1).[5] This means that vectors need to be used a bit differently than simple data types.

DOI: 10.1201/9781003345916-33

Vectors are intended to be used with method calls, not with the standard mathematical operators (+, -, * and /); for instance, to add two vectors (Code 4).

Code 4

```
PVector vectorRect1 = new PVector(10, 40);
PVector vectorRect2 = new PVector(50, 20);

PVector vectorCombined = PVector.add(vectorRect1, vectorRect2);

rect(vectorRect1.x, vectorRect1.y, 15, 15);
rect(vectorRect2.x, vectorRect2.y, 15, 15);
rect(vectorCombined.x, vectorCombined.y, 25, 25);
```

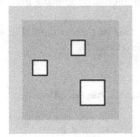

Note that the sizes of the squares are only used for dramatic effect.

Actually, one could use the standard mathematical operator + to add two vectors if one does it by hand, i.e. component by component (Code 5, changes are highlighted).

Code 5

```
PVector vectorRect1 = new PVector(10, 40);
PVector vectorRect2 = new PVector(50, 20);

PVector vectorCombined = new PVector(0, 0);
vectorCombined.x = vectorRect1.x + vectorRect2.x;
vectorCombined.y = vectorRect1.y + vectorRect2.y;

rect(vectorRect1.x, vectorRect1.y, 15, 15);
rect(vectorRect2.x, vectorRect2.y, 15, 15);
rect(vectorCombined.x, vectorCombined.y, 25, 25);
```

Similar to the example of adding two vectors in Code 4, one can subtract (Code 6), multiply (Code 7) and divide vectors (Code 8).

Code 6

```
PVector vector1 = new PVector(80, 40);
PVector vector2 = new PVector(50, 20);
PVector vectorCombined = PVector.sub(vector1, vector2);

println(vector1);
println(vector2);
println(vectorCombined);
```

  Output:

```
[ 80.0, 40.0, 0.0 ]
[ 50.0, 20.0, 0.0 ]
[ 30.0, 20.0, 0.0 ]
```

Code 7

```
PVector location = new PVector(20, 35);
float scaleBy = 2;
PVector vectorScaled = PVector.mult(location, scaleBy);

rect(location.x, location.y, 15, 15);
rect(vectorScaled.x, vectorScaled.y, 20, 20);
```

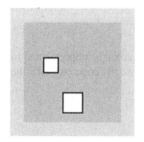

Code 8

```
PVector speed = new PVector(80, 60);
float divideBy = 2;
PVector vectorDivided = PVector.div(speed, divideBy);

line(0, 0, speed.x, speed.y);
strokeWeight(3);
line(0, 0, vectorDivided.x, vectorDivided.y);
```

For most vector operations, both *static* and *instance* method calls work; for others, only *instance* method calls work. Static method calls (such as PVector vectorCombined = PVector.add(vectorRect1, vectorRect2)) do not modify the vectors given as arguments, and return the result of the operation in a return value (a vector; assigned to vectorCombined in this case). Instance method calls (such as vector1.add(vector2)) modify the vector instance (vector1, in this case) and have no return value.

The above examples for add(), sub(), mult() and div() all use static method calls. But instance calls work as well (Code 9–Code 12).

Code 9

```
PVector vec1 = new PVector(10, 40);
PVector vec2 = new PVector(50, 10);
println(vec1.add(vec2));
```

Code 10

```
PVector vec1 = new PVector(50, 40);
PVector vec2 = new PVector(10, 20);
println(vec1.sub(vec2));
```

Code 11

```
PVector vector = new PVector(20, 40);
float scaleBy = 2;
println(vector.mult(scaleBy));
```

Code 12

```
PVector vector = new PVector(20, 40);
float divideBy = 2;
println(vector.div(divideBy));
```

To make full use of the power of vectors, several more operations are conveniently implemented in *Processing* (in other languages one might need to import a math library, or write the code oneself); the PVector class offers, for instance, the following functionality:

mag() – Returns the length (magnitude) of a given vector

```
PVector vector = new PVector(70, 60);
println(vector.mag());
```

normalize() – Scales a vector to length (or magnitude) 1, but preserves its direction

```
PVector vector = new PVector(20, 50);
println(vector.normalize());
```

dot() – Calculates the dot product of two vectors (both static and instance calls are possible)

```
PVsector vector1 = new PVector(20, 50);
PVector vector2 = new PVector(70, 10);
println(PVector.dot(vector1, vector2));
println(vector1.dot(vector2));
```

cross() – Calculates the cross product of two vectors

```
PVector vector1 = new PVector(20, 50);
PVector vector2 = new PVector(70, 10);
println(vector1.cross(vector2));
```

Code 13 demonstrates some of the mathematical operations in an interactive program.

Code 13

```
void setup()
{
  size(320, 240);
  strokeWeight(3);
  noFill();
}
void draw()
{
  background(140, 180, 45);
  PVector pointerLocation = new PVector(mouseX, mouseY);
  ellipse(pointerLocation.x, pointerLocation.y, 40, 40);
  text("Pointer is at coordinates " + pointerLocation.x + ", " +
  pointerLocation.y, 10, height - 55);
  text("Distance pointer to origin is " + pointerLocation.mag() + " pixels", 10,
  height - 35);
  text("Angle is " + degrees(pointerLocation.heading()) + " degrees", 10,
  height - 15);
  PVector scaledLocation = pointerLocation.div(2);  //to scale by half
  line(0, 0, scaledLocation.x, scaledLocation.y);
}
```

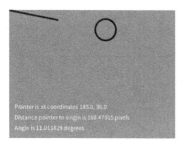

Chapter End Exercise

0. Are Vectors any Good

   Draw something on the screen using two ints. Then revise the code and use a vector instead. What is the advantage of using a vector? What is the advantage of using two ints?

Notes

1. Vectors are also very popular in, for instance, *Unity* scripting with *C#*, so it is useful to be aware of them.
2. Vectors are also an improvement over arrays, because many mathematical graphical operations are readily available on vectors (discussed earlier in this chapter).
3. In programming lingo, `null` denotes a void pointer which leads nowhere. *Processing* does not have pointers.
4. To have the `PVector` hold values of type `float` makes some sense, because the coordinates of most things that move are probably of type `float`.
5. For info on classes, see Chapter 25.

34

ArrayLists

Here we discuss ArrayLists which
are more versatile (but also
more expensive) than arrays

ArrayLists are an upgrade on arrays. Both ArrayLists and arrays store a number of indexed values of a single data type (or objects). The essential difference is that ArrayLists can change in size.[1] While the size of arrays needs to be set when they are created, and is then fixed,[2] in ArrayLists items can be added and removed at run-time. One can start with an empty ArrayList and add items, or start with a full ArrayList and then remove items, or one has an ArrayList which dynamically reacts to what happens in the program.

In a 2D action game, for example, an ArrayList can hold the bullets that are being fired, and bullets are dynamically added and removed as they are fired and as they hit a target or exit the screen. In a card game such as *Blackjack*, the players' hands (the cards they hold) could be implemented as ArrayLists, as can the stack of cards from which new cards are drawn (point to blackjackarraylists demo code online book website).

For ArrayLists, the luxury of having a variable size comes at a cost, though; plain arrays are cheap and fast because they cause very little organisational overhead. ArrayLists are a bit more costly. For them, the computer cannot, as it can for arrays, reserve a single, continuous piece of memory of fixed size that is used for as long as the array exists, because any item can be removed at any time from an ArrayList, and items can be added to it.[3] One should consider if this functionality is actually needed in every specific case.[4]

For some data types, *Processing* offers specialised kinds of ArrayLists: There is an IntList, a FloatList and a StringList.

Code 1 demos a bullet array; the next code snippet then shows how the program could look when using an ArrayList.

Code 1

```
//main program:
Bullet[] bullets = null;
void setup()
{
  size(320, 240);
  noStroke();
  bullets = new Bullet[10];
  for (int i = 0; i < bullets.length; i++)
  {
    bullets[i] = new Bullet(i);
  }
}
```

DOI: 10.1201/9781003345916-34

```
void mousePressed()
{
  for (int i = 0; i < bullets.length; i++)   //find an empty spot in the array
  for the new bullet
  {
    if (!bullets[i].isOn()) { bullets[i].add(mouseY); break; }
  }
}
void draw()
{
  background(0);
  for (int i = 0; i < bullets.length; i++)
  {
    bullets[i].update();
    bullets[i].display();
  }
}

//class definition:
class Bullet
{
  int id = -1;
  float posX = 0;
  float posY = 0;
  boolean isOn = false;
  Bullet(int n)
  {
    id = n;
  }
  void add(int y)
  {
    posX = 0;
    posY = y;
    isOn = true;
    }
  boolean isOn()
  {
    return isOn;
  }
  void display()
  {
    if (!isOn) { return; }  //only display bullets that are on
    fill(((128 + (17 * id)) % 256), ((128 + (57 * id)) % 256), ((128 + (111 *
    id)) % 256));
    rect(posX, posY, 10, 6);
    ellipse((posX + 10), (posY + 3), 6, 6);
  }
  void update()
  {
    if (!isOn) { return; }  //only update bullets that are on
    posX += 5; //not yet time-fixed, obviously, but it should be
    if (posX >= width) { isOn = false; }
  }
}
```

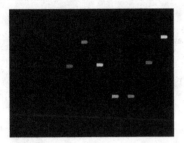

Note that in the above implementation, it is possible that there is no space for a new bullet, if there are already many active bullets. Two possible ways to handle this situation are either to not care (for instance, if it is computer opponents that fire at the player, that would be fully acceptable in many games; this is done in the code example above) or to randomly overwrite an existing bullet with the new one (for instance, if it is the player firing; the player certainly would want something to happen when he or she presses the fire button).

Code 2 uses an `ArrayList` to store the bullets. Bullets are added to the `ArrayList` when the mouse button is pressed, and removed from it when they exit the screen.

Code 2

```
//main program:

ArrayList<Bullet> bullets = null;

void setup()
{
  size(320, 240);
  noStroke();
  bullets = new ArrayList<Bullet>();   //now there is an empty arrayList
}

void remove(Bullet b)
{
  bullets.remove(b);
}

void mousePressed()
{
  bullets.add(new Bullet(mouseY));   //on every mouse button press we add a
  bullet to the arrayList
}

void draw()
{
  background(0);
  for (int i = 0; i < bullets.size(); i++)
  {
    bullets.get(i).display();
    bullets.get(i).update();
  }
}

//class definition:
class Bullet
{
  int colour = 0;
  float posX = 0;
  float posY = 0;
```

```
Bullet(int y)
{
  posX = 0;
  posY = y;
  colour = int(random(10));
}
void display()
{
  fill(((128 + (17 * colour)) % 256), ((128 + (57 * colour)) % 256), ((128 +
  (111 * colour)) % 256));
  rect(posX, posY, 10, 6);
  ellipse((posX + 10), (posY + 3), 6, 6);
  }
void update()
{
  posX += 5;  //not yet time-fixed, obviously, but it should be
  if (posX >= width) { remove(this); }  //uses a function in the main
  program
}
}
```

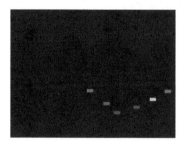

Note that in the Bullet class, the constructor is now combined with the add() method, and the boolean variable to reflect the status of the bullet is gone, of course (and the colouring of the bullets is now random). The removal of the bullets is a bit awkward because the bullet object cannot remove itself (in the update method); it uses a function in the main program to do this.[5]

In draw(), the calls to the update() and display() methods have been swapped because removing bullets is done in update(); if update() is called before display(), and a bullet is removed, display() tries to access an object that does no longer exist (one could also use two separate loops and keep the order).

With ArrayLists, instead of the usual *for* loop, one can also use a more fancy *for* loop:

```
for (Bullet bull : bullets)
{
  bull.display();
}
```

When using this enhanced syntax, items cannot be removed within the loop.

Chapter End Exercise

0. Who Comes to Dinner?

Create a program that writes out (to the console) all elements from an arrayList which contains ten names (i.e. strings). The output should be in random order, without repeating any elements. Potential extra feature: A mouse click should repeat this, again in a random order.

Notes

1. Resizable arrays are known under different names in different languages; they are called `ArrayLists` in *Processing* and *Java*, `Vectors` in *C++*, and `Lists` in *Python*, for instance.
2. In established programming languages, arrays have a fixed size. In *Processing*, the size of arrays can factually be increased (with the `append()` and `expand()` functions), and decreased (with the `shorten()` function; see Chapter 13).
3. It is not documented how `ArrayLists` are internally managed by *Processing*. Two possibilities are a linked list, where each item knows the next item in line (and probably the previous), or an array. That means either the links between items need to be updated when changes happen, or the whole array needs to be relocated (new memory space allocated, contents copied, the old memory position freed). Whatever happens, it takes effort.
4. The author is quite a fan of low-tech, and uses arrays everywhere. The author doesn't feel that the fixed size of arrays is a major limitation. Usually, the author knows, as the designer and programmer of his own game, for instance, roughly how many aliens, bullets, stars or bonus items there will be. The array items that are currently unused in, for instance, a bullet array, the author marks as being 'off' with a `boolean` variable in the class.
5. A possibility would be to introduce a boolean variable in the class that is set to true when the bullet should be removed; the main program could then ask each bullet (e.g. after the call to `display()`) if needs to be removed and remove it, if necessary. But then one could use an array in the first place...

35

Recursion

Recursion can be extremely elegant and efficient; and in some cases the best thing one can do. It is not used extensively in game design, but if one has never seen it before, it might be hard to recognize. So it's better we have it covered!

Recursion happens when a function calls itself.[1] It is often used when dealing with (large) data structures, such as a database or the Internet. Also, some mathematical functions can be described recursively. Many interesting (chaotic, self-similar) shapes can be produced when recursion is applied to graphics. Recursion is also just another type of loop, but often conceptually or intuitively close to what one wants to do, and it can be a very elegant way to approach a challenge.

There are three distinct forms of recursive functions. The first is essentially a loop. A function is called, does something, and calls itself at the end. The first example Code 1 demonstrates this. It does its work *on the way in*. A variation is a function that is called, first calls itself, and then does something. The examples Code 2 to Code 4 are of this type. These do their work *on the way out*. This form could also be easily formulated as a loop. The two first forms can also be combined (Code 5). The third form of recursion is a branching function (Code 6).

Code 1 demonstrates recursion which is very similar to a loop.

Code 1

```
void setup()
{
  size(170, 100);
  drawRect(8);
}

void drawRect(int n)
{
  if (n==0) { return; }  //stop recursion
  rect(width - (n * 20), 10, 10, (n * 10));
  drawRect(n - 1);
}

void draw() { }
```

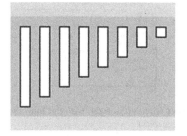

DOI: 10.1201/9781003345916-35

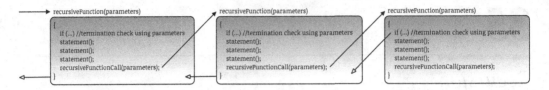

FIGURE 35.1   The first variant of recursion (depth 3); program execution goes from left to right, executing statements (black arrows), and then back, doing nothing (white arrows)

The `width - (n * 20)` part is used to draw the rectangles from left to right. The vertical size of the rectangles indicates how many more will be drawn.

Figure 35.1 shows the program flow; first left-to-right, following the black arrows; then back, following the white arrows.

Code 2 is modified from Code 1 and demonstrates the second form of recursion, which does its work on the way out (or right to left).

Code 2

```
void setup()
{
  size(170, 100);
  drawRect(8);
}
void drawRect(int n)
{
  if (n==0) { return; }  //stop recursion
  drawRect(n - 1);
  rect(width - (n * 20), 10, 10, (n * 10));
}
```

Figure 35.2 shows the program flow; first left-to-right, following the black arrows; then back, following the white arrows.

The rightmost rectangle is drawn first.

The author implemented a *Processing* version of the popular turtle graphics (originating in the 1967 *LOGO* programming language) to demonstrate some graphical recursive algorithms. To run the following example code, get his turtle implementation from the book's website at (the download is called *Nurtle*).[2]

The following example (Code 3) is structurally identical to the example in Code 1. It draws a rectangle and then starts a slightly smaller rectangle which is rotated 5° inside the first. The graphics is intended to show how recursion *goes into*.

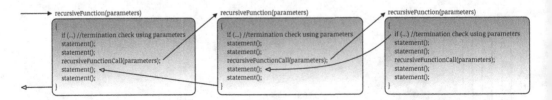

FIGURE 35.2   The second variant of recursion (depth 3); program execution goes from left to right, with the function recursively calling itself (black arrows), and then back, executing statements (white arrows)

Code 3

```
void vBox(int sideLen) {
  if (sideLen > 5) {  //check if recursion should continue
      nurtle.forward(sideLen);
      nurtle.left(90);
      nurtle.forward(sideLen);
      nurtle.left(90);
      nurtle.forward(sideLen);
      nurtle.left(90);
      nurtle.forward(sideLen);
      nurtle.left(90);
      nurtle.up();
      nurtle.left(45);
      nurtle.forward(sideLen * 0.1);
      nurtle.right(40);
      nurtle.down();
      vBox( sideLen - 15);
  }
}
```

This is the `draw()` function of the code. The Nurtle needs to be initialised and stopped:

```
void draw() {
  nurtle.start();
  vBox(100);
  nurtle.end();
}
```

A kind of snaky blocky maze pattern is drawn by Code 4; in this case, it makes sense to use recursion because it is close to how one thinks about the task (it would be possible but hard to do the same thing with e.g. a *for* loop):

Code 4

```
void vMaze(float n)
{
  if (n < 10) { return; }  //stop recursion
  nurtle.forward(n);
  nurtle.right(90);
  vMaze(n * 0.9);
}
```

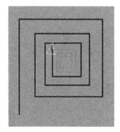

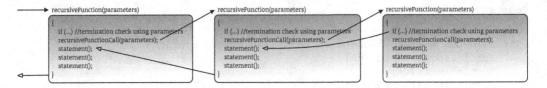

FIGURE 35.3 Sketch showing function calls on the way in (black arrows) and on the way out of the recursion (white arrows)

The above graphics is created with an argument of `100`:

```
vMaze(100);
```

A mix of the first and second forms of recursion is demonstrated by the example in Code 5. It is a spiral that is first winding in, and then winding out. It can be seen in the code. First, all the ingoing segments are drawn (upper half of the function, above the recursive call, shown in blue), then, on the way out, all the outgoing (lower half, shown in green; Figure 35.3). Again, it would not be impossible to implement this in other ways, but tricky.

Code 5

```
void vSpiral(float f) {
  if (f < 10) { return; }  //stop recursion
  nurtle.forward(f * 0.5);
  nurtle.left(35);
  vSpiral(f * 0.8);
  nurtle.forward(f * 0.5);
  nurtle.right(35);
}
```

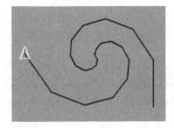

This is the call that starts it:

```
vSpiral(100);
```

Experiment, and try to draw patterns or shapes, such as the following tree. Adding random numbers (in moderation) can have interesting effects.

Code 6 demonstrates the third form of recursion: A function is called and calls itself several times (it *branches*). The tree that is drawn also shows the recursive structure of the program: Every twig that is drawn is a recursive function call.

Code 6

```
void vTree(float n)
{
  if (n < 10) { return; }  //stop recursion
  nurtle.forward(n);
  nurtle.left(25);
```

```
  vTree(n * 0.7);
  nurtle.right(50);
  vTree(n * 0.7);
  nurtle.left(25);
  nurtle.backward(n);
}
```

This is the call that starts it:

```
vTree(90);
```

Figure 35.4 shows the program flow of a branching recursion of depth 3.

Chapter End Exercises

0. Image Crawler

   A potential application area for a branching recursive function (as in Code 6) might be web-sites. Implement a web crawling program; its central part is a function that gets a URL and a depth, saves all the images the web page contains (or rather, points to), and triggers a further recursive call for every URL it finds on the page, by calling itself (with depth -1) if depth is not 0 (so the recursion will end at some point).

   The program is sketched in pseudo code (Code 7; see the section 'Pseudo Code' in Chapter 3). It can probably be implemented with moderate effort (of course, many technicalities will pop up, such as wonky html code, dead links and links to other types of files than text (html)). [See the demo program mini browser on the book's web site]

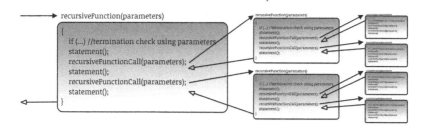

FIGURE 35.4   Branching recursion; the way in (black arrows) and the way out (white arrows)

Code 7

```
void checkPageAndSaveAllImages(String url, int stepsToGo)
{
  println("Now looking at URL " + url + ", and there are " + stepsToGo + "
  steps to go");

  //load html page source

  //go through it

    //if image is found (identify by <img> tag), save it to disk

    //if link is found (identify by <a href> tag), and stepsToGo is not 0,
    call checkPageAndSaveAllImages(link, stepsToGo - 1)

}
```

Notes

1. 'Recursive is like Russian dolls', as Julian Oliver says (Networkshop, ITU, March 2014, my notes). A directory entry on recursion that says: 'Please see directory entry recursion.' would also be recursive, but would also never stop – this would be a problem for the computer.
2. Or readers can create their own implementation of turtle graphics?!

36

Basic Game AI and Enemy Behaviour

Here we see different possibilities to get
some semi-intelligent reactions from the
computer, for instance, in games

Historically, Artificial Intelligence (AI) in digital games started out as a substitute for a potentially absent second player. Already in 1956, there was a tic-tac-toe playing AI (Montfort/Bogost 2009:38).

Certainly, the computer promoted the idea of automated, and more or less complex responses to player actions. Before computers, games had, at most, very simple reactions built-in. For instance, at a certain event, a player would draw a card in a board game that describes a random intervention (such as for players to pay a fee for each of their houses and hotels for 'street repair' in *Monopoly*[1]; or environmental events in *Forbidden Island*). Other (board) games may have included simple, automated movements (such as the monster token moving towards the closest player token). These were either hard-wired reactions or random events controlled by, for instance, throwing dices or drawing cards.

Early Games

Early two-player games such as *Pong* often did not contain computer-controlled players. Single-player games regularly included computer-controlled players, often in the form of an immense mass of faceless, idiotic and pretty suicidal opponents, e.g. in platform games (*Mario*), space shooters (*R-Type* (Irem 1987), *Katakis* (Rainbow Arts 1987), Uridium (Graftgold 1986)) or maze games.

In the most simple of these games, the computer-controlled entities fully ignore what the player does. For instance, computer-controlled enemies may walk back and forth on platforms, or fly across the screen from right to left. The robotic opponents in *Space Invaders* who move sideways and down, reverse (horizontal) direction when colliding with the screen border, and shoot randomly with a certain frequency (similarly, enemies in *Centipede* (Atari 1980)). Computer-controlled cars in *Out Run* (Sega 1986) drive with a certain speed and swerve back and forth across the track, whatever the player does (except when the player collides with them, but they resume their movement pattern immediately after).

Slightly more sophisticated, but still rather predictable behaviours include enemies moving towards the player (such as the ghosts in *Gauntlet*, Atari 1985) or aiming shots at players (such as the lobbers in *Gauntlet*, and the enemy soldiers in *Ikari Warriors* (SNK 1986) and in *Cabal* (Taito 1988)). More advanced are computer-controlled enemies that follow rather simple decision trees to guide their

DOI: 10.1201/9781003345916-36

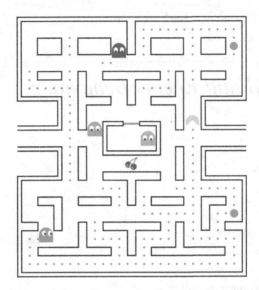

FIGURE 36.1   Sketch of an in-game situation: Each of the four ghosts in *Pac-Man* (Namco 1980) behaves differently

behaviours, based, for instance, solely on the distance to the player. And that usually works well enough to facilitate interesting gameplay (e.g. in *Gauntlet*). Such behaviours are regularly not too hard to implement and both sufficiently complex for players to be engaged and at the same time to be somewhat predictable for them. It appears that in most action games, it is quite uncommon to include even readily available data such as energy levels, available weapons, location of (other) enemies or number of enemies.

Pac-Man's Ghosts

Let's look at *Pac-Man* (Figure 36.1) as a classic example of a relatively early game with computer-controlled enemies that behave in cleverly designed, non-trivial ways, controlled by not overly complex programming. Toru Iwatani, the designer of *Pac-Man*, comments that 'there's not much entertainment in a game of eating, so we decided to create enemies to inject a little excitement and tension [...] [t]he enemies are four little ghost-shaped monsters, each of them a different colour – blue, yellow, pink and red', and each of the enemies was to have 'its own character' (qtd. in Birch 2010). *Pac-Man* is to traverse each level and collect (i.e. eat) all the dots, and he loses a life if he collides with one of the ghosts. In each level, there are four ghosts; they are popularly known as Blinky (red), Pinky (pink), Inky (blue) and Clyde (orange).

All ghosts are in one of three modes: *Chase, scatter* or *frightened* (Pittman 2009). In the chase mode, they hunt *Pac-Man*, in the scatter mode, they head for their home corners, and in the frightened mode, they evade *Pac-Man*. The ghost modes automatically alternate four times between scatter and chase at the start of each level (for a few seconds each), before staying permanently in chase mode. The frightened mode is triggered when *Pac-Man* eats an anti-ghost pill. Iwatani explains that he 'felt it would be too stressful for a human being like Pac Man to be continually surrounded and hunted down'; as a consequence, he designed the 'monsters' invasions to come in waves [...] [t]hey'd attack and then they'd retreat', which he believed was 'more natural than having constant attack' (qtd. in Birch 2010).

The ghosts move around the level, and need to make navigational decisions at the crossings (they never move backwards into the spot they came from, except under special circumstances, such as mode changes). That each ghost has its own movement strategy is, Iwatani believes (qtd. in ibid.), 'the heart of the game'.

Blinky aims to get to the spot in the level where *Pac-Man* is. At a crossing, Blinky thus selects the movement option that gets it closer to *Pac-Man* (measured in a straight line). Birch (2010) explains:

> If two or more potential choices are an equal distance from the target, the decision between them is made in the order of up > left > down. A decision to exit right can never be made in a situation

where two tiles are equidistant to the target, since any other option has a higher priority. [...] Since the only consideration is which tile will immediately place the ghost closer to its target, this can result in the ghosts selecting the 'wrong' turn [...] [with an] overall [longer] path [...].

Blinky speeds up twice per level by 5% when *Pac-Man* has eaten a number of dots (Birch 2010). Birch (ibid.) notes that Blinky in addition also changes 'his behavior in Scatter mode'. With the change, Blinky does not retreat to his (upper-right) corner in scatter mode but keeps chasing *Pac-Man* (ibid.).

Pinky aims to move not to the spot where *Pac-Man* currently is, but 'look[s] at Pac-Man's current position and orientation, and select[s] the location four tiles straight ahead' (Birch 2009). Birch (ibid.) notes that '[o]ne important implication of Pinky's targeting method is that Pac-Man can often win a game of "chicken" with him'. He (ibid.) explains that 'if Pac-Man heads directly towards him, Pinky's target tile will actually be behind himself once they are less than four tiles apart', and Pinky will then 'take any available turn-off in order to loop back around to his target [tile]'.

Inky bases its movement on *Pac-Man*'s position in the level, as well as on Blinky's position. Inky's target tile is twice the length of the vector from Blinky's position to the tile two tiles ahead of *Pac-Man*'s position (Birch 2019). Birch (2019) observes that thus 'Inky's target can vary wildly when Blinky is not near Pac-Man, but if Blinky is in close pursuit, Inky generally will be as well'.

Clyde's movement strategy varies, depending on its distance from *Pac-Man*. If Clyde is more than eight tiles away, it moves towards *Pac-Man*'s position (similar to how Blinky moves; Birch 2009); if Clyde is closer to *Pac-Man*, the target is its home (bottom-left) corner. Birch notes that '[t]he combination of these two methods has the overall effect of Clyde alternating between coming directly towards Pac-Man, and then changing his mind and heading back to his corner whenever he gets too close'.

AI's Comin', in Just Five More Years

A basic level of AI support is today often taken for granted in everyday applications. Google, Apple and Amazon each have an AI assistant built into their products, several manufacturers (from both the automotive and technology sectors) develop and experiment with self-driving cars, AIs developed using Google's *DeepMind* technology are competently playing many classic Atari games (see, e.g., Morelle 2015), and Open AI's *ChatGPT*[2] produces texts that are hard to distinguish from texts written by humans.

Obviously, there have been tremendous successes in the history of the development of AI. Two such high-profile, landmark events were when elite human players were beaten by computers at both, chess (IBM's *Deep Blue* beats Garry Kasparov in 1996) and *Go* (DeepMind Technologies' *AlphaGo* beats Lee Sedol in 2016). While the computer's triumph in chess was somewhat predictable, and essentially enabled by a rule-based, hardcoded heuristic on (increasingly) powerful hardware, the victory in *Go* might be conceptually more interesting because the software was based on a self-learning neural network. In any case, these events arguably were, for many members of the general public, substantial (and somewhat understandable) achievements, and clear signals that AI was progressing quickly. But the well-publicised progress of AI is often overrated in the public discourse, it appears. The idea that after one can create machines that can play games such as chess and *Go*, one would understand and be able to create human-level intelligence has, so far, not been realised. Research is ongoing, but predictions that the lessons learned could be readily (and somewhat speedily) applied to other areas beyond such games have yet to be facilitated.

'Attempts to simulate cognitive processes on computers have [...] run into greater difficulties than anticipated', Hubert Dreyfus writes in 1965 (p. iii). Eminent academics such as him, Joseph Weizenbaum and Noam Chomsky have been arguing for decades that conceptually, general, human-level intelligence is unrealistic to be technically achieved. Ever. Even Marvin Minsky (qtd. in Stork 1996), who certainly cannot be accused of being hostile towards new technologies or of harbouring romantic ideas about human intelligence, points out that 'the true majesty of general intelligence still awaits our attack', and that so far only 'collections of dumb specialists in small domains' have been created. This is still the case many years later; Chomsky (qtd. in Al-Sibai 2023) seconds the opinion that AI can only be 'useful [...] in some narrow domains', and asserts that the recent advances in AI research do not signal the technical realisation of 'artificial general intelligence', despite 'what can be read in hyperbolic headlines and reckoned by injudicious investments'. Chomsky (ibid.) explains that '[t]he human mind is not, like ChatGPT and its ilk, a lumbering statistical engine for pattern matching, gorging on hundreds of terabytes of data and extrapolating the most likely conversational response or most probable answer to a scientific question', but 'a surprisingly efficient and even elegant system that operates with small amounts of information; it seeks not to infer brute correlations among data points but to create explanations'.

Although considerable efforts have been expended, and the emergence of a general AI has been predicted and expected every five or ten years since the 1950s, for the moment, it appears to be elusive. Ask *ChatGPT* about this.

AI's Uncanny Valley

AI faces challenges not only on both ends of the spectrum of performance but, interestingly, also in its centre. From a game design perspective, the development of game AI appears thus to encounter a challenge similar to the visual 'uncanny valley' phenomenon that has been observed in technical representations of humans (first formulated by Masahiro Mori in 1970; see Hsu 2012, Perera 2023).

On the lower end of the performative spectrum, it is hard to imagine too trivial AI (re-) actions to facilitate play. Even with minimal levels of performance, Non-Player Characters (NPCs[3]) in games can already be conductive to engaging and exciting gameplay. *Pac-Man*'s ghosts are perfectly acceptable to players, however, primitive and predictable their behaviours are. Nobody expects the other *Space Invaders* to flee when one of them is shot. Even the most primitive interactions can facilitate play, and many of the greatest and most popular games are, arguably, somewhat basic.

AI needs a minimal level of performance, but, probably counter-intuitively, it should not be too capable, either. On the upper end of the performative spectrum, NPCs run the risk of being too perfect, and thus facilitating one-sided and, ultimately, boring gameplay. Playing chess against a chess computer, program or app may be intimidating rather than enjoyable for many ordinary players; bots in a FPS game can likely easily outperform most human players.

Interestingly, there appears to exist a strip of middle ground between the extremes that is problematic, as well. When NPCs get smarter (than, say, the ghosts in *Pac-Man*) and start to pretend to act intelligently and to look like (representations of) humans, as many NPCs in popular games now do, they run the risk to disappoint players' expectations and thus to substantially compromise the playing experience.

Warpefelt et al. (2013) report multiple instances of unexpected, irrational and unlogical behaviours of NPCs in games that do not align with player expectations. They describe enemy archers in *Dragon Age: Origins* who do not move into position to fight the players, hostile soldiers in *Mass Effect 3* who 'leave an advantageous position in cover in order to take up positions in worse cover, where they are in the crossfire between the player and his companions', players being able to enter 'into private residences and sleep in people's beds' in plain sight of the residents without any consequences in *Morrowind*, and players being able to shoot at friendly NPCs in *Space Marine* who simply 'continue [...] with what they were doing as if nothing [was happening]'. One player complains about similar NPC behaviours in *Skyrim*; he or she describes that 'NPCs, both friendly/neutral and hostile (like bandits) just don't care when someone gets sneak-killed right next to them'. He or she also reports that 'sometimes NPCs are hostile on sight[,] even if it doesn't make sense, and sometimes they aren't hostile[,] when [he or she] would expect them to be'.[4] In the game *Naval Action* (Game-Labs 2019), one player observes that 'NPCs have always been Incredible Intent on constantly Sailing Straight with their Face into the Wind. For whatever reason they really Love to do just Turn away and Drive Straight against the Wind rather than trying any actual Maneuvers.'[5] Another player replies that he agrees, and that 'the behavior of the AI, as described, is really idiotic and sweep off a lot of fun and immersion in that game, actually'.[6]

So, What Can We Do in Games, Then?

Usually, it is neither attempted nor required to model a fully-capable human intelligence within or without the application area of digital games. Winograd and Flores (1986:137) assert for the design of productivity tools, that the belief in artificial intelligence by 'projecting human capacities onto the computer' is a fallacy. They see the 'key to design' in 'understanding the readiness-to-hand of the tools being built, and in anticipating the breakdowns that will occur in their use'. Rather than designing systems 'that provide [...] a limited imitation of human facilities [and] will intrude with apparently irregular and incomprehensible breakdowns', they recommend to 'create tools that are designed to make the maximal use of human perception and understanding'.

Games or game genres are closed systems and limited domains. In such well-defined areas, computers have certainly made advances towards semi-intelligent behaviours. Behaviours of entities in games can be implemented with and benefit from various AI techniques (see the section 'Different Types of AI Implementation' later in this chapter). AI can thus be an interesting part of game design.

However, the term 'AI' in game development regularly refers to something relatively basic. The majority of games (even those hailed for their intelligent AI) often use very simple decision making for any computer-controlled entities. These entities are often given particular data (such as their position, the player position, their previous action, amount of ammo, and amount of health) that they can use to determine their next action (such as to chase the player, take cover, reload). The resulting behaviours can be appropriate and convincingly enough in games, and reasonably simple to design and implement. For example, for enemies in many action games, decision trees with one variable or a low number of variables can be perfectly sufficient.

One strategy to facilitate interesting gameplay can be, to not aim for general or optimal on-task performance of computer-controlled entities in games, or to pretend something that they cannot feasibly deliver; but to design NPCs with specific skills and (exploitable) weaknesses. And this is actually a quite common, popular and successful approach in game design. For instance, the opponents in *Yie Ar Kung-Fu* (Konami 1984) and *Shufflepuck Cafe* (Broderbund, 1989) have certain strengths and weaknesses and can be beaten with specific (often simple) strategies. Strategy games such as *The Perfect General* (Quantum Quality Productions 1991) regularly feature computer-controlled opponents which are modelled on (in-) famous military commanders and presumably simulate (some of) their professional characteristics.[7] Sports games often feature multiple competing teams or opponents of various strengths; in *Tennis Cup*, there are '32 possible opponents, each with their own qualities, defects and tactics' (Loriciel ca. 1989:1).

Different Types of AI Implementation

There are numerous different models how AI can work and how it can be implemented. To give a very broad and general overview, here are briefly sketched: Heuristic methods, Brute Force approaches, probabilistic methods, data-based methods and Neural Networks. Hybrids exist, for instance, a heuristic AI combined with a database, or with a Brute Force algorithm (such as *Deep Blue*). Each of these methods and approaches has certain properties and requirements and is suited to specific applications.

Heuristics

Heuristic AI uses expert systems, where human designers create a set or series of conditions or cases and responses or reactions (or questions and answers).[8] This set is then queried by the AI at run-time to decide how to react. With a static set, the AI does not change or modify its behaviour over time (reproducible responses are an asset rather than a problem in many applications and contexts). Heuristics typically react within a reasonable (and usually predictable) time frame; they have deterministic output given a specific input, and they do not use significant computing resources and slow the program down. They work robustly and reliably within their limits (e.g. medical diagnosis, enemies in games). However, the approach requires domain experts, is labour-intense to set up and to maintain, and is only practically feasible for quite limited and well-explored domains.

An example is a *Blackjack*-playing AI. The optimal strategy to play the game varies slightly between different rule variants but is generally fairly well-established. The ideal actions for all in-game situations can be stored in a table.[9] During the game, the AI can look up what to do.[10]

This is the type of AI probably most popular in games, and the type that is covered here (see the section Our First 'AI' later in this chapter).

Brute Force Approaches

Brute Force approaches try to solve problems without sophisticated (e.g. heuristic) strategies. The approach does not try to be clever (or selective) in its attempts, but it simply calculates everything in a deterministic, systematic and comprehensive fashion, hoping to find a solution eventually (e.g. in code-breaking). An advantage is, that the programmers do not need to know (or anticipate) a lot about the subject domain; a drawback is the often massive amount of resources needed (such as hardware, time and energy). Brute Force AIs can slow a program down considerably, depending on the breadth (how many possibilities are there in one step?) and depth of a search (how many steps are there?). Because they require many resources, and can thus only be used in few, limited contexts, Brute Force attempts are often seen as the least desirable. Depending on the game, implementing this type of AI can also involve a large programming overhead as the AI must be given the ability to simulate the game states as well as a way to rank its choices so it can figure out how to act.

Chess is a game for which AI is typically implemented as a brute force approach (usually combined with a heuristic to limit the search space). The task appears to be a technically relatively simple challenge that can be solved by the use of massive computational resources (i.e. repeating a well-defined and well-understood mathematical task very often). In the AI's turn, it calculates some possible moves from its pieces in the current position, and then also some moves from the player's pieces from some of the resulting positions, and then decides on one of the moves by assessing the quality of the resulting positions.

Probabilistic Methods

The problem is that there exist many search spaces in interesting subject domains that are far too extensive to be feasibly traversed in an exhaustive manner within a reasonable and acceptable timeframe by Brute Force approaches, even on fast hardware, and no suitable (or sufficiently capable) heuristics exist. One such application is the game of *Go* which 'has many more moves available to the player than in chess, and each of those moves can have major effects 50 to 100 moves ahead', which 'makes the game trees in Go much wider and deeper which vastly increases the complexity' (Magnuson 2015).

For application in such domains, and as an alternative to Brute Force approaches, statistical sampling has been proposed. The currently most popular method appears to be Monte Carlo Tree Search (MCTS). Magnuson (ibid.) explains that 'Monte Carlo methods use repeated random sampling to obtain results', and that '[i]n MCTS, the random sampling is in the form of random simulations which are used to expand the game tree'. The AI then decides on its move based on the game tree. Because MCTS is a probabilistic algorithm, 'it will not always choose the best action, but it still performs reasonably well' (ibid.).

Data-Based AIs

AI can also be realised as database systems that understand nothing about a given subject domain but are guided by a dataset of past events. In a specific game situation, they act by identifying a similar past situation and pick an action that has led to desirable outcomes before. Data-based AIs require a substantially large data set to function properly. The AI can start with a base data set but also continue to add to the data set in order to improve (an example is probably Google's ranking algorithm). AIs can use this approach to play, for instance, poker without actually performing any (intelligent) reasoning, solely by harvesting a database of previous games.

Neural Networks

A Neural Network is a specific implementation of Machine Learning (or Deep Learning) AI, that is inspired by how human brains (might) work. The network is built up of nodes and connections that mimic some basic characteristics of the human brain's neurons and synapses. For Machine Learning, a self-learning algorithm is fed much data together with desired outcomes, and one hopes that the system can somehow learn how to decide things, and apply this capability outside of the training data set (e.g. *AlphaGo* was trained with *Go* matches played by professional (human) players).

One problem for Neural Networks is that the quality of their performances hinges on the training data. Regularly, training data sets are skewed and unrepresentative (e.g. most representative of the developers of such systems, e.g. white males).

Another problem with Neural Networks is, that even if some desirable behaviours emerge from a network, it is usually opaque what specifically goes on, and why. The internal processes are super complex and almost impossible to follow or retrace (which is exactly the idea, one wants the network to do the work, not to program a heuristic). Specific undesirable behaviours are regularly hard to prevent (because there are no rules that could be adjusted – only a trained network).

Other problems are that Machine Learning needs large amounts of energy for training, to be able to generate even the most basic results. If the model changes, the system needs to be retrained. Applications outside of the original, specific domain are often difficult and problematic, and unforeseen (and thus untrained) events usually lead to a system breakdown.

Our First 'AI'

In this section, we are looking at very simple AIs that can act based on a very small amount of data. The first example (Code 1) is rather similar to code snippets from the beginning of this book (e.g. Code 12 from Chapter 6) as it only contains a very simple class that compares two numbers (the tiredness and hunger levels of the 'AI') to decide what it wants to do.

Code 1

```
//Tired AI, by Max Wrighton

//main program

SimpleAI ai = null;

void setup()
{
  size(200, 100);
  ai = new SimpleAI();
  ai.randomiseValues();
}

void draw()
{
  background(50);
  text(ai.writeThoughts(), 10, 20);
}

void keyReleased()
{
  ai.randomiseValues();
}

// SimpleAI class

class SimpleAI
{
  int tiredness = 0;
  int hunger = 0;

  String writeThoughts()
  {
    if (tiredness > hunger) { return "I want to go to bed"; }
    else if (tiredness < hunger) { return "I want to eat"; }

    return "I don't know what to do";
  }
```

```
void randomiseValues()
{
  tiredness = (int)random(0, 100);
  hunger = (int)random(0, 100);
  println("tiredness: " + tiredness + "   hunger: " + hunger);
}
}
```

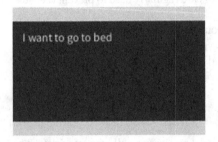

Output:

```
tiredness: 84          hunger: 69
```

Depending on which number is greater, the AI either wants to sleep or to eat (if both values are equal, the AI does not know what to do).

Already with only two variables we have created a decision tree with multiple outcomes. If these variables were set up to drain over time, and the SimpleAI could do something about it (e.g. sleep or eat) then we would already be on our way to a *The Sims*-like system. We can also use player manipulating variables (such as mouse position) as input and have the AI react to this.

Code 2 is a class definition for an AI that will move towards a given point as long as it has energy. If the class object reaches the point or runs out of energy, it rests and recovers its energy.[11] The complete project is available from the book's website.

Code 2

```
//GoToMouseGetTired AI, by Max Wrighton

class Wanderer {
  float xPos = 200.0;
  float yPos = 200.0;
  float walkSpeed = 40.0;
  float energy = 100.0;
  float energyReplenishmentSpeed = 10.0;
  boolean resting = false;
  float closeToPointThreshold = 15.0; // if the wanderer is within 15 pixels
  of the mouse it will stop and rest

  void update(float timeDelta, int goToX, int goToY) {
    if (goToX < 0) { goToX = 0; }
    else if (goToX > width) { goToX = width; }

    if (goToY < 0) { goToX = 0; }
    else if (goToY > height) { goToY = height; }

    float dirX = goToX - xPos;
    float dirY = goToY - yPos;
    float directionVectorLength = sqrt((dirX * dirX) + (dirY * dirY));

    if (directionVectorLength <= closeToPointThreshold) { // check if the
    wanderer is close enough to the mouse
        resting = true;
    }
```

```
    if (resting) { // if resting we increase our energy
        energy += energyReplenishmentSpeed * timeDelta;

        if ((energy > 80.0) && (directionVectorLength > closeToPointThreshold))
        { resting = false; }
        else if (energy > 100.0) { energy = 100.0; }
    }
    else { // otherwise we follow the mouse
        dirX /= directionVectorLength;
        dirY /= directionVectorLength;

        xPos += dirX * walkSpeed * timeDelta;
        yPos += dirY * walkSpeed * timeDelta;
        energy -= abs(((dirX + dirY) * 5) * timeDelta); // 5 is a Magic Number

        if (energy <= 0.0) { resting = true; }
    }
  }
  void display(){
    if (resting){ fill(0, 0, 255); } // fill is blue when resting
    else{ fill(255, 0, 0); } // fill is red when not resting
    ellipse(xPos, yPos, 25, 25);
    text("ENERGY: " + (int)energy, 5, 15); // print the energy level in the
    top left of the screen
  }
}
```

Code 3 is for an object that follows a predefined path given to it on initialisation. The path is made up of an array of x coordinates and an array of y coordinates (both arrays should be of the same length). The guard objects instantiated from the class can be set to loop around or backtrack through their patrol routes. The complete project is available from the book's website.

Code 3

```
//GuardPatrol AI, by Max Wrighton
class Guard
{
  int[] patrolXPositions = null;
  int[] patrolYPositions = null;
  boolean patrolLoops = false;

  float xPos = 0.0;
  float yPos = 0.0;
  float walkSpeed = 75.0;
  int currentNodeToWalkToo = 0;
  float nodeThroeshold = 7.5;
  boolean walkingBack = false;
```

```
Guard(int[] xPositions, int[] yPositions, boolean looping)
{
    patrolXPositions = xPositions;
    patrolYPositions = yPositions;
    patrolLoops = looping;

  // the guard starting pos is the first pos on the patrol
  xPos = patrolXPositions[0];
  yPos = patrolYPositions[0];
  currentNodeToWalkToo = 1; // setup the first goal point as node 1;
}

void update(float timeDelta)
{
  // calculate the movement direction based on the node we are heading too
  float dirX = patrolXPositions[currentNodeToWalkToo] - xPos;
  float dirY = patrolYPositions[currentNodeToWalkToo] - yPos;
  float directionVectorLength = sqrt(pow(dirX, 2) + pow(dirY, 2)); //[12]
  dirX /= directionVectorLength;
  dirY /= directionVectorLength;

  // move the guard
  xPos += dirX * (walkSpeed * timeDelta);
  yPos += dirY * (walkSpeed * timeDelta);

  // check the distance to the target node and update the target node if we
  are close enough to it
  float sqrDistanceToTargetNode = pow((patrolXPositions[currentNodeToWalkToo] -
  xPos), 2) + pow((patrolYPositions[currentNodeToWalkToo] - yPos), 2);

  if (sqrDistanceToTargetNode < pow(nodeThroeshold, 2))
  {
     if (walkingBack) // walking back means we are going back the way we
     came until we get to point 0
     {
        currentNodeToWalkToo--;

        if (currentNodeToWalkToo < 0)
        {
           currentNodeToWalkToo = 1;
           walkingBack = false;
        }
     }
     else // otherwise we are going forwards so we want to make sure we
     don't go past the last point in the array
     {
        currentNodeToWalkToo++;

        if (currentNodeToWalkToo >= patrolXPositions.length)
        {
           if (patrolLoops) // if we are going past the last point in the
           array we are either setting the target point back to 0 for a
           looped patrol
           {
              currentNodeToWalkToo = 0;
           }
           else // or starting to walk back the way we came
           {
              currentNodeToWalkToo = patrolXPositions.length - 2;
              walkingBack = true;
           }
        }
     }
  }
```

```
    }
  }
  void display()
  {
    fill(255, 0, 0);
    ellipse(xPos, yPos, 20, 20);
  }
}
```

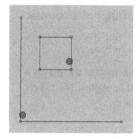

Code 2 and Code 3 could be combined to make a Guard object that chases the player.

On the book's website, a program is available in which stationary guards constantly look for the player but cannot see through walls. The guards store the last known position of the player which is represented by a red circle on the map. The program does this by checking if a line connecting the player and guard (line of sight) intersects with any walls on the map. If an intersection is found, the player can't be seen; if no intersection is found, the player can be seen.

Computing power increased massively over the years, that is, speed and memory, and approaches got quite sophisticated. But conceptually and philosophically, computers are not more intelligent today than they were in 1950, as far as I can tell - bring your Interceptor 12A EMP laser in case you are not sure

Chapter End Exercises

0. The *Ludo* AI

    Create a game of *Ludo* that is played by four AIs. Every player has four tokens. Tokens can be kicked out when another token lands on them directly. Players roll two dice; rolling doubles gives an extra turn. The house has to be reached directly (no left over points).

    As a minimum requirement, the AI should check the following conditions (in this order):

    1. Can I move a token into the house?
    2. Can I kick a token out? If there is more than one token that can be eliminated, pick the one from the leading player; if there is not one player leading, pick the token that is closest to its house.

    Optimisations are possible (e.g. move a token outside the reach of another token, or bring another token into play to trail another player's token to increase chances to be able to kick it out).

1. *Connect 3* AI

    Create a simplified version of *Connect 4* that is played between a human player and the computer (check out exercise 3 in Chapter 26 for a description of the game). The computer AI always plays second and should make its moves in a semi-intelligent way. That is, the AI should check through the following cases from top to bottom and execute the first condition that applies:

1. Place a winning move if it can line up three tokens of its colour;
2. Block the player if they have a winning move on their next turn;
3. Place a token that will create a line of two tokens either horizontally, vertically or diagonally; or
4. Place a token randomly.

The game displays 'Winner: Player', 'Winner: Computer', or 'Draw' depending on the outcome of the game, then waits for a click to restart.

Potential extra features:

- When placing a token under the conditions 3 or 4, the computer avoids to give the player a winning move in the next turn (i.e. the computer checks what would happen if the player were to place their token above the token the computer is about to place);
- Animate the tokens sliding down the columns;
- Setup a short wait time so the computer does not make its move a split second after the player has played;
- Sound; and
- Create a menu to choose a one-player game against the computer or a two-player game.

Notes

1. 'You are assessed for street repair. $40 per house. $115 per hotel' (Community Chest card in classic *Monopoly* (2008 to 2021), US version, qtd. in to Jenni Fielding. List of all Monopoly Chance & Community Chest Cards (Including New Cards!). Post on *Monopoly Land*, March 11, 2022, www.monopolyland.com/list-monopoly-chance-community-chest-cards (January 21, 2023)).
2. chat.openai.com (January 28, 2023).
3. The notion of NPCs is to include all computer-controlled entities in games, such as enemies, allies, opponents and bots.
4. Semako. Best mods for believable NPC behaviour? Post. *Reddit*, June 9, 2021. www.reddit.com/r/skyrim/comments/nw3gdb/best_mods_for_believable_npc_behavior (May 31, 2023).
5. Sunleader. Thread 'Pls do Something about Idiotic NPC Ship behaviour.' Post. *Game-Labs Forum*, January 13, 2018. forum.game-labs.net/topic/24384-pls-do-something-about-idiotic-npc-ship-behavior (May 31, 2023).
6. Holm Hansen, ibid., January 13, 2018.
7. For a brief discussion of properties of AI opponents in (early) digital games, see Montfort/Bogost 2009:38–41.
8. A special case are mathematically solvable games; then an optimal solution can be calculated by an algorithm.
9. See e.g. Exchange Blackjack Strategy. Online. Exchange Games, n.d. exchange-games.com/exchange-blackjack-strategy (November 21, 2019).
10. To further increase the odds of winning, one would need to count cards (to estimate which cards are still in the deck or decks) and might be drawn.
11. Note that the (movement) time fix is located in the main program (not in the class) in Code 2f.
12. Recall, pow() is a power of function (e.g. pow(4, 2) == 4^2 == 4 * 4 == 16) and sqrt() is calculating the square root (e.g. sqrt(16) == 4).

37

Programming Libraries, and Using an Audio Library

Outline

- Setting Up the Audio Library *Minim*
- Playing Audio Tracks from Disk (or URL)
- Playing Samples from Memory

Programming languages usually have a basic selection of functionality built-in. Most languages allow other functionality to be added in the form of libraries. The basic functionality covers core programming; libraries support more niche or special applications.

Different languages prioritise different functionalities. For instance, *C* only offers bare-bones functionality out of the box; everything, from math to graphics to fonts to audio to network, can be added in the form of libraries. This makes it very lightweight, versatile and adaptable to many application contexts. It can, however, be time-consuming to set up, that is, to find, get and install all required libraries e.g. when one receives the source code of a program, and one wants to run it or make changes. *Processing* includes much more functionality as part of the basic installation, such as graphics and fonts. For other functionality, *Processing* can use its own *Processing* libraries and all *Java* libraries.

There is no benefit in every programmer developing the same specialised algorithms and procedures e.g. for sound or networked communication. Collections of code are thus shared that provide specific functionalities. These collections of code are called libraries. Importing a library into a project is similar to adding extra functions to a project. *Processing* has a `rect()` function built-in, but it has no simple built-in commands, for instance, for playing sounds or for handling live video unless one imports a library. A multitude of libraries for many purposes are made and shared. Many libraries can be browsed in and downloaded from the *Contribution Manager* (see also the section 'Finding and Downloading Libraries' in Chapter 23).

Setting Up the Audio Library *Minim*

There are several audio libraries available for *Processing* (and *Java*). As an example of a library, I here use *Minim* which its developers describe as 'audio library that provides easy to use classes for playback, recording, analysis, and synthesis of sound'. To import a library into a *Processing* sketch, select the menu command Sketch > Import Library... > Manage Libraries. This opens the Contribution Manager on the Libraries tab, and one can search for the *Minim* library (Figure 23.3 in Chapter 23). After installing the *Minim* library, one can either select the import menu command (Sketch > Import Library... > Minim) or add all or some of the following to the current project's main program (Code 1).

Code 1

```
import ddf.minim.*;
import ddf.minim.analysis.*;
import ddf.minim.effects.*;
import ddf.minim.signals.*;
```

DOI: 10.1201/9781003345916-37

```
import ddf.minim.spi.*;
import ddf.minim.ugens.*;
```

These lines of code add new classes to the project that offer audio capabilities. One does not always need to import all of these; for sound basics, one only really needs ddf.minim.*.

Here, the basics of playing sounds in games are covered, but the official documentation is much more comprehensive.[1]

In any program that is to use *Minim*, first import the library, then declare and instantiate a minim object. One should also stop the minim object on the program close (Code 2).[2] This code should thus be *added to all projects* that use *Minim* (such as Code 4 and Code 5 below):

Code 2

```
import ddf.minim.*;
Minim minim = null;

void setup()
{
  minim = new Minim(this);   //instantiating the minim object on startup
}
void stop()
{
  minim.stop();   //stop the minim object before exiting
  super.stop();   //trigger cleanup routines
}
```

Playing Audio Tracks from Disk (or URL)

Minim offers an AudioPlayer class to play audio files. This class is intended for and should be used for (relatively) large files or long tracks (such as a game's title screen music) because the file is played from the hard disk (e.g. from a file in the program's data folder) or streamed from a URL, rather than (pre-) loaded into the computer's memory.

Code 3 shows how one would play looping theme music for a game with an AudioPlayer.[3]

Code 3

```
import ddf.minim.*;
Minim minim = null;
AudioPlayer audioPlayer = null;

void setup()
{
  minim = new Minim(this);   // instantiating the minim object on startup
  audioPlayer = minim.loadFile("track.mp3");   // mp3 oder wav file is needed

  audioPlayer.loop();   // loop starts the track if it isn't already playing,
  one can use .play() to play a track but it will not play again after the
  track ends
}
void stop()
{
  minim.stop();   // stop the minim object before exiting
  super.stop();   // trigger cleanup routines
}
void draw()
{ }
```

Music and sound effects can make a huge
difference for the playing experience of a
game. But never play looping music -
players will get sick of it in no time

Code 4 plays a mp3 file (e.g. from disk), and shows a visualisation based on the audio buffer.

Code 4

```
//MP3 Player, by Max Wrighton

import ddf.minim.*;
Minim minim = null;
AudioPlayer audioPlayer = null;

void setup()
{
  size(512, 256);
  stroke(255);

  minim = new Minim(this);
  audioPlayer = minim.loadFile("track.mp3");  // mp3 oder wav file is needed
  audioPlayer.play();
}

void draw()
{
  background(0);

  float step = audioPlayer.bufferSize() / TWO_PI;

  float x1 = 0.0;  // these variables are only used locally in the loop
  below, but I rather declare them here once, than to declare them a million
  times
  float y1 = 0.0;
  float x2 = 0.0;
  float y2 = 0.0;

  for (int i = 0; i < audioPlayer.bufferSize() - 1; i++)
  {
    // setup the left spiral
    float left1 = audioPlayer.left.get(i) * 350.0;
    float left2 = audioPlayer.left.get(i + 1) * 350.0;

    x1 = 128 + (sin(step * i) * left1);
    y1 = 128 + (cos(step * i) * left1);
    x2 = 128 + (sin(step * (i + 1)) * left2);
    y2 = 128 + (cos(step * (i + 1)) * left2);

    line(x1, y1, x2, y2);

    // setup the right spiral
    float right1 = audioPlayer.right.get(i) * 350.0;
    float right2 = audioPlayer.right.get(i + 1) * 350.0;

    x1 = 384 + (sin(step * i) * right1);
    y1 = 128 + (cos(step * i) * right1);
    x2 = 384 + (sin(step * (i + 1)) * right2);
    y2 = 128 + (cos(step * (i + 1)) * right2);

    line(x1, y1, x2, y2);
  }
}
```

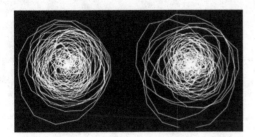

The bufferSize of the audioPlayer is the number of samples stored in memory. For each draw, the program steps through these samples (separately on the left and right channels, to be able to visualise stereo audio) in a loop connecting the amplitude of the samples in a spiral shape using sin() and cos(). The use of variables x1, y1, x2 and y2 is optional; one could do the calculations of the endpoints of the lines in two (long) lines without the use of the variables:

```
line((128 + (sin(step * i) * left1)), (128 + (cos(step * i) * left1)), (128 +
(sin(step * (i + 1)) * left2)), (128 + (cos(step * (i + 1)) * left2)));

line((384 + (sin(step * i) * right1)), (128 + (cos(step * i) * right1)), (384 +
(sin(step * (i + 1)) * right2)), (128 + (cos(step * (i + 1)) * right2)));
```

But Code 4 is more clear (if much longer) because it shows how each position is calculated individually.[4]

Playing Samples from Memory

Audio files (such as mp3 files) as in the above example (Code 4) are often large, and are typically played only once (or with large time gaps, e.g. on every game over); *Minim*'s audioPlayer thus only loads the file piece by piece, as needed to play it but does not keep the whole file in memory. Short sound effects, in contrast, do not take up much memory, their playback is usually highly time-critical, and often the same sample is played multiple times.[5]

Code 5 plays sound effects on button press with the Sampler class. The class loads the samples into memory and supports multiple voices, i.e. simultaneous playbacks of the same sample (the number of simultaneous playbacks is limited by the second argument, see the class constructor in Code 5). Playback of a Sampler object is initiated by calling its trigger method.

Code 5

```
//Sample Trigger, by Max Wrighton
//Revised to use the Sampler class, by dace

// main program

import ddf.minim.*;
import ddf.minim.ugens.*;   // needed for the Sampler class
Minim minim = null;
AudioOutput out = null;

Hero hero = null;

void setup()
{
  minim = new Minim(this);
  out = minim.getLineOut();

  hero = new Hero();
}
```

```
void keyPressed()
{
  if ((key=='w') || (key=='W')) { hero.jump(); }
  if ((key=='s') || (key=='S')) { hero.shoot(); }
}

void draw()
{ }

// hero class

class Hero
{
  // audio samples can also be declared and initialised in classes so each
  // class can handle it's own sounds
  Sampler jumpSample = null;
  Sampler shootingSample = null;

  Hero()
  {
    jumpSample = new Sampler("jump.wav", 2, minim);  // load file; two
    simultanious voices should suffice...
    shootingSample = new Sampler("shoot.wav", 2, minim);  // ...if the sample
    is very short
    jumpSample.patch(out);  //connect sampler to line out
    shootingSample.patch(out);
  }

  void update()
  {
    // update the hero's x and y position based on their movement speed, y
    velocity, and/or gravity
    //...
  }

  void display()
  {
    // draw the hero to the screen based on their current x and y position
    //...
  }

  void shoot()
  {
    shootingSample.trigger();  // and create a projectile in front of the
    hero
  }

  void jump()
  {
    jumpSample.trigger();  // and add y velocity to the hero
  }
}
```

Hint: If a sound effect is to be played in reaction to an in-game event, such as collecting a diamond or shooting a weapon, one should trigger the sound effect first, before doing anything else, such as initiating a graphical effect (e.g. a particle explosion). Audio is very time critical, playing a sample takes some time, and a few ticks can make a big difference in effect.

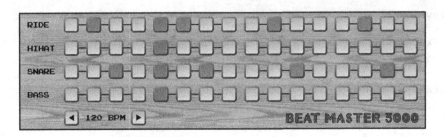

FIGURE 37.1   Drum machine screen layout sketch

Chapter End Exercises

0. The Musical Keyboard

   Make a musical keyboard. Assign the notes of an organ (or a similar instrument) to letter keys on the computer keyboard. A sound plays as long as its key is pressed. Import and use the *Minim* library. Play a tune.

1. The Drum Machine

   Implement a basic, step-sequenced drum machine (Figure 37.1) with 16x4 positions and only four instruments (e.g. ride, hi-hat, snare, bass drum). The speed (beats per minute, bpm) can be adjusted (e.g. using buttons). Playback is constantly running. All functions can be triggered by mouse. Use the *Minim* library for audio; do not use other libraries. Use classes (specifically, the positions/buttons should be objects).

Notes

1. See the *Minim* documentation at `code.compartmental.net/minim` (June 5, 2023).
2. *Minim*'s documentation advises that one 'must call [`stop()`] to release all of the audio resources that Minim has generated' if *Minim* is used 'outside of Processing' (Minim documentation. Minim : : Minim : : stop, code.compartmental.net/minim/minim_method_stop.html (December 7, 2022)).
3. Never, ever, play looping music in a game... players will get sick of it in no time.
4. There is also an example that shows the drawing of a waveform in the Minim documentation: code.compartmental.net/minim/audioplayer_method_buffersize.html.
5. *Bfxr* (available for *Windows* and *Mac*, www.bfxr.net) is a super useful tool for creating 8-bit style sounds quickly. It is funded through *Patreon* and free to use.

Glossary

Application Programming Interface (API): A protocol (such as a language with commands) for applications to interface and interact with each other.

***Arduino* (hardware):** A little computer on a chip, popularly used in DIY or Making projects, usually programmed in the *Arduino* language (see Arduino (language)).

***Arduino* (language):** Basically *C*.

Array: A variable that can hold multiple values of the same data type, which are numbered for access (they are indexed); it is often convenient to access values by index (in loops, for instance).

ASCII (American Standard Code for Information Interchange): Encoding for letters, numbers, symbols and control codes; originally developed for teleprinters in the 1960s. 7-bit ASCII encodes 128 characters, including all letters used in English.

Assignment: Putting a value into a variable.

BASIC: High-level programming language aimed at learners, developed in the 1960s.

Blitting: Copying a piece of graphics from memory to the screen.

C: Widely-used, bare-bones, lean, mean programming language, originally developed by Dennis Ritchie in the early 1970s.

C#: A more comfy and accessible version of *C++*, so far mostly limited to *Windows*.

C++: Improvement on *C*, the most essential being the addition of classes, the focus is on performance (i.e. speed; not e.g. on convenience or stability).

Comment: Brief texts in a program that are not executed or even read by the computer, and are aimed at the human reader of the code.

Compiler: Tool to translate human-readable code into gibberish that the computer can execute.

Data type: There are different kinds of variables, some hold numbers in different formats, some text, etc. These different kinds are called data types.

Debugger: Programming tool to support the process of identifying and locating errors in programs.

Declaration: Introduction of a variable with data type (but no value yet).

Event-driven programming: A style of programming in which the flow of a program mirrors the flow of the interaction between a user and the system.

Godot: Free and open source game engine (godotengine.org).

Header: In programs, headers typically contain the title of the program, the name of coder, date information and probably a brief description of what the program does, how to use it, and what does not work (yet).

Hotkey: The key to trigger an action with a single button press, such as Ctrl-S to save a file or project.

Instance: object.

Instantiating: making an object from a class.

Integrated development environment (IDE): Kind of text editor that usually integrates writing code, compiling and debugging.

Magic number: Literal value written out in the code. Should be avoided.

Non-player character (NPC): Computer-controlled entities in games, such as enemies, allies, opponents and bots.

Particle system: Set of many small things that do some simple stuff, and look intriguing because they are so many. Particle systems can be used, e.g. to visually simulate explosions, smoke, bubbles, rain and rocket boosts.

Pixel: One element of a raster display; such displays consist of a limited number of pixels, that define the visual resolution of the device.

Polygon: Shape defined by straight lines; in computer graphics, most polygons are triangles, because of efficiency reasons.

Processing: Programming language popular with artists and designers; based on *Java*.

Pseudo code: Sketches what a program should do in plain English before it is written out in proper code.

Python: Programming language, mostly aimed at data-heavy applications, such as data analysis, scientific calculations and machine learning; not at interactive applications (although everything is possible, e.g. with the *pygame* library).

Recursion: Recursion happens when a function calls itself. It is often used when dealing with (large) data structures, such as a database or the Internet. Also, some mathematical functions can be described recursively. Many interesting (chaotic, self-similar) shapes can be produced when recursion is applied to graphics. A glossary entry on recursion that says: 'Please see glossary entry recursion' would also be recursive, but would also never stop.

Scripting: Scripting is a method to interact with applications. It is used, for instance, to automate repetitive tasks in *Photoshop* or to define complex behaviours in *Unity*. Scripting is usually done in some well-known language such as *JavaScript* or *C#*.

Simple DirectMedia Layer (SDL): Free programming library for *C++* (it works also for *C#* and *Python*) based on *OpenGL* and *Direct3D* with a focus on interaction and graphics (libsdl.org).

Sprite: Little pieces of (often animated) graphics, such as a spaceship in a shooter, or a little figure running and jumping in a platformer (see tile).

Sprite sheet: Collection of images in one file for entities in a game.

Syntax highlighting: Feature of virtually all IDEs, to colour-code different syntactical parts of a program. Different parts of the code such as comments, function names, loops, literal Strings are then visually marked in different colours.

Tile: Little piece of (often not animated) graphics, such as platforms, walls, tree and diamonds (see sprite).

Tile sheet: Collection of images in one file for e.g. level objects in a game.

Tiling: Assembling e.g. level graphics from small (often square) parts; popular in 2D games.

Time fix: Code to make interactive or animated programs such as games run with the same speed on different hardware.

Uncanny valley: The phenomenon that an almost human-looking figure may look creepy or eerie (in contrast to figures that are more abstracted); observed and popularised by Masahiro Mori in the 1970s.

Unicode: Encoding for letters and numbers that accommodate thousands of symbols. Extends and improves on ASCII (see ASCII).

Unity: Popular game engine, can be used to make 3D or 2D games, is used by amateur and professional game designers.

Unreal: Game engine.

Uniform resource locator (URL): More colloquially, an online link.

References

Al-Sibai 2023 Noor Al-Sibai. Noam Chomsky: AI Isn't Coming For Us All, You Idiots. *The Byte*, Mar 9, [2023, presumably]. futurism.com/the-byte/noam-chomsky-ai (June 1, 2023).

ASCII History 2017 ASCII History. www.liquisearch.com/ascii/history (March 3, 2017).

Ashcraft, Breitzman 2012 Catherine Ashcraft, Anthony Breitzman. Who invents IT? Women's participation in information technology patenting, 2012 Update. *National Center for Women & Information Technology (NCWIT)*, 2012.

Badal 2014 Sangeeta Badal. The Business Benefits of Gender Diversity. *Gallup*, January 20, 2014, www.gallup.com/workplace/236543/business-benefits-gender-diversity.aspx (August 10, 2019).

Barta et al. 2012 Thomas Barta, Markus Kleiner, Tilo Neumann. Is there a payoff from top-team diversity? *McKinsey Quarterly*, April 2012.

Bezroukov 2014 Nikolai Bezroukov. The History of the Development of Programming Languages. February 19, 2014. www.softpanorama.org/History/lang_ history.shtml (Feb 4, 2015).

Birch 2010 Chad Birch. Understanding Pac-Man Ghost Behavior. *GameInternals*, Dec 2, 2010. gameinternals.com/understanding-pac-man-ghost-behavior (Jun 1, 2023).

Blackman 2017 Andrew Blackman. 10 Key Advantages of Promoting Diversity in Your Business. *Envato Tuts+*, February 24, 2017. business.tutsplus.com/tutorials/advantages-of-promoting-diversity-in-your-business-cms-28259 (August 10, 2019).

Bohnacker et al. 2012 Hartmut Bohnacker, Benedikt Gross, Julia Laub. *Generative Design: Visualize, Program, and Create with Processing*. Ed. Claudius Lazzeroni. Transl. Marie Frohling. New York: Princeton Architectural Pr., 2012.

Catalyst 2018 Catalyst. Quick Take: Why Diversity and Inclusion Matter. *Catalyst*, Aug 1, 2018. www.catalyst.org/ research/why-diversity-and-inclusion-matter (August 10, 2019).

Collins 2022 Sarah Collins. The life of Pi: Ten years of Raspberry Pi. News item on Cambridge web site, February 28, 2022. www.cst.cam.ac.uk/life-pi-ten-years-raspberry-pi (Apr 22, 2023).

Dizikes 2014 Peter Dizikes. Study: Workplace diversity can help the bottom line. *MIT News Office*, October 7, 2014, news.mit.edu/2014/workplace-diversity-can-help-bottom-line-1007 (August 10, 2019).

Dobbin, Kalev 2016 Frank Dobbin, Alexandra Kalev. Why Diversity Programs Fail. *Harvard Business Review*, July–August 2016, hbr.org/2016/07/why-diversity-programs-fail (Augugust 10, 2019).

Dreyfus 1965 Hubert L. Dreyfus. *Alchemy and Artificial Intelligence*. Memo. Santa Monica: RAND Corp., 1965.

Granlund 2019 Torbjörn Granlund. *Instruction latencies and throughput for AMD and Intel x86 processors*. Online, 2019.

Grayson 2016 Nathan Grayson. Overwatch player gets highest possible rank despite losing every match. Article. *Kotaku*, September 12, 2016. kotaku.com/overwatch-glitch-catapults-korean-player-to-highest-pos-1786538765 (September 5, 2018).

Greenberg 2007 Ira Greenberg. *Processing: Creative Coding and Computational Art*. Berkeley: Apress, 2007.

Hearthstone Science 2015 Hearthstone Science. [Hearthstone Science] Divine Spirit Rounding Bug and Maximum Possible Health. Online video. *YouTube*, July 12, 2015. www.youtube.com/watch?v=VwwtzER5ewc (September 16, 2022).

Hsu 2012 Jeremy Hsu. Why "Uncanny Valley" human look-alikes put us on edge. Article. *Scientific American*, April 3, 2012. www.scientificamerican.com/article/why-uncanny-valley-human-look-alikes-put-us-on-edge (May 31, 2023).

LearnCpp 2016 LearnCpp.com – Teaching you how to program in C++ since May 25, 2007. *Floating point numbers*. www.learncpp.com/cpp-tutorial/25-floating-point-numbers (February 3, 2017), October 28, 2016.

Loriciel n.d. Loriciel. *Tennis Cup Manual*. Game manual. N.d. (ca. 1989).

Magnuson 2015 Max Magnuson. Monte Carlo Tree Search and its applications. *Proceedings UMM CSci Senior Seminar Conference*, May 2015, Morris, MN., n.p.

Maher 2020 Cian Maher. Actually, The bug that made Gandhi drop nukes in Civilization is just a myth. News item. *The Gamer*, October 29, 2020. www.thegamer.com/nuclear-gandhi-meme-civilization (September 3, 2022).

Marckmann 2019 Maya Marckmann. *Creativity and Critical Reflection with the BBC micro:bit. A Study on the Introduction of the BBC micro:bit in Danish Primary Schools from a Constructionist Perspective.* Master's thesis, ITU, 2019.

Meier 2020 Sid Meier. *Sid Meier's Memoir! A Life in Computer Games*. London: WW Norton, 2020.

Montfort/Bogost 2009 Nick Montfort, Ian Bogost. *Racing the Beam. The Atari Video Computer System.* Cambridge, MIT Pr., 2009.

Morelle 2015 Rebecca Morelle. Google machine learns to master video games. Article. *BBC News*, 25 February 2015. www.bbc.com/news/science-environment-31623427 (Jun 1, 2023)).

Noble 2009 Joshua Noble. *Programming Interactivity: A Designer's Guide to Processing, Arduino, and open-Frameworks.* Cambridge: O'Reilly, 2009.

Odewahn 2011 Odewahn. Codebox: Handling exceptions in Processing. In: *Make*, Jan 5, 2011, makezine. com/2011/01/05/codebox-handling-exceptions-in-proc (April 17, 2015).

Oliver 2014 Julian Oliver. Networkshop. Workshop. ITU, Copenhagen, Personal Communication, March 2014.

Perera 2023 Ayesh Perera. Uncanny Valley: Examples, Effects, and Explanations. Online article. *SimplyPsychology*, April 24, 2023. www.simplypsychology.org/uncanny-valley.html (May 31, 2023).

Phillips 2014 Katherine W. Phillips. How diversity makes us smarter. *Scientific American*, October 1, 2014, www.scientificamerican.com/article/how-diversity-makes-us-smarter (August 10, 2019).

Pittman 2009 Jamey Pittman. The Pac-Man Dossier. Blog entry. *Game Developer*, February 23, 2009. www. gamedeveloper.com/design/the-pac-man-dossier (Jun 1, 2023).

Plunkett 2014 Luke Plunkett. Why Gandhi Is Such An Asshole In *Civilization*. Article. Kotaku, November 3, 2014. kotaku.com/why-gandhi-is-such-an-asshole-in-civilization-1653818245 (January 4, 2016).

Processing 2016 Processing online documentation. PImage/Reference/Processing.org. 2016. processing.org/ reference/PImage.html (March 5, 2016).

Processing 2023 Processing online documentation. map()/Reference/Processing.org. processing.org/reference/ map_.html (March 12, 2023).

Reas, Fry 2007 Casey Reas, Ben Fry. *Processing: A Programming Handbook for Visual Designers and Artists.* Cambridge: MIT Pr., 2007.

Reas, Fry 2010 Casey Reas, Ben Fry. *Getting Started with Processing.* Cambridge: O'Reilly, 2010.

Reas, Fry 2014 Casey Reas, Ben Fry. *Processing: A Programming Handbook for Visual Designers and Artists*, 2nd ed. Cambridge: MIT Pr., 2014.

Regan 2012 Rick Regan. Exploring Binary. *Why 0.1 Does Not Exist in Floating-Point.* www.exploringbinary. com/why-0-point-1-does-not-exist-in-floating-point (February 3, 2017), September 6, 2012.

Sack 2019 Warren Sack. *The Software Arts.* Cambridge: MIT Pr., 2019.

Shiffman 2008 Daniel Shiffman. *Learning Processing: A Beginner's Guide to Programming Images, Animation, and Interaction.* Burlington: Morgan Kaufmann, 2008.

Stork 1996 David G. Stork. Scientist on the Set: An Interview with Marvin Minsky. In: David G. Stork (Ed.). *Hal's Legacy: 2001's Computer as Dream and Reality.* MIT Press, 1996, www-mitpress.mit.edu/e-books/Hal/chap2/two1.html to …/two6.html (May 14, 2002).

Tero 2012 Paul Tero. Unicode, UTF8 & Character Sets: The Ultimate Guide. In: *Smashing Magazine*, June 6th, 2012 (www.smashingmagazine.com/2012/06/all-about-unicode-utf8-character-sets (March 3, 2017)).

Viegas 2020 Daniel Viegas. Civilization Gandhi nuclear aggression bug is a myth, says Sid Meier. News item. *Game Rant*, Sep 9, 2020. gamerant.com/civilization-gandhi-nuclear-aggression-bug-myth (September 3, 2022).

Walker 2020 Ian Walker. Civilization Creator Shoots Down Our Memories of a Nuke-Happy Gandhi. Article. *Kotaku*, September 9, 2020, kotaku.com/civilization-creator-shoots-down-our-memories-of-a-nuke-1845006305 (June 12, 2023).

Warpefelt et al. 2013 Henrik Warpefelt, Magnus Johansson, Harko Verhagen. Analyzing the believability of game character behavior using the Game Agent Matrix. *Proceedings of DiGRA 2013: DeFragging Game Studies*, 2013.

Weinmann/Lourekas 2012 Elaine Weinmann, Peter Lourekas. Photoshop CS6 Fundamentals: Color Modes. (Adapted from *Photoshop CS6: Visual QuickStart Guide.* Peachpit Press, 2012) Available online www. graphics.com/article-old/photoshop-cs6-fundamentals-color-modes (April 4, 2016).

Wholley 2019 Meredith Wholley. 10 Diversity Statistics That Will Make You Rethink Your Hiring Decisions. *ClearCompany*, Updated Apr 2019. blog.clearcompany. com/10-diversity-hiring-statistics-that-will-make-you-rethink-your-decisions (August 10, 2019).

Wikipedia 2017 Wikipedia. Slash (punctuation). 2017. en.wikipedia.org/wiki/Slash_(punctuation)#Programming (last edited March 15, 2024).

Winograd/Flores 1986 Terry Winograd, Fernando Flores. *Understanding Computers and Cognition*. Boston: Addison-Wesley, 1986.

World Population Review 2016 World Population Review. New Zealand Population (2017), November 20, 2016. worldpopulationreview. com/countries/new-zealand-population (February 11, 2017).

Code Index

Note: Page numbers in **bold** and *italics* refer to tables and figures, respectively.

--, 67
-=, 53, **54**
; (statement terminator), 165–166
! (logical operator), 58–60
!= (relational expression), 53, **54**
(int), 84–85
[] (array), 88
[][] (array, multi-dimensional), 90
*=, 177
/* */, 26
//, 25
/=, 301
&& (logical operator), 55–58
% (operator, modulo), 52
^ (power), **218**
++, 67
+=, 68
< (relational expression), 53, **54**
<= (relational expression), 53, **54**
= (assignment), 64, 71
== (relational expression, check for equivalence), 45, 167
> (relational expression), 53, **54**
>= (relational expression), 53, **54**
|| (logical operator), 55–58

A

add() (PVector), 279
alpha(), 140
append(), 93, 286
arc(), 271
ArrayIndexOutOfBoundsException, 87
arrayList, 93, 279–285

B

background(), 94
beginShape(), 129–131
BEVEL (drawing mode for vertex), 127
bezier(), 14–16
bezierVertex(), 271
blue(), 140
boolean (data type), 20, 31
BOTTOM (vertical text alignment), 7, 55
Break, 24, 45–46
brightness(), 140
byte (data type), 30

C

CENTER
    drawing mode for rectangle and ellipse, 126–127
    horizontal text alignment, 143
    vertical text alignment, 143
char (data type), 30
char(), 30, 92
charAt(), 92
circle(), 22
CLOSE (argument for endShape()), 130
color (data type), 136
color(), 136, 140
continue, 37
CORNER (drawing mode for rectangle and ellipse), 126–127
cos(), 112
createFont(), 143, 225
cross() (PVector), 277
cursor(), 153
curve(), 271
curveVertex(), 271

D

data (folder), 23
day(), 149
degrees(), 280
div() (PVector), 279
dot() (PVector), 280
double (data type), 260
draw(), 106–108

E

ellipseMode(), 126
else, 51
else if 48–51
endShape(), 129
ENTER (key), 146
EOFException, 164
expand(), 159

F

false, 30, 54
FileNotFoundException, 164
fill(), 17–18, 98
float (data type), 70, 81

Subject Index

Note: Page numbers in **bold** and *italics* refer to tables and figures, respectively. Page numbers followed by 'n' refer to notes.

0, division by, 171

A

Access, 86–91
Accuracy, 34n3, 64–65, 69–70, 167–168
Adaptability, 176–177
Addition (+), 63, 67
Additive colour model, 137
Adventure Game Studio, 4, 256
Alien, space, 84, 115, 179, 182
AlphaGo, 295
Animation
   editor, 221
   frame-based, 238–239
   geometrical, 241
Application programming interface (API) documentation,
   161
Arduino boards, xv, *xv–xvi,* 3, 5n6, 22n7, 93n8
Arguments, 8, 9, 95
   function, 9
   passing, 97–98
Arraylists, 282–286
Arrays, 104n7, 234
   access, 86–91
   declaration, creation and assignment of values,
     84–86
   definition, 182
   multi-dimensional, 88–89
Artificial intelligence (AI) in digital games, 293,
     295–297
   Brute Force approaches, 298
   data-based, 298
   heuristics, 297
   levels, 298–303
   neural networks, 298–299
   probabilistic methods, 298
ASCII Codes, 217–218
Assignments, 64–66
   operator (=), 64
   of values, 85–86
   (=) vs check (==), 167
Atom, 159–160
Audio, *see* Minim
AudioPlayer, 306–308
   bufferSize, 308
Autocompletion, 157, *158*
Autofire, 201–202
Autoformat, 156
Avatar, 256

B

Bad Cat, 256
Ball, 89, 120
BASIC, xvii
BBEdit, 159
BEVEL, 127
Bézier curve, 14–16, *15*
Billiards simulator, 125
7-bit ASCII Table, **218**
Blackjack, 282
Boolean variable, 115n2
Bounding box, *see* Collision detection, basic
Braces (), 72
BreakOut (game), 187, 189, 191–193
Brick, 88 89
Brute Force approaches, 298
Bubble, 103, 185
Bugs, xx, 25, 31, 33, 34n15, 163; *see also* Errors

C

C#, 4, 5n7, 92n4
Cannonball, 108
Capitalization, 171
Case sensitivity
   processing, 10
   and whitespace, 10
Casting, type, 69–71
CENTER, 126, *126–127*
Centipede, 293
Characters and character codes, 168–169
Checks, 1
Chess, game, 203–205, 234, 295–296, 298
Clarity, 176
Classes, 179
   array, 183
   example applications, 179–182
   inheritance, 193–197
   multiple objects with array, 183–188
   programming structure, 129
   syntax, 180
   'this' prefix, 188–189
CMYK colour mode, 136, 138
Code, creation of, 2
Code completion, *see* Autocompletion
Coded keys, 215–217
Code highlighting, *see* Syntax highlighting
Coding, 175
   rules in professional life, 178